🌿 *Young Frederick Douglass* 🌿

Publisher's Note

Works published as part of the Maryland Paperback Bookshelf are, we like to think, books that have stood the test of time. They are classics of a kind, so we reprint them today as they appeared when first published many years ago. While some social attitudes have changed and knowledge of our surroundings has increased, we believe that the value of these books as literature, as history, and as timeless perspectives on our region remains undiminished.

Also available in the series:

The Amiable Baltimoreans by Francis F. Beirne
The Bay by Gilbert C. Klingel
Tobacco Coast by Arthur Pierce Middleton
Watermen by Randall S. Peffer

Douglass, ca. 1845, shortly after he left Maryland

Young Frederick Douglass
THE MARYLAND YEARS

Dickson J. Preston

The Johns Hopkins University Press
Baltimore and London

Originally published, 1980
Maryland Paperback Bookshelf edition, 1985

The Johns Hopkins University Press
701 West 40th Street
Baltimore, Maryland 21211
The Johns Hopkins Press Ltd., London

The paper in this book is acid-free and meets the guidelines for permanence and durability of the Committee on Production Guidelines for Book Longevity of the Council on Library Resources.

Library of Congress Cataloging in Publication Data

Preston, Dickson J.   1914-
Young Frederick Douglass: The Maryland years.

Bibliography: pp. 209-11.
Includes index.
1. Douglass, Frederick, 1817?-1895—Childhood and youth.
2. Abolitionists—United States—Biography.
3. Slavery in the United States—Maryland.   I. Title

E449.D75P74   973.8′092′4 [B]   80-7992
ISBN 0-8018-2439-7 (hardcover)
ISBN 0-8018-2739-6 (paperback)

❧ Contents ❧

⚴ Foreword ⚴

In the years when I was working on my novel about the Chesapeake Bay, I had the good fortune to meet Dickson Preston, a retired newspaperman living on the Eastern Shore. I gathered such a favorable opinion of his scholarship and attitudes that I invited him to read my manuscript and protect me from making gross errors of fact about the region's history. He agreed, and found much about which he wanted to argue. Almost always his strong feelings and solid documentation prevailed, so I was much indebted to him.

As we worked together I learned that he was engaged on a job of his own. "I have always been fascinated by Frederick Douglass and the spectacular role he played not only in the antislavery movement but in American social reform generally," he said. "I've been curious as to what made him tick—what lay behind his spectacular rise from slave boy to a man of international fame."

"What are you doing about it?" I asked, and he informed me he had outlined an in-depth study of Douglass, who had grown up in the same county in which we both now lived. It emphasized remarkable new facts that Preston had uncovered in local courthouse and newspaper files. I asked if I might see the manuscript; so while he read my novel, I read his study of this great slave propagandist. It was very good. I told him, "Dick, I'm convinced this book will find a publisher," and we devised various tactics to locate one.

What impressed me in the manuscript? It deals intelligently with the youth of one of America's outstanding men, placing him securely in his social, political, and physical setting. Whole new areas of understanding are presented to illuminate the development of Douglass's challenging and sometimes difficult personality.

But perhaps best of all, the manuscript comes to grips with the real Eastern Shore, that remarkable enclave overlooked by history. Previous books have centered on the scintillating life of the romantic squires and their ladies, with little attention given to what occurred in the slave quarters whose inhabitants enabled the masters to live their gracious lives.

As late as 1940 the newspapers of this region refused to acknowledge that blacks existed, even though they comprised a large percentage of the population, except as comic characters involved in laughable petty crimes. As late as 1970, some of the fashionable schools of the area were still segregated. So the Douglass document will prove invaluable, I believe, in bringing such disparities into a better balance. Subsequent books on the region will have to take into account the data provided by this work.

But as I read I found that, even though I was attracted by the social implications of Preston's study, I liked even more the manner in which Douglass's personality emerged. Unusually handsome, gracious, clever, and always on the lookout for the dramatic stroke, he was destined to cut a wide swath through antislavery circles. It was inevitable that he would become the movement's most eloquent speaker; but what may surprise many is that after emancipation was achieved, Douglass went right on fighting for a wide variety of reforms in the areas of black voting rights, urban betterment, pacifism, social justice, and, especially, women's suffrage. His interests were universal and he spent himself willingly in their promotion. In this he was the prototype of the modern liberal. By bringing out the moral climate of his childhood, and especially the influence of his grandmother and of his beloved "Miss Sopha," Preston demonstrates how and why these facets of his mature character were molded.

In following his development, Preston does not spare Douglass. He subjects every statement Douglass made about his youth to cold examination in the light of available evidence, and at numerous points he identifies instances in which Douglass distorted facts, or suppressed them, or even invented them. Most notable was his oft-repeated claim that as a child he was subjected to constant cruelty and mistreatment; on the contrary, as Preston's study shows, while young Frederick did undergo some suffering, in the main he was recognized as a child of exceptional ability and given opportunities not open to other blacks of his time.

But even in the light of this critical examination, Douglass comes out as a solid, honest social revolutionary, patiently assembling in his youth the material that would be useful in a lifelong fight against slavery and its successor, discrimination. People like me who vaguely know of Douglass forget what a significant role he played in American politics of the post–Civil War period. He was controversial, arrogant, insistent, brilliant in debate, and adroit at utilizing leverage. Indeed, he reminds me more of a nineteenth-century Andrew Young than of a nineteenth-century Martin Luther King, Jr.

Preston performs a useful service in trying to place Douglass in perspective, and some of the data he offers will surprise. In an era of different racial attitudes, Douglass might have been a United States senator or a member of the cabinet. He did achieve the highest public office of any black up to his time, and he became the liberal front for a score of worthy causes.

Any book about Douglass or any other slave, no matter how glamorous their later lives, must face the gnawing question: What was it like to be a slave? Here Preston provides real guidance. Using chiefly such records as he has been able to uncover himself, he creates a factual, nonhysterical portrait of slavery on the Eastern Shore in the eighteenth and nineteenth centuries. He offers challenging answers to such questions as: Was cruelty endemic on the plantations? If slaves were happy, why did so many try to run away? and What was the impact of the sudden arrival of slave traders from the Deep South in the 1820s on the patterns of black life in Maryland?

Following as I did my friend's researches into these subjects, I was startled to learn how rich the Maryland records are in factual information. Old newspapers, letter files, court records, diaries, and journals throw surprising light on many phases of slave existence, and particularly upon individual black families. By merely concentrating his digging in likely spots, Preston has uncovered substantial material on young Frederick's family history. Douglass himself thought that "genealogical trees did not flourish among slaves," but the records show that a black family's genealogical history is as complete as that of the average white family of that time and that region.

Blacks who may have thought that tracing their slave ancestors was a hopeless task will be surprised and encouraged by the amount and quality of the information that lies hiding, waiting to be utilized. At the conclusion of his digging in the Douglass materials, Preston felt that almost any black family whose slave ancestors had lived in Maryland, and especially on the Eastern Shore, would stand a good chance of uncovering just about as much data on their progenitors as he did on Douglass.

One personal note: In fighting to find a home for this manuscript, which I knew deserved to be published, I was confronted by an ugly situation that needs to be ventilated. Two different editors told me: "Regardless of its merits, we've reached the point in our cultural history when any book about Frederick Douglass must be written by a black. We can't run the risk of offering one by a white man." I would agree, as I know Preston would also, if they had changed the phrase "must be written" to "ought to be written." Of course it would be valuable to have a reassessment of Douglass from the hand of some perceptive black scholar who could empathize with his subject and bring the weight of black hopes and intentions to bear in his treatment.

But meanwhile, this obvious and natural preference should not exclude a scholar like Preston from reporting his significant discoveries and trusting that somewhere down the line a black writer will find and use his material in some bold new way. Perhaps only a black can know the full meaning of discrimination; but in significant research there is no room for reverse discrimination. It is good to learn that not all publishers take this attitude. We cannot have artificial barriers either way; we must all work together to throw the light of truth a little farther, a little deeper. This book does that.

James A. Michener
The Eastern Shore

❧ Preface ❧

In the 1840s Frederick Douglass came storming out of Maryland slavery, an angry young giant, to astound his white contemporaries with his oratorical brilliance and his intellectual capabilities. For half a century after that he was the gadfly of America's conscience, a black man who dared to challenge the doctrine of white supremacy on its own grounds, a former slave who put the lie to the myth of inherent Negro inferiority, an uncompromising advocate of human rights whether in the sphere of women's suffrage or political and social equality between the races. At his death in 1895 he was not only the most honored Negro in American history but, as one eulogist noted, probably the best-known American throughout the world since Abraham Lincoln.

His contemporaries were at a loss to explain him. They could not reconcile his genius with the nineteenth-century stereotype of the shuffling, childlike southern "darkey." Some called him "a white man trapped in a black man's skin" and attributed his superior qualities to the blood of his unknown white father. Others refused to believe that he was what he said he was, a slave-born product of what were thought to be the dregs of society in rural Talbot County on the Eastern Shore of Maryland. Even his abolitionist friends found it difficult to take him at face value. In Massachusetts he was advised to "have a little of the plantation" in his speech, to stop the rumors that he had never been south of the Mason-Dixon line; in Great Britain he was obliged to kink up his hair, making it as "woolly looking" as possible, so that he could pass for "half a Negro at any rate." Throughout his life his statements about his Maryland background were challenged, both by those who thought him too talented to have come from such lowly beginnings and by those who charged he had falsified his experiences to make a stronger case against slavery. But no one, during his lifetime or since, tried to look behind his own account to see how much of what he said could be verified—or disproved—by independent evidence.

So this book began as an adventure in what might be called historical detective work. I had read his vividly written first autobiography, the *Narrative of the Life of Frederick Douglass, an American Slave*, and had been deeply moved by its stark recital of the grimmer side of Eastern Shore slavery. I had also read—and heard, for they are still spoken on the Eastern Shore—the denials, the insistence that Douglass was a charlatan who had made up most of his life story or had had it written for him by his northern white benefactors. But what were the facts? How much could be learned from external sources about Douglass's Maryland experience?

From the beginning of my search it was evident that, even as a child, Douglass had been a keen observer and a good reporter. Writing from memory without access to records about events that had occurred many years earlier, he had done a remarkable job of recalling them in detail, especially in his second autobiography, *My Bondage and My Freedom*. It was true that he had misspelled names, confused dates—including his own birth date—and in some cases distorted incidents in his antislavery zeal; but in the main his story checked out. Places, happenings, historical events, and people, even down to the identities of obscure slave children he had known only casually, could be verified from existing public and private documents. While the atrocities he described—the alleged beatings, tortures, and murders—were not susceptible of proof one way or the other, the participants he named had been actual people, identifiable on the basis of outside evidence. It became abundantly clear that Douglass had been writing about real individuals he had known, and events he had witnessed or had been told about. My chief contribution in this respect was to correct his spelling of names, straighten out his misstated dates, and add salient details not available to him.

Meanwhile, however, a broader and deeper vision was emerging of the boy who became Frederick Douglass. He had not sprung full-grown out of nowhere, as his contemporaries seemed to think; his black ancestors, for a century or more before his birth, had been a strong and closely knit kin group with family pride and traditions that were handed on to him by his part-Indian grandmother, Betsey Bailey. His roots were anchored deeply in the earliest American experience. Although they were illiterate Eastern Shore slaves, the Bailey clan into which he was born were far from being "dregs of society." They were part of a culture group, too often overlooked, that had been thoroughly Americanized by long and intimate association with the dominant Eastern Shore whites. Their values were American, not African; and the Eastern Shore, by virtue of long and uninterrupted tenure, was their beloved homeland.

It also became evident that the common picture of Douglass's boyhood as one of deprivation and cruelty was largely a myth, fostered at least in part by Douglass himself. He dwelt so much on his bad experiences—being forced to go naked, to eat like a pig from a trough, to sleep on a cold dirt floor in an old corn sack, to suffer the agonies of the "slave-breaker's'' lash—that readers and hearers could not be blamed if they thought those were the rule rather than the exception in his youth. The impression grew, and prevails, that young Frederick was the victim of brutal masters who half-starved him, whipped him unmercifully, and angrily opposed his efforts at self-improvement. That made his rise to prominence seem even more miraculous.

The truth, careful study shows, was exactly the reverse. Far from being a deprived child, Frederick was an exceptionally privileged one. From early childhood he was recognized by his white masters as an unusually gifted boy and, within the limits of their conditioned attitudes as slaveholders, he was treated as such. He was given opportunities open to few, if any, other young blacks. At the Lloyd plantation he was the chosen companion of Colonel Lloyd's son Daniel, and this was a relationship that greatly broadened his horizons. For the seven most formative years of his youth he lived in virtual freedom, under a mistress who regarded him as a foster son, in the intellectual ferment and commercial bustle of Baltimore. His playmates there were the white boys of his Fells Point neighborhood, with whom he associated as an equal and to whom he later acknowledged a great indebtedness for their efforts in helping him learn to read and write. On three occasions his masters had to make major decisions affecting his future; each time their conclusion was to send him to Baltimore to live with the gentle ''Miss Sopha,'' who was the dominant mother-figure of his life.

Douglass was well aware of this, as his private correspondence shows. But there were in fact two Frederick Douglasses: the public figure, overflowing with wrath against the institution of slavery and willing to make use of anyone and anything in his zeal to destroy it; and the private human being, warmly sentimental about his Maryland boyhood and filled with love for the people who had been part of it. ''I ran away . . . not from you but from slavery. . . . Indeed, I feel nothing but kindness for you all,'' he wrote to Hugh Auld twenty years after his escape. But the public Douglass, meanwhile, had made the names of Hugh and Thomas Auld objects of scorn and ridicule on two continents.

In the same vein was his feeling about his native state of Maryland. It was not Maryland he hated, but slavery in Maryland. The distinction is important. He loved Maryland, where his roots were, with a deep and abiding affection that was obscured by his public testimony against the evils he had observed while living there, and he spoke out so vehemently against the evils that they were mistaken for the state itself, just as his carefully selected memories of mistreatment were mistaken for the whole story of his childhood.

For example, so much attention has been paid to his experiences on the Lloyd plantation that it is difficult to remember he was there only eighteen months out of his twenty Maryland years, and that even then, by his own account, his sufferings were at the hands of the sadistic "Aunt Katy," herself a slave, rather than his master. And only for one brief period, during his first seven months under Edward Covey, was he subjected to the full horrors of slavery as it was experienced by many, if not most, other blacks. Bad as they were, these two short interludes in an otherwise relatively free childhood were not enough to brutalize him or dull his sensitivity and intelligence.

Viewed in this light, his rise to greatness becomes remarkable but not inexplicable. Douglass was a man of superb talents and powerful emotional drive. It is entirely to his credit that when the opportunity arose to escape from the cesspool of slavery, he had the wit and fortitude to take advantage of it. But it should be kept in mind that he had helping hands along the way, and that not all of them were black.

⚜ *Acknowledgments* ⚜

Many persons contributed to the research and writing of this book. I thank them all, but special acknowledgments must be made to the following:

Carl G. Auld, for access to much information and numerous documents on the Auld family, and for his long and unflagging enthusiasm for the project.

James A. Michener, whose advice and encouragement from the start kept me from giving up.

Dr. Benjamin Quarles, whose professional comments and constructive criticisms were far more helpful than he is willing to admit.

Dr. John W. Blassingame and the staff of the Frederick Douglass Papers project at Yale University, and particularly Lawrence N. Powell and Clarence Mohr, former associate editors of the project.

Mrs. Elizabeth Carroll, director of the Talbot County Free Library, and Mrs. Arthur N. Starin, curator of the library's excellent Maryland Room.

William N. Thompson, for permission to use a genealogical chart he prepared of the Skinner family.

William and Jean Sears, for Sears family material and photographs.

The Maryland Hall of Records, for access to Anthony papers in the Dodge Collection and much other material; the Library of Congress, Manuscript Division, for its vast collection of Douglass papers; the Moorland-Spingarn Research Center, Washington, D.C., for letters and photographs from its Frederick Douglass Collection; and the Maryland Historical Society for permission to use the Lloyd Papers.

Also, Norman Harrington, for his splendid help with photographs; Karl de Rochefort-Reynolds, for useful comments; Dr. William Calderhead of the United States Naval Academy, for information on Austin Woolfolk; Mrs. Morgan Schiller of Wye House; Norman Rukert, for a crash course in Fells Point history; Mrs. Arretta Cooper, for information on Stephen Bailey and his descendants; Helen Barrett; H. Chandlee Forman.

And finally my wife, Janet.

I have made up my mind, wherever I go, I shall go as a man, and not as a slave. —Frederick Douglass

Faneuil Hall, Boston, May 31, 1849

Part I

A Boy Named Frederick

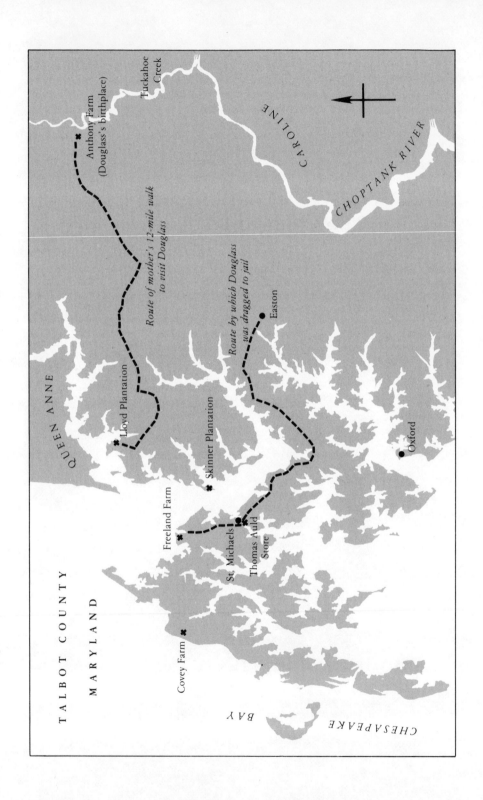

TALBOT COUNTY

MARYLAND

QUEEN ANNE

CAROLINE

CHOPTANK RIVER

Tuckahoe Creek

Anthony Farm (Douglass's birthplace)

Route of mother's 12-mile walk to visit Douglass

Route by which Douglass was dragged to jail

Easton

Lloyd Plantation

Skinner Plantation

Freeland Farm

St. Michaels

Thomas Auld Store

Oxford

Covey Farm

CHESAPEAKE BAY

❧ *Chapter One* ❧

The Bailey Heritage

The Family

In mellow middle age, Frederick Douglass grew nostalgic about the Eastern Shore of Maryland, scene of his birth and childhood as a slave.

"I am an Eastern Shoreman, with all that name implies," he proclaimed proudly to an 1877 audience. "Eastern Shore corn and Eastern Shore pork gave me my muscle. I love Maryland and the Eastern Shore." [1]

Race-proud, tradition-bound Eastern Shore whites who heard him may have sneered at such presumption by a Negro, but Douglass had every right to make the claim. His ancestral roots went deep into the Eastern Shore's early history. Not only was he born there, but all available evidence indicates that his black as well as his unknown white ancestors had lived on the Eastern Shore almost from its beginnings as a part of the Maryland colony.

The public record of his black forebears dates from June 1746, thirty years before the American Revolution, when the name of his great-grandmother, Jenny or Jeney, appeared in an inventory of slaves belonging to one Richard Skinner, a tobacco planter in the Miles River Neck district of the Eastern Shore's Talbot County. [2]

Jenny was a nursing infant, six months old, when the inventory was taken. Only two adult women, Sue and Selah, were listed as Skinner property; clearly, therefore, one of them must have been her mother. And there was only one adult male, a man named Baly. In the absence

3

of other evidence, he can be presumed to have been Jenny's father. All the other blacks named in the inventory were children ranging in age from five months to nine years, undoubtedly the offspring of Sue and Selah. Thus it is almost certain that Richard Skinner's slaves constituted a family or clan grouping—a man, two women, eight children—that had been established for some years in Talbot County.

The progenitor of the family appears to have been Baly, born about 1701, for it was from him that the family surname of Bailey, by which Douglass first was known, eventually was taken. Where Baly was born, or who his parents were, are questions left unanswered in the mists of recorded early Maryland history. He may well have been descended from slaves who had been in Talbot almost from the time of the county's first settlement around 1660.[3] Or he may have been imported, as were many Talbot County blacks of his generation, from Barbados or some other English colony in the West Indies. As I document later, it is most unlikely that he came directly from Africa. The fact that he bore a common English name suggests that he had been associated with English-speaking whites from his childhood; Baileys, under various spellings, had been among the first white settlers of Talbot County.[4]

Considering that he was a black slave on the rural Eastern Shore, a surprising amount of information can be gleaned from existing records about Baly. He was about forty-five years old in 1746, when he was recorded as living on the Skinner plantation, and was evidently considered an able worker, since he was valued at forty-five pounds, current money of Maryland. He was still there, an eighty-year-old man, in 1781. Strong circumstantial evidence indicates that he had two wives, and numerous children and grandchildren; but because fatherhood was seldom recognized in Maryland slavery, that must remain speculation.

Even the surroundings in which he spent his adult life can be visualized. The Skinner plantation, on what was then known as Bear Point Creek (now Leeds Creek), was not an especially large or wealthy one, as such estates went in colonial Talbot County. The main house, still extant but now incorporated into a larger mansion called Fairview, was a frame structure with two brick chimneys and gable ends. It was forty-one feet long and twenty wide. There was a separate kitchen, almost as large, with an attic and cellar; the tobacco house, roofed with featheredged shingles, was the largest building on the plantation.

The "quarter" in which Baly and the other slaves lived was built of logs and was probably windowless, with bunks along the walls for sleeping. It was twenty-five by sixteen feet, with a large fireplace at one end used for both heating and cooking, and a substantial brick chimney. Here from ten to sixteen blacks were crowded in communal squalor.[5]

Other buildings on the place were a brick meathouse, ten feet square; a milkhouse; a "chaise house" (carriage house); a long, narrow barn and shed; a necessary house; two corn cribs; a workshop; and a stable. About forty of the three hundred or so acres were "low swamp," and most of the tillable land had been denuded of trees, but there was a fine orchard with more than a hundred apple and twenty cherry trees. At the upper end of the plantation, away from the creek, was a smaller dwelling with its own orchard, tobacco barn, and other outbuildings. [6]

In the 1740s, when Richard Skinner was master, he owned, in additon to 11 human chattels, 108 sheep, 25 cows and calves, 5 steers, 2 bulls, and about 60 swine. As a measure of how blacks were regarded in the eighteenth century, it is worth noting that the same inventory account which listed his slaves by name also gave the names of all his horses: Dragon, Lyon, Squirrel, Maloony, Fenia, Bony, and Sorrel. He had one white servant, bound to him for a term of years, who undoubtedly acted as his overseer. [7]

In such a setting Baly and the large clan that eventually took his name lived with little or no disruption for more than half a century. Their world, though harsh, was a stable and dependable one. They had nothing to fear from changes of ownership; in all that time no Skinner slave was ever sold away from the Eastern Shore, and only one was ever sold outside the family. [8] Slaves in eighteenth-century Maryland were too valuable, both as productive workers and as status symbols, to be sold or given away lightly; instead, they were handed down from generation to generation, like family heirlooms.

Baly's ancestors had been torn from Africa and subjected to the unknown terrors of slavery in a strange environment; his descendants, in Frederick Douglass's generation, would face similar uprooting. But in Baly's time, at least, slave life had a stability that made it bearable. Security was in the land on which one was born, lived, and died, the seasons that served as calendar, the "white folks" to whom one owed loyalty, and the submerged but tenacious allegiance to a black family.

How strong this family loyalty was among the Baly-Baileys can be surmised from one bit of tangible evidence: the persistence with which given names were passed on from mother to daughter, and even from unacknowledged father to son, through successive generations. While some Eastern Shore slaves, in mockery of their natural dignity, were arbitrarily given such ridiculous names by their masters as Caesar, Pompey, Cato, Jupiter, and the like, the naming of many was left to their slave mothers; and often the name of a beloved older person was the only possession a mother could bestow to give her child a sense of belonging to a particular clan group or family.

Beginning with the original Baly, that name appeared in five successive generations under various spellings (Baly, Bealy, Bail, Baley, Baily) until it finally emerged as Bailey, the family surname. Other given names also turned up with a regularity that could scarcely be coincidental. In addition to the Jenny born in 1745, there was a Jenny who was a young girl in 1781, and another Jenny, granddaughter to the first one, who was a sister of Douglass's mother, Harriet. In at least three generations there were boys named Phil or Phill, and indications are that they were probably father, son, and great-grandson. Selah emerged later as Sillah and Priscilla. [9] Harry-Henry, Bett-Betty-Betsy, Isaac, Sarah, and Sue all were used in one generation after another. Even Augustus, Douglass's original second name, came to him from an uncle who had died shortly before the boy Frederick was born. [10]

In part, this clan feeling among blacks can be linked to their ancestral experience in Africa, where the kin group played a key role in the social structure. [11] But in Maryland, at least, it also reflected their long and intimate contact with an aristocratic white society that placed supreme emphasis on "breeding" and pride of family. However it originated, identity with the kin group was important to eighteenth-century Talbot County blacks, and no family unit is more clearly defined over a longer period than the Baly-Bailey clan. Although its existence had no official recognition, its members were well known to one another. Ancestors were remembered and honored, and children were taught to emulate the skills and virtues of beloved parents, grandparents, aunts, and uncles. The Baileys were a strong and, in their own way, prideful family, with deep roots in their Eastern Shore soil and a long tradition of courage and endurance. That makes it less surprising that they produced, out of the sordidness and poverty of slavery, the flowering genius of a Frederick Douglass.

As noted earlier, the family first appeared in written records in June, 1746, when an inventory was made of the goods and chattels of the late Richard Skinner. At its head was Baly. The women were Sue and Selah; and there were eight young children: Stepney (age not given); Jacob, aged nine; Baly, six; Jem (Jim), five; Phill, two; Harry, eighteen months; Jeney (Jenny), six months, and Dol, five months. [12]

The bare record, unfortunately, gives no clues by which the two mothers can be linked to their respective children. All that can be said is that Jenny and Dol certainly had different mothers, since they were only a month apart in age. That means Sue was the mother of one child and Selah of the other. Which of the two women was Douglass's ancestor cannot be established. Nor can any more be said than that Baly *might* have been Jenny's father.

Earlier Talbot County records have been searched in vain for any hint as to where Richard Skinner had acquired Baly, Sue, and Selah, or how long he had owned them. The Skinner family had possessed their Talbot County plantation since the 1660s, but neither Andrew Skinner I, the family founder, nor his sons are known to have had black slaves. Their plantation labor was performed by white indentured servants. [13]

In his will Richard Skinner gave the boy named Baly to a son, Daniel, along with land in Dorchester County, and gave Jem and Jacob to his two young daughters. [14] But the rest of the blacks remained on the Skinner estate. Most of them were still there thirty-five years later, when an inventory was made of the estate of the late Hugh Rice, who had married Richard's widow, Katharine, and had thus become owner of record of her slaves and other property. [15]

The Hugh Rice inventory, recorded March 16, 1781, [16] reveals amazingly little change among the blacks in more than a third of a century. Old Baly was still there, his age now given as eighty, and his name for the first time spelled as the family later would spell it, Bailey. Being far past working age, he was valued at only four shillings (about one dollar). Sue was sixty. Selah's name was missing (presumably she had died), but Phill and Harry, who had been small boys in 1746, were now adults approximately thirty-five years old; and there was a new pair of boys named Phill and Harry, possibly their sons. There was also yet another Baly (this one spelled Bealy), aged fourteen, who represented the third successive generation to bear the name.

Jenny was now an adult woman with children of her own. At least one of the four young children named in the inventory can with certainty be assigned to her: a girl, Bett, aged six, who grew up to be Betsey Bailey, the beloved grandmother with whom Douglass lived as a child. At least two other girls, Hester and little Jenny, probably belonged to the elder Jenny also. [17]

Of the ten adults credited to Rice in the inventory, no less than five (Bailey, Sue, Phill, Harry, and Jenny) can be identified both by name and approximate age with their counterparts in the Richard Skinner estate thirty-five years earlier. This is far too many to leave any doubt that, despite the absence of surnames, the Skinner blacks of 1746 and the Hugh Rice blacks of 1781 belonged to the same closely knit family unit. Two other adults, Isaac and Sarah, bore names later associated with the Bailey family, as did all the young children, Bealy, Phill, Hester, Harry, Bett, and Jenny.

A third document, this one an unpublished private record, provides the key that links all the family members together and establishes beyond question that they were in fact the direct ancestors of Frederick Douglass. It is a handwritten table compiled in part by Aaron Anthony, Douglass's first master, who had married Ann Skinner, Richard Skinner's grand-daughter, and through her had acquired ownership of some of the Skinner slaves. The couple were married in 1797; a few years after that, Anthony began a tabulation of the names, ages, and maternal parentage of all the blacks in his possession, carrying it back in some cases as far as the third generation. Presumably Anthony got the information from his wife or her family; he could not have known the detailed history of his acquired slaves. The table was continued by Anthony descendants, who kept it up to date almost to the time of the Civil War. Thus it became a document almost unique in black genealogy—a record of a slave family extending over more than a century, from which relationships can be traced back to colonial times and forward to the present day.[18] Luckily for Douglass scholars, the family was that into which he was born; the table contains the only known written record of his birth, which it dates as February, 1818.[19]

The table is headed "My Black People." Analysis of it reveals that the thirty blacks Anthony owned at his death in 1826 fell into two separate family groupings, not closely related except through intermarriage, which apparently occurred fairly often. One group was descended from a couple named "Emblem and Phil" (this document provides note of a rare instance in which male parentage was recognized). The other, much larger, is composed of descendants of the woman Anthony named as "Jinny" (Jenny) through her daughter "Bets," whose birth date is given as May, 1774. This dovetails precisely with the girl called "Bett" who was six years old when the Hugh Rice inventory was taken on March 16, 1781. "Bets" is given as the mother of Harriet, and Harriet, of Frederick Augustus. When it is recalled that Ann Skinner Anthony was High Rice's step-daughter, and that some of the slaves credited to him actually were held in trust for her, we have positive confirmation that the "Jinny" of the Anthony table, the "Jenny" of the 1781 inventory, and the "Jeney" of the 1746 inventory all were the same person, and that she was Frederick Douglass's great-grandmother.

"My Black People" provides much other information of which Douglass himself may not have been aware. He wrote that his grandmother Betsey had five daughters and one son; the table shows that she had nine daughters, three sons, and at least twenty-five grandchildren.[20] He knew little about his mother; the table records her birth date, February 28, 1792, and shows that she had at least five other children in addition to him: Perry, Sarah, and Eliza, older than he was, and Kitty and Arianna, younger sisters.

To sum up, a combination of various sources provides a maternal ancestry for Douglass, in large part confirmed by independent evidence, that reaches back five generations into the early history of the Eastern Shore. In genealogical terms, it may be expressed as follows:

First generation: Baly, born ca. 1701, presumed father of Jenny (Jeney, Jinny), born ca. December, 1745. Sue, born ca. 1721, or Selah, mother of Jeney.

Second generation: Jenny (Jeney), born 1745, mother of Bets (Bett, Betsey), born May, 1774.

Third generation: Bets, born 1774, mother of Harriet (Hariet, Harriott), born February 28, 1792.

Fourth generation: Harriet, born 1792, mother of Frederick Augustus, born February, 1818.

Fifth generation: Frederick, born 1818, took the name Frederick Douglass.

Unfortunately for his peace of mind, Douglass never saw either the private or public records of his birth and ancestry. [21] If he had he would have found answers to questions that haunted him all his adult life: who he was, when he was born, whence he came. And he would have had additional support for his argument that black Americans should not be shut out from the national heritage; for his roots, if he had only known it, went as far back into the beginnings of the American experience as did those of almost any Anglo-Saxon white.

For that matter, they may have reached back even further, into American prehistory. A substantial body of evidence suggests that Douglass was part Indian. Strong family tradition supports this view; "Your cousin Tom Bailey ... told me that your grandmother [Betsey Bailey] was of Indian descent," Lewis Douglass wrote his father while visiting Eastern Shore relatives in 1865. [22]

Certainly Douglass looked Indian, with his broad forehead, heavy cheekbones, and yellow-brown skin. While he never publicly confirmed that he had an Indian ancestor, perhaps because he wasn't sure the family tradition was true, he gave broad hints of it in his speeches and writings. On one occasion he appeared to boast of an Indian background. In a speech at the Carlisle Indian Institute, he told the assembled student body, "I rejoice beyond expression at what I have seen and heard at this Carlisle School for Indians. I have been known as a Negro, but I wish to be known here and now as Indian." [23]

There are other indications. When Frederick was a child, his master, Aaron Anthony, called him his "little Indian boy." [24] As an adult, he wrote, he was often asked "whether I was not part Indian as well as African and Caucasian?" [25] Douglass did not say how he answered the question, but he did record his answer when he was accosted by a stranger on a Hudson River steamer "who took me for one of the noble red men of the far West." When Douglass replied that he was not an Indian chief but a Negro, he said the man turned away in disgust. [26]

Douglass described his mother, who died when he was about seven, as "of dark, glossy complexion"; but his memory of her suggests that she had an Asian rather than black African cast of features. In the 1850s he came across a drawing of the head of an Egyptian pharaoh, Rameses the Great, in a book on anthropology. "The features . . . so resemble those of my mother that I often recur to it with something of the feelings which I suppose others experience when looking upon the likenesses of their own dear departed ones," he wrote. The author, James Cowles Prichard, cited the head of Rameses as a type that "approaches the Hindoo" rather than the European or African. [27]

Whether or not there was an American Indian strain, Douglass's ancestry was solidly based in an American rather than an African tradition. His black forebears had lived in Talbot County for many years, perhaps more than a century, before his birth. They were thoroughly acclimated to their environment, and their black subculture was attuned to the dominant white society of which they were a subservient part. Inevitably, their group attitudes were absorbed by the boy who was born into the Bailey family in 1818, and were reflected in the character of the mature Douglass. In turn, those attitudes reflected the peculiar social and economic patterns of Talbot County and the Eastern Shore during the colonial period.

The Setting

In the first half of the eighteenth century Maryland's Eastern Shore, today an isolated outpost, was the most prosperous and thickly settled region of the young colony, which then occupied two narrow strips of tidal land along the east and west coasts of the Chesapeake Bay.

At the heart of the Eastern Shore, both geographically and symbolically, was Talbot County. It was there the courts sat, and there the governmental business of the eastern half of Maryland was conducted. It was there, too, that most of the powerful families which dominated Eastern Shore social, economic, and political life—the Lloyds, Tilghmans, Goldsboroughs, Hollydays, and their kinfolk—had their principal seats of residence.

The seventeenth-century founders of these families had been English adventurers who had, for one reason or another, received large grants of Eastern Shore land from the Calverts. Their descendants parlayed this good fortune into social virtue. Within a few decades, the children and grandchildren of the first arrivals created for themselves a tightly knit aristocracy that has been described as perhaps the purest ever existing in America. Its base was land, and its source of wealth the universal crop, tobacco; but its lifeblood, without which it could not have survived, was a plentiful supply of cheap labor.

As they acquired capital, the more affluent planters began investing it in servants. At first these were almost entirely white; the trend toward black slave labor developed much more slowly in Talbot County than it did on the Western Shore of Maryland. As late as 1712 Talbot County had only 492 blacks in a total population of more than 4,000, compared with 1,559 blacks out of 5,000 people in Anne Arundel County. [28] Not only were blacks more costly, but immigrants from the London slums, convicts from British prisons, and Irish and Scottish rebels were considered superior workers.

The few blacks who were imported came not directly from Africa but from the West Indies, principally the English island colony of Barbados. Not until June, 1742, is there a record of a slave ship arriving at Oxford, Talbot County's port of entry, with a cargo that can be linked directly to Africa. [29] While there probably were some African imports earlier, the great majority of early blacks reached Talbot County in small lots, "seaven, eight, nine, or ten in a Sloope," from the West Indies. They traveled as deck cargo, along with West Indies rum, sugar, molasses, and salt, to be swapped for the tobacco, timber, and furs of the Eastern Shore. Oxford port records spell out the pattern: the brig *Two Brothers*, out of Barbados, three Negroes, November 8, 1731; brig *Hannah & Frances*, out of Barbados, five Negroes, December 4, 1732; sloop *Peggy*, out of Barbados, eleven Negroes, July 19, 1732; and so on. As late as 1746, when large scale African imports were becoming the rule elsewhere, merchant Robert Morris advertised for sale in Oxford "a parcel of negro men, women, boys and girls," just arrived by the ship *Cunliffe* from Barbados. [30]

With few exceptions, therefore, the blacks who reached Talbot County before 1750 were not, in fact, transplanted Africans, but transplanted West Indians of African background. Many were already long removed from direct contact with native African culture; even before their arrival in Maryland, these blacks had developed distinctive behavior patterns that set them apart from the mainstream of black slave life in America. They were well into the process that, for want of a better term, has been called *creolization,* defined as "the transformation of the African into the Afro-American." [31]

In effect, life on Barbados was an apprenticeship for life on the Eastern Shore. The island colony, first settled by the English in 1627, had developed a large slave population much earlier than either Maryland or Virginia (by 1690 it had 60,000 blacks to 20,000 whites), and it not only served

Douglass wrote that this drawing of an Egyptian pharaoh closely resembled his mother as he recalled her.

as the principal early source of supply to the mainland, but also provided the model on which the Maryland and Virginia slave systems were based. [32]

Barbados slaves worked under English masters and learned to speak a form of English. Sugar dominated the Barbados economy much as tobacco dominated that on the Eastern Shore, and while the type of labor involved was different, basic working conditions were similar. New arrivals underwent a period of "seasoning" which ensured that those who survived—by expert estimate 30 to 50 percent did not—were hardy specimens, inured to long hours of work, disease, and humid climate. [33]

Much of the Barbados legal code also was echoed in the slave code later adopted in Maryland. No slave could leave his plantation without a pass. If a slave offered "any Violence to any Christian," he was to be whipped for a first offense, branded for a second, and punished even more severely for a third. Petty theft was punished by forty lashes; arson, murder, robbery, burglary, and stealing of livestock could be punished by death. Runaways could be slain by whites with impunity. No black could testify against a white person, and blacks had no other legal rights in court. [34]

Even the basic racial attitude expressed in Barbados law was strikingly

12

similar to that adopted in Maryland. The island's "Act for the Governing of Negroes," drafted in 1688, stated that blacks "are of barbarous, wild, and savage Natures, and such as renders them wholly unqualified to be governed by the Laws, Customs and Practices of our Nation." Maryland's "Act for the most effectual Punishing of Negroes," which remained on the books until 1809, stated that blacks "have no Sense of Shame, or Apprehensions of future Rewards or Punishments," and therefore English law was not sufficient to deter them. [35]

Thus a black arriving at Oxford from Barbados would not be a terrified stranger in an unknown world. He would know the rules; he would probably speak the language; he would be accustomed to hard work under the eyes of an overseer; he would be part of a community of blacks of similar background; and he would be familiar with the social and moral customs of English colonists. He would be well on his way toward becoming a black American rather than an African in America.

The process was accentuated by Eastern Shore conditions. Most Talbot County slavery was of the domestic rather than the plantation type throughout the eighteenth century. A slave family lived in close proximity with the white family; the women were cooks, house servants, nurses to the children, as well as field workers on occasion. A typical slaveholding consisted of a man and wife, their children, and perhaps one or two elderly relatives. Large plantation operations, such as that which Douglass described on the Lloyd estate, were rare exceptions. In the early part of the century more than 90 percent of those who owned black slaves had five or fewer; even as late as 1790 only 37 Talbot County heads-of-families out of 1,434 had more than twenty. [36]

In such an intimate relationship, there was a constant interchange of cultural values. Not all of it was from white to black; James Hollyday, later a prominent attorney, was so entranced by the music his mother's slaves made on their primitive stringed instruments that he sent several of the instruments, along with a transcribed scale, to a cousin in England, and thus introduced the "Maryland banjeau" to London society. [37] In general, however, blacks emulated the customs of their white masters and adapted them to their own needs, so that their African heritage was further diluted.

At the same time, undeniably, there was a literal mixing of bloodlines. Many second and third generation slave children were sired by white fathers, a fact of life on the Eastern Shore that was tacitly and sometimes even legally recognized. There were also cases, especially in the early years, of children born of a white mother and black father. [38]

Thus the traditions and values prized by Douglass's maternal ancestors, and that he inherited, were fundamentally different from those later

13

developed by the slaves of the Deep South. The two cultures had little except skin color in common. Baly and his clan undoubtedly held themselves to be superior to the "Guinea niggers" who were imported directly from Africa, who spoke what seemed gibberish, and who appeared to be little better than animals. Douglass himself provided evidence that this class distinction continued as late as the 1820s. When he was taken as a boy to live on the Lloyd plantation, he found the "Guinea dialect" spoken there almost impossible to understand. He discovered that there were slaves whose parents had been born in Africa and even some who had been born there themselves. This was a revelation to him; clearly it was something entirely outside his family experience. All his life he would have difficulty in relating to blacks who did not share his cultural background. [39]

The Law and the Church

The legal code under which Baly and his clan lived was far harsher than even the cruel English code that governed whites, which prescribed death by hanging for crimes as minor as stealing a loaf of bread. Under the dictum, first expressed in 1729, that Negroes had no sense of shame and therefore could not be governed by the laws that applied to Englishmen, Maryland provided a remarkable punishment for a black slave convicted of murder or arson. At the discretion of the justices, he could be sentenced "to have the Right Hand cut off, to be Hanged in the usual manner, the Head severed from the Body, the Body divided into Four Quarters, and Head and Quarters set up, in the most publick Places of the County where such Fact was committed." [40]

Such executions were rare, but Baly may have witnessed one, or at least have seen the gruesome remains set up in the courthouse square as a warning to blacks. A slave who had stabbed his overseer to death was mutilated, hanged, drawn, and quartered in Talbot County in June, 1745, the year Douglass's great-grandmother Jenny was born. [41]

Other laws were scarcely less severe. A slave who allegedly was trying to escape could be shot to death by any lawful pursuer. In practice, as Douglass later would point out, the killing of a black by a white was not considered a crime in Talbot County. The white could always plead "extenuating circumstances" such as self-defense without much fear of being refuted, since no Negro or Indian (free mulattos excepted) could testify in a legal case involving a "Christian white person." [42]

Gatherings of slaves were severely restricted for fear the blacks might plot insurrection. "Tumultuous meetings" on the Sabbath were to be broken up by local constables, who were empowered to use the whip or other weapons if necessary. A slave found on a plantation other than his own without a permit was presumed to be there for no good reason, and could be whipped at the discretion of the plantation owner. In later years, even church meetings were forbidden unless a white minister or some other "responsible person" (a code phrase for whites) was present throughout the meeting. Masters and overseers had almost godlike powers; they could administer whippings for many minor infractions without recourse to judge, jury, or even a hearing. Capital crimes included burglary, robbery, and horse-stealing, although death sentences for these were often commuted by the governor. A slave who struck his overseer was to be punished by having his ear cropped; not until 1818 was this modified to thirty-nine lashes.

There were also laws providing punishment for masters who mistreated their slaves, but whether these were ever enforced is doubtful. One such, enacted in 1715, provided a fine of up to 1,000 pounds of tobacco for underfeeding or overworking slaves or beating them excessively. It remained in effect until slavery ended, but the very fact that as late as 1860 its fine was still expressed in pounds of tobacco indicates how thoroughly it was ignored in practice. [43]

Religious training, if blacks received any, was scanty, and religion was probably practiced in secret. Jesuit priests, themselves under severe legal restrictions, converted hundreds of Talbot County blacks to Roman Catholicism in the 1750s, a fact which so shocked Colonel Edward Lloyd III, a wealthy slaveholder, that he wrote an outraged letter about it to London. [44] One Anglican rector, the Reverend Thomas Bacon, preached a series of sermons about 1750 contending that blacks were human beings with souls capable of being saved. He castigated his parishioners for leaving their slaves, even those who had been in Maryland for many years, "as entirely ignorant of the principles of religion, as if they had never come into a Christian country." Bacon even started an industrial school at which blacks were to be admitted alongside whites, said to have been the first integrated industrial school in America. [45] But only a few Talbot Countians agreed with his advanced views. Most held to the belief that if slaves became indoctrinated with Christian teachings they would demand their freedom. [46] The practice of setting aside gallery pews in churches for blacks did not arise until after the Revolution.

There were, of course, exceptions to these general rules. The Eastern Shore produced humane masters and mistresses as well as callous or cruel ones. In practice, the harsh letter of the law was often ignored. Some owners encouraged their slaves to learn to read, [47] to raise and sell garden crops and other products on their own initiative, or to "hire out" their own labor and keep a portion of the proceeds. Even Douglass conceded that slaves in Maryland were better treated than those elsewhere, because of relatively enlightened public opinion.[48] Many Eastern Shore planters could boast with perfect truth that they never mistreated their "black families"; the necessary brutality was left to overseers, while the owners enjoyed the "foppery, idleness and dissipation" of life at their town houses in Annapolis, considered the giddiest capital in colonial America.[49] And many slaves had a genuine affection for the whites they served, even if they hated the cruel overseers.

The overriding quality of black slave life on the Eastern Shore in the eighteenth century was its stability. Existence was hard but predictable. Even the rigid legal code provided a framework within which it was possible to endure. A black knew where he stood, what he must do to survive. Punishment for transgressors was swift and certain. And he knew there was no escape. The safety valve of flight to the North to freedom had not yet evolved, but neither had the threat of being "sold South" to a far worse existence on a cotton plantation. Both were almost entirely nineteenth-century developments.

Such was the atmosphere in which Baly and his contemporaries lived out their lives in peaceful poverty and ignorance. The clumsy tobacco hoe, a heavy slab of iron wedged to a wooden handle as thick as a man's arm, was their daily companion; with it they chopped the sunbaked soil, grubbed out weeds and rotting tree roots, broke new fields to feed the voracious appetite of "King Tobacco," tended the corn crops that fed both slaves and animals.

In more than half a century the Skinner slaves seldom, if ever, ventured off their home plantation. It was their land; they possessed it through their labor at least as much as the various owners who, in that period, paraded in and out of the "big house."[50] The life of the girl Jenny was typical. She was born, grew up, worked, loved, gave birth to children, and eventually died within sight of the familiar "log quarter" with its mud-daubed walls and brick chimney. It is possible, even likely, that in all her forty or more years she never once set foot off the Skinner plantation.

If turbulent winds of revolution blew across America during her lifetime, if men in Philadelphia declared that all men were created equal, if a war was fought for something called "independence," what did that mean to her? She was an Eastern Shore slave; in the brave new world of "liberty" and "equality," she and her kind were not included.

In 1797, a sudden and disruptive change broke up the long placidity of life on the Skinner plantation. Ann Skinner married Aaron Anthony, and Anthony promptly moved the slaves she had inherited away from the land where they had been born, and where their ancestors had lived, to a farm on Tuckahoe Creek, fifteen miles distant. Included were the woman called Bets or Betsey, now twenty-three years old, and her two young daughters, Milly and Harriet. It was the first serious breach in the family circle in many years.

Betsey Bailey

From all indications, Betsey must have been a handsome woman at this time. She was tall, straight-backed, and strong, more brown than black in complexion, with regular features and, one can imagine, flashing black eyes that reflected her Indian background.

Although technically a slave, she neither lived nor behaved like one from 1797 on. Throughout her adult life she displayed remarkable self-reliance and independence of mind. One can only speculate whether her mother, Jenny, or her unknown father possessed these same characteristics, although it seems probable; but certainly Betsey passed them on to her children and grandchildren. She was a recognized leader in the black community, a figure of strength in holding together her large family, and a lifelong source of inspiration to the many children she helped to train. Her favorite grandson may have been Frederick, and certainly her influence on his emotional development was enormous, but he was by no means the only child she cared for who later reflected Betsey's strength of character. [51]

Soon after the move to Tuckahoe, if not before, she was considered married to Isaac Bailey, a free black man who worked as a sawyer, cutting firewood and dressed timbers from the many trees—loblolly pines, oaks, locusts, maples, sweet gums, and walnuts—that grew in profusion along Tuckahoe Creek. They set up housekeeping, not in the communal quarter, but in a little cabin in a woods clearing not far from the bank of the Tuckahoe.

The cabin had few pretensions as a home. It floor was packed clay; its chimney was made of mud and straw; its log walls had no windows. Its downstairs area was a single room, above which was a tiny attic, reached by a crude ladder, with a floor of split rails on which was laid straw-filled bedding. Outside was a shallow well into which a bucket was dipped by means of a wooden beam suspended in the fork of a dead tree. There was also a nearby spring, in a wild ravine known as "Kentucky," and a path that led down to the creek bank at a spot called "muddy shore," the fishing ground where shad and herring were trapped in seine nets during their annual spring runs to spawn in the fresh upper reaches of the Tuckahoe. [52]

17

Here Betsey and Isaac lived for many years, and here they raised the children who came along rapidly after 1797: Jenny, named for her grandmother, born in 1799; young Betty, in 1801; Sarah, in 1804; Maryann, in 1806; Stephen, in 1808; Esther, in 1810; Augustus, in 1812; Cate, in 1815; Priscilla, in 1816; and Henry, Betsey's last, born when she was nearly forty-six years old, in 1820. Here, too, when her daughters became old enough to work, Betsey took in their children along with her own, so that at times there were a dozen youngsters playing around the cabin door and sleeping in front of the fireplace or upstairs in the tiny attic. [53]

Long after Isaac had died and her children and grandchildren were scattered, Betsey stayed on in the little cabin, lonely but still self-reliant, until at last she became blind and unable to care for herself. It is a tribute to the force of her personality that, many years after her death in November, 1849, the site where the cabin had stood was still known to whites as well as blacks as "Aunt Bettie's Lot." [54]

Isaac Bailey was as self-reliant in his way as Betsey was in hers. He was an independent operator who had business dealings with Aaron Anthony over a period of thirty years, and his work as a sawyer was so prosperous that on at least two occasions he was able to hire a slave to help him by the year. Both times the slave was "Bealy" (also called "Bale" and "old Henry Baly" in various records), a son of the Skinner-owned couple named Emblem and Phil. Isaac rented him for the year 1797 from Aaron Anthony for eighteen pounds, fifteen shillings (about fifty dollars), and again for the year 1812 for thirty-five dollars. [55]

Isaac's connection with other members of the Baly-Bailey clan is obscure. Douglass in his autobiographies barely mentioned him, although he wrote eloquently and at length about Grandmother Betsey. For that matter, it is by no means certain that Isaac was Frederick's natural grandfather; the record is silent on whether he and Betsey lived together before 1792, when Frederick's mother, Harriet, was born, or whether they met afterward. Douglass described him as "quite dark" in complexion, but nothing else about his physical characteristics is known.

Local records reveal only tantalizingly inconclusive clues to Isaac's history. There was an Isaac, aged twenty, among the slaves owned by Andrew Skinner, Ann Skinner Anthony's father, at Skinner's death in 1769, and an Isaac, aged thirty, who may have been the same person, in the Hugh Rice inventory of 1781. But if this was the man later known as Isaac Bailey, he was much older than his wife, since Betsey was only six in 1781. [56] Nor has any hint been found as to when and from whom Isaac obtained his freedom. He was described as "Isac Baley, free negrow" in Aaron Anthony's ledger book in 1797. [57]

Granting of manumissions was exceedingly popular in Talbot County in the post-Revolutionary decades. Both economic and moral considerations were involved. The decline of tobacco culture, which gave way to wheat during the Revolution, made slaves less valuable as workers; and the rise of Methodism, which in early years condemned slavery as "contrary to the laws of God, man and nature," stirred many converts to free their slaves as an act of conscience. Quakers, who were numerous in Talbot County, also were forbidden to hold slaves on pain of expulsion after 1776. By 1800 Talbot had the largest population of free blacks of any Maryland county, and probably the highest ratio of free to slave blacks of any similar area in America.[58]

Although detailed manumission records were kept during these years, none has been found that appears to fit Isaac Bailey. Four men named Isaac were granted freedom, all with no apparent connection,[59] and there was a "Bail" whose owner, Margrett Robertson, set him free effective January 1, 1796, with a ringing declaration of conscience: "I Margrett Robertson of Talbot County, state of Maryland, do think it wrong and oppressive to hold negroes in abject slavery when it is clearly against the law and government, the dictates of reason, the common maxims of equity, the law of nature, the admonition of conscience, in short the whole doctrine of natural religion."[60] It would be gratifying to think the man set free by those eloquent words was Frederick Douglass's grandfather, but there is no real reason to believe so.

At any rate Isaac was certainly free by 1797, when his name first appeared in Aaron Anthony's ledger in connection with the rental of "Bale." In the years that followed references to Isaac were numerous: credit for sawing walnut planks; charges for bacon, corn, rent, cash paid out; an account rendered "per his wife Betty" in tacit recognition of the couple's marital status. The final item, dated June 6, 1826, a few months before Anthony's death, was a charge of seventy cents to Isaac's account for "1 bush. of corn to old Betty."[61] Isaac also worked for Colonel Edward Lloyd, Anthony's employer. In 1810 he was paid a dollar a day for four days as a reaper during the peak of the wheat harvesting season in July.[62]

Betsey's status remained suspended between slavery and freedom. Legally she was a slave, so that Anthony could claim ownership of her large and valuable brood of children and grandchildren; but in fact she was the wife of a free man and her life was one of considerable freedom. She worked on her own account, making and selling seine nets with such skill that they were in demand as far away as Denton and Hillsboro in Caroline County.[63] There is no record that Anthony ever hired her out, as he did her daughters, to work as a field hand. On the contrary, he paid her $2.40 per birth for her services as a midwife; his ledger for 1809 credited Isaac with $26.50 '' by acc't rendered per his wife Betty As Midwife with 11 women.''[64]

She was also highly esteemed throughout the Tuckahoe area for her skills as a fisherwoman and gardener. According to Douglass, her status was ''far higher than is the lot of most colored persons in the slave states.'' He wrote of her:

> I have known her to be in the water waist deep, for hours, seine-hauling. She was a gardener as well as a fisherwoman, and remarkable for her success in keeping her seedling sweet potatoes through the months of winter, and easily got the reputation of being born to ''good luck.'' In planting time Grandmother Betsey was sent for in all directions, simply to place the seedling potatoes in the hills or drills, for superstition had it that her touch was needed to make them grow. This reputation was full of advantage to her and her grandchildren, for a good crop, after her planting for the neighbors, brought her a share of the harvest.[65]

In fact, Betsey's ability to make sweet potatoes grow owed less to a ''magic touch'' than to traditional skills she had learned from older members of the family as a girl. She was careful not to use seed potatoes that had been bruised in digging; she protected them from winter frost by burying them deep in the earthen floor of her cabin; at planting time she took equal care to see that the seedlings were neither too deep nor too shallow in the hills. Her inherited knowledge was indirect but telling evidence of the family's West Indian background: sweet potatoes, erroneously called yams, were unknown in Africa, but were native to tropical America, where they were widely cultivated.[66]

Her new surroundings on Tuckahoe Creek undoubtedly were something of a shock to Betsey after the comforting familiarity of the Skinner plantation. Tuckahoe was the poorest district in Talbot County and one of the poorest on the entire Eastern Shore. It has no tidewater mansions, no well-to-do white families with pretensions to aristocracy, no large slave communities. The land was unproductive, the farms neglected, the inhabitants poverty-ridden whites, mostly tenants, who scratched out a bare living with the help of even poorer blacks hired as free laborers or rented by the year from absentee owners. East of the creek (actually a tidal estuary in this area) great stretches of marsh bred malarial mosquitoes by the millions. Douglass described the district aptly as ''thinly populated, and remarkable for nothing that I know of more than for the worn-out, sandy, desert-like appearance of its soil, the general dilapidation of its farms and fences, the indigent and spiritless character of its inhabitants, and the prevalence of ague and fever.''[67]

Even Aaron Anthony, who had grown up in the district east of the Tuckahoe, regarded the land he acquired as nothing but an investment and a place to keep his slaves. He and his family never lived on the Tuckahoe property; their home was a rent-free house on Colonel Edward Lloyd's palatial estate, a dozen miles westward on Wye River, where Anthony served as chief overseer. Anthony paid only five dollars an acre for his farm. He equipped it with secondhand farming tools, put some battered furniture in the small house, added a few head of livestock, and thereafter either leased it—and the slaves on it—to tenants or had it farmed by a hired overseer.[68] When he bought more land just to the north of the Tuckahoe property a few years later, he daubed the house on it with red clay from a nearby hill, named the new place the Red House Farm to distinguish it from the Holme Hill Farm, and leased it out also.[69]

The blacks he rented out to various neighbors went a long way toward supplementing his income. In 1801 his annual pay as Colonel Lloyd's overseer was eighty pounds Maryland money a year (about $215), while his "neat proseedes . . . by the hier of my people" came to twenty-two pounds. Sarah, Bale, and Harry all were rented out regularly, and as soon as Betsey's daughters grew big enough to work, they also were put to "hier" as field hands.

In 1808, the year the girl named Harriet reached the age of sixteen, she was rented for six months to Nathan Malony. In 1809 she and her older sister Milly both worked the full year for Athel Steuart, netting their master forty dollars. In 1810 Harriet was rented to John Nabb; in 1812 to John Malony; and in 1813, John Malony having died, to his widow, Elinor Malony, who was Anthony's sister.[70]

That was the year Harriet's first child, the boy Perry, was born. Harriet was twenty-one years old, like all of Betsey's daughters a good-looking woman, described as "tall and finely proportioned, of dark, glossy complexion, with regular features, and amongst the slaves . . . remarkably sedate and dignified." Reportedly she could read, a rare accomplishment among slaves and one not achieved by a good many of her white contemporaries.[71]

Harriet continued to work for the widow Malony in the years 1814 through 1816, along with her younger sister Jenny. Anthony collected only twelve dollars annually for both girls in those years, far below the standard rate for female slaves. Perhaps he gave a bargain price to his widowed sister; or perhaps Harriet's efficiency was reduced by continued childbearing. Her daughter Sarah was born in August, 1814, Eliza, in March, 1816, and sometime after that Harriet discovered she was pregnant again.

✣ Chapter Two ✣

Father Image: Aaron Anthony

Old master very early impressed me with the idea that he was an unhappy man.
Even to my child's eye, he wore a troubled, and at times, a haggard aspect. His
strange movements excited my curiosity, and awakened my compassion. He seldom
walked alone without muttering to himself; and he occasionally stormed about, as
if defying an army of invisible foes. "He would do this, that, and the other; he'd
be d----d if he did not," was the usual form of his threats. Most of his leisure was
spent in walking, cursing and gesticulating, like one possessed by a demon. Most
evidently, he was a wretched man, at war with his own soul, and with all the world
around him.

Frederick Douglass, *My Bondage and My Freedom*

Those words, based on the observations of a boy of six or seven, form
the only portrait history provides of the man who was Frederick Douglass's
first master and who may well have been his natural father. As Douglass
recalled him, Aaron Anthony was the epitome of evil, a real-life Jekyl and
Hyde who could pat Frederick on the head with paternal affection at one
moment and savagely beat a slave girl who had spurned his advances at
the next.[1] He comes down to us as a sadistic, half-mad old man, drunk
on a slavemaster's power and consumed by the fires of frustrated lust.

There is no reason to doubt the literal accuracy of this picture as far as
it went. Even in childhood, Douglass was a remarkably acute observer;
while his account of Anthony's behavior cannot be independently verified,
it bears the ring of truth.

22

And for nineteenth-century antislavery readers, the portrait was a sufficient one. Aaron Anthony owned slaves; therefore he was an evil man. That thousands of Maryland slaveholders did not go around muttering to themselves, did not act if possessed by demons, did not put beautiful slave girls to the lash, was beside the point. So were the classic symptoms of deepening mental illness that Douglass's recollections revealed. The world had not yet been exposed to Sigmund Freud; if Anthony behaved like a man on the edge of insanity, Douglass's readers, like Douglass himself, blamed it all on slavery.

Yet there was far more to Aaron Anthony than these glimpses of him at the age of fifty-seven bring to view. He was not a fictional character, not a Jekyl and Hyde, nor even a Simon Legree, but a human being with human strengths and weaknesses. He had come to the point at which Douglass knew him by a long, hard road. Moreover, Douglass's own words reveal a curious ambivalence toward the man who was a dominant figure of his early childhood. He loved him and hated him, admired him and feared him, felt compassion for him even while he turned away from him in horror.

Even at a young age, Frederick no doubt had heard the slave quarter gossip that Anthony was his father; and he may have believed it then, although as he grew older he came more and more to doubt if it was true. In his first autobiography, written in 1845, Douglass recorded the rumor in these words: "My father was a white man. He was admitted to be such by all I ever heard speak of my parentage. The opinion was also whispered that my master was my father; but of the correctness of this opinion, I know nothing; the means of knowing was withheld from me."

In *My Bondage and My Freedom* (1855) he repeated the "whisper" but added, "it was only a whisper, and I cannot say that I ever gave it credence. Indeed, I now have reason to think he was not." He also qualified the earlier statement that his father had been white, writing: "My father was a white man, or nearly white," although in another passage he spoke of "my admitted Anglo-Saxon paternity." In *Life and Times of Frederick Douglass* (1881) he omitted all reference to Anthony in this connection, saying merely, "Of my father I know nothing."[2]

The question is obviously one that cannot be answered now. But whether or not the gossip was true, it seems certain that Aaron Anthony was Frederick's first father image, a man with character traits that the adult Douglass would extoll and emulate as well as flaws from which he would recoil.

Like Douglass, Anthony was preeminently a self-made man, of a type that Douglass would praise from the lecture platform as the finest product of the American way of life.[3] Like Douglass, he rose by his own efforts from an environment of ignorance and poverty that in many ways was the white equivalent of black existence. Like Douglass, he lived by a stern moral code: "Through faith I am determined to conquer tho I dy." Like Douglass, he had pride, self-discipline, ambition, and a lifelong concern for thrift. He drove his sons as hard as he drove himself. "Violate not the sacred command of god," he wrote in the Bible he bought for them. "Reade and keep them holy. Walk upright & honourably before god and man." He also had considerable good luck, just as Douglass did; but by one means or another, he came from nowhere to achieve security, respectability, and, by the standards of his time, a substantial share of worldly goods.

If in the end it came to nothing, if by the time Frederick knew Aaron Anthony he was a lonely, tired old man, tortured beyond endurance by the shameful sin of lust, that too can be understood if not condoned. In a system that gave him godlike powers over human lives, the wonder is that he didn't do worse.

In 1767 James and Ester (or Esther) Anthony were living in the flat, marshy district east of Tuckahoe Creek known as Tuckahoe Neck. They were poor farming people, owning neither land nor slaves, and both signed their names with an *X*. The region, then a part of Queen Anne's, but later incorporated into Caroline County, was populated largely by poor whites "of the lowest order, indolent and drunken to a proverb," and by even poorer blacks, slave and free.[4]

Where Esther's family had come from is unknown; but James, at least on his mother's side, was the product of English emigrants who had been in Maryland for many years. James's mother was born Elinor Leonard. In the late 1600s her ancestors appear to have lived in Baltimore County on the Western Shore; but by 1715 her father, John Leonard, had established himself in Tuckahoe Neck. In that year he bought a plantation there called Hackton, comprised of two hundred acres, adjoining another small plantation, Millford, where he lived. At his death Hackton was divided between his daughters, Elinor and Rebekah, while his other lands went to his sons; so Elinor Leonard Anthony had only one hundred acres to share among her own children.[5]

It was probably on Hackton that James Anthony struggled to feed his large family. The land was not his—his mother outlived him—and no trace of his Anthony ancestors has been found; nor is there any indication that they possessed land. Born on November 11, 1767, Aaron was James and Esther Anthony's seventh and last child.[6]

James died before Aaron's second birthday, leaving not much to show for his life except children and unpaid bills. His will, probated on October 5, 1769, bequeathed "unto Ester my well beloved wife all my personal

Estate to raise my small children upon and to pay my just Debts.'' The estate could not have amounted to much, since it included no land or slaves, and the widowed Esther must have faced a difficult time. Five of her seven children were under the age of seventeen when their father died.[7]

Thus Aaron Anthony, like Frederick Douglass, grew up a fatherless child. Somehow he got a little schooling: he learned to read, write, and do simple arithmetic, although the art of spelling eluded him to the end of his days. He also learned to handle boats, probably as a deckhand aboard one of the numerous sloops and schooners that hauled cargo on the Choptank River and Chesapeake Bay. He saved his money, bought a lot in the new Caroline County seat called Denton, and built a house on it and then sold it at a profit. He bought a farm and sold it, and acquired a ledger book, the first of several in which he would keep accounts for the next thirty years.[8]

He evidently learned seamanship well; by the time he was twenty-seven he was ready for one of the most prestigious commands on Chesapeake Bay. On March 7, 1795, he made a proud entry in his ledger: ''This day entered on Board the schooner Elizab. & Ann the property of the hn. E. Lloyd at the rate of 76/10/0 per year.''

The new post was a big step upward for an orphan boy from Tuckahoe Neck. Not only did it carry a good salary (the equivalent of $200 a year) and the title of ''captain'' (which Anthony would carry for the rest of his life), but it was aboard the *Elizabeth & Ann,* the most luxurious schooner on the bay. Her owner, his new employer, Colonel Edward Lloyd, was the Eastern Shore's richest man and one of the wealthiest men in America, with vast estates and hundreds of slaves in addition to a handsome town house in Annapolis. Colonel Lloyd had spared no expense a few years earlier in outfitting the *Elizabeth & Ann* with the finest English-made equipment. He wrote to his London agent:

Be pleased to send me a compleat Sett of American Colours for a Pleasure-Boat of about 60 Tons burthen. Ensign and Pennant with 15 stripes; my Arms painted thereon, the Field azure, the Lion Gold; let these Colours be full sized. Six brass Guns with hammers, screw &c compleat to fix on Swivels and to act in such a manner as to give the greatest report; with the letters E. Ll. thereon, fitted to fire with locks. Powder-horns, pricking-wires & charges, showing the quantity of powder for each gun; and 200 ball, fitted to the size of the Bore. Have the guns full proved before purchasing.[9]

For the next three years Anthony served as master of this handsome craft, transporting members of the Lloyd Family between their Wye River plantation and their Annapolis town house while they reclined on rugs

25

and pillows beneath gaily striped awnings, and supervising the sounding of a splendid salute from the brass cannon as the schooner entered Annapolis harbor. When no member of the family was aboard, he had more mundane duties, hauling tobacco, wheat, and livestock to the Baltimore markets with a slave crew. Colonel Lloyd, fourth of the family to bear the name of Edward, died in agony of gout in 1796, but his son, Edward Lloyd V, retained Anthony as master of the *Elizabeth & Ann.*

Shortly afterward came another upward step. On January 16, 1797, Anthony married Ann Catherine Skinner, a member of a prominent Talbot family and a woman who, through her Massachusetts mother, traced her ancestry to Elder William Brewster of the Mayflower Company. Considering the rigid caste lines of Eastern Shore society, it was a remarkable coup for a landless schooner captain. But there were unusual circumstances: a son, Andrew Skinner Anthony, was born six weeks after the wedding.[10]

Young Edward Lloyd V saw to it that the newlyweds started married life in comfort with their son. The youthful colonel (all Edward Lloyds became militia colonels as soon as they took title to the family estates) provided living quarters for them at Wye House, his home plantation, and gave Anthony a raise to eighty pounds ($213.60) a year. Anthony noted the rent-free accommodations in his ledger as "a house gardain pastur for two creaters wood lot," and so on. Not long afterward Colonel Lloyd promoted him from schooner captain to chief overseer of the entire Lloyd empire, which included thirteen farms containing nearly ten thousand acres in Talbot County alone, and more than five hundred slaves.

For Anthony, it was a classic case of "poor boy makes good." The orphaned son of an illiterate tenant farmer now had a socialite wife, a growing family (five more children came along by 1804), a rent-free house, and a responsible job he performed so well that he retained it for nearly three decades.

For a number of years things went smoothly. Anthony's temperament was well suited to the role of top lieutenant for the politically and socially active Colonel Lloyd. He was tough minded and trustworthy, necessary traits in a man who had full charge of the estate during Lloyd's frequent absences in Annapolis and Washington as legislator, Maryland governor, congressman, and United States senator. He was a good administrator, holding costs down, keeping track of the number of hogs, sheep, cattle, horses, mules, and slaves on each farm, recording the sales of wheat and tobacco, maintaining the blacks at the barest subsistence level. Colonel Lloyd, an able businessman himself, required plenty of money for his fighting cocks, his stable of racing horses, his political career, his two mansions, and his reputation as a lavish host who possessed Maryland's finest wine cellar.

Anthony's own first passion was money. He treated it with the respect natural to a man who had seldom seen any in his youth. He recorded the cost of almost everything. In the family Bible is a note that it was purchased for nine dollars in 1803; in one of the ledger books is the inscription "Aaron Anthony his Book Bought of huett Elk Warf Cost 5/2." In listing the family's fifty-volume library, he set down the value of each book beside its title. The one that perhaps interested him most was a well-thumbed copy of "The Pleasant Airt [Art] of Money Catching," valued at a shilling and sixpence. Even his modest charities went into the ledgers: "Two bushels of corn to a begger man @ 75¢"; "small coffin for negro child," fifty cents.

Everyone and everything were expected to pay their way. Not only were his Tuckahoe slaves rented out, but his two sons were apprenticed for five years each to learn trades, Andrew to a cabinetmaker, Richard to a blacksmith. When he hired James Smith as a live-in schoolmaster for his family, he required Smith to help earn his keep by doubling as shoemaker. And even after Thomas Auld, who was master of Colonel Lloyd's new sloop, the *Sally Lloyd*, married Anthony's daughter, Lucretia, Anthony charged a $2.50 weekly board bill to the colonel whenever his son-in-law stayed at the Anthony home.[11]

As the money accumulated, Anthony invested it in land. He bought Holme Hill Farm, which he recorded as "204½ achors," from Colonel Lloyd for about $5 an acre in 1802; earlier he apparently had received the use of the land rent free. In 1805 he purchased "105 achors" north of it, which became Red House Farm, as well as a one-sixth interest in the mill that stood between the two farms, for $600. In 1806 he acquired the 41 acres of wild and untillable land called "Kentucky," near where Betsey Bailey's cabin stood, for virtually nothing. Other acreage was added later; before he was through, this son of landless parents owned 597½ acres, an estate nearly as large as that his wife's proud Skinner ancestors had held.[12]

He had no need to purchase slaves; Betsey Bailey and her prolific daughters were producing them in plenty for him. Between 1799 and 1826, in addition to the ten children born to Betsey, her daughter Milly had seven, Harriet, at least six, Jenny, three, young Betty, three, and Hester, one. Kate, the Emblem granddaughter, bore seven children during that same time. At his death Aaron Anthony was master of thirty slaves, all of them home bred, conservatively valued by his executors at $3,065.[13]

In the spring of 1808 Anthony remodeled the old house in which he and his family lived on the Lloyd plantation, charging at least part of the cost to Colonel Lloyd. It was an ancient structure that had been a wing or dependency of the original Lloyd mansion, built shortly after 1660, but it was falling apart, and the Anthonys needed more room. Aaron had it rebuilt, and a new north wing was added; he recorded part of the cost thus: "McCalloster and amos hail to 4 weakes Board while laying brick and plastering at my house they say E. Lloyd is to paiy thare Board $8.00." C. J. Kirby built a separate kitchen, "smoak house," and other structures for £37.10.0, also charged to the colonel. The Anthonys moved back in on May 10, 1808.[14]

The kitchen, a wooden building, was the one in which Frederick later lived. No trace of it remains today, but the main house is still standing, though it has again been remodeled. It is now known as the "Captain's House," reputedly for Captain Anthony.

Three of the six children born to Ann Skinner Anthony died in infancy. The two who survived, besides Andrew, were Richard Lee, born on June 4, 1800, and Lucretia Planner, December 7, 1804. Anthony recorded in his nine-dollar Bible a warning to them that reveals something of his own stern moral outlook: "Through Faith I am determined to conquer tho I dy. It is my desire for this book to remane in the possession of My Son Richard and his ares without interruption. All you my children violate not the sacred command of god ritten in this Book. Reade and keep them holy. Walk upright & honourably Before god and man that you may be ares to the kingdom of heaven and meet me on the Banks of Deliverance and long Dwell together."

There are indications, however, that Aaron did not always live up to his ideals. Like many a Marylander before and since, he fudged at least a little on his taxes. In the 1817 Talbot County tax assessment he acknowledged ownership of only seven slaves, valued at a paltry $700, when actually he owned twenty, worth more than twice that much. In 1826 he charged himself with nineteen slaves but "forgot" ten others, including Frederick, who was away at the time, living in Baltimore. He also seems to have had a bad head for the ages of black children; all were reported younger than they really were, thus lowering their value for tax purposes. But he was meticulous in reporting the names, ages, and values of the slaves belonging to his employer, Colonel Lloyd.[15]

He didn't always pay bills promptly. Thomas Perrin Smith, editor of the *Republican Star & General Advertiser,* had to wait two and a half years to collect on an ad Anthony had run in the fall of 1825. By the time Smith got his money, the total, including interest and two years of unpaid subscriptions, came to $10.39.[16]

The "Captain's House" on Lloyd Plantation. Aaron Anthony lived here. Frederick lived in the kitchen, now gone, at the rear.

His religious affiliations, if he had any, are not known, but among his fifty books were several devoted to Methodism, including (in his spelling) "the experience and travils of free Born Garrettson," Wesley's "Jornels," and seven volumes of the works of Bishop Law, in addition to numerous hymn books, sermon collections, and two Bibles. The books on Methodism may have been Ann's; certainly Anthony was not influenced by the strictures of early Methodist leaders against keeping slaves.

The substance of Anthony's life seemed to crumble in his later years. Ann became an invalid and died in 1818, the year Frederick was born. The Anthony boys did not turn out well. Andrew, after his apprenticeship with cabinetmaker James Neall of Easton, went west to seek his fortune in Indiana, coming back instead with a new wife and a taste for gambling and liquor. There is no indication Richard ever practiced his trade as blacksmith, although he did buy a secondhand set of blacksmith tools. Finally, there was gossip, at least among the blacks, about Anthony's relationships with Betsey Bailey's attractive daughters.[17]

When Frederick knew him, in the years 1824 to 1826, Anthony was clearly not a well man. The details of the incidents described in the

Douglass autobiographies (discussed in chapter 5) add up to a classic case of deepening mental illness. Toward Frederick, especially, he was kind and affectionate, "almost fatherly . . . gently leading me by the hand . . . patting me on the head, speaking to me in soft, caressing tones and calling me his 'little Indian boy.'" On occasion he gave Frederick "a regular whipping, such as any heedless and mischievous boy might get from his father," but otherwise did not mistreat him. "I have nothing cruel or shocking to relate of my own personal experience . . . at the home of my old master," Douglass wrote.[18]

Yet the old man's mood could change in an instant. His gestures would turn violent, "ending with a threatening shake of the head, and a sharp snap of his middle finger and thumb." At such times Frederick learned to stay well away from him, for he tended to take out his rage on the nearest object, whether bush, tree, or small boy.

Anthony's handling of his adult slaves was even more unpredictable. In routine dealings his attitude was much like that he adopted toward his own sons—harsh and unyielding, but not unfair according to his code. He protested vigorously when Colonel Lloyd failed to punish one of his overseers for shooting down a black man who had fled to avoid a whipping.[19] But his own mood could be equally vengeful. When two of his slaves ran away to the North, he ordered their young children, aged seven and six, to be sold to a firm of Alabama slave traders. When one of the girls from his Tuckahoe farm pleaded for his protection after being beaten by a drunken overseer, he refused to intervene, telling her she deserved the beating. And in the case of Hester, whose "crime" was that she preferred a young black man to him, he completely lost control and gave her a savage lashing that more than any other incident revealed him as a sexually frustrated, mentally unstable man.

By 1826 Anthony had lost everything he cherished except his money and his land. He had been replaced by a younger man in the job he had held for nearly thirty years. His daughter, Lucretia, had moved to Hillsboro where her husband, Thomas Auld, was now operating a store. Frederick, his "little Indian boy," was in Baltimore, living with the family of Thomas Auld's brother Hugh. Sons Andrew and Richard were grown and gone. In the lonely house on the Lloyd estate there was no one to keep him company except the demons that tormented his soul.

That fall old Aaron made a visit to Hillsboro to see Lucretia and his little grandchild, Arianna Amanda, born in January. And there, on November 14, 1826, three days after his fifty-ninth birthday, he died. He was buried in an unmarked grave not far from that of Harriet, Frederick's mother, on the Holme Hill Farm he had labored so hard to acquire.[20]

❧ Chapter Three ❧

Frederick's Birth

Douglass's Birth Date

The forces that went into the making of the boy who became Frederick Douglass were linked together almost by chance at the place called Holme Hill, the more southerly of Aaron Anthony's two Tuckahoe Creek farms. There is no question about the location; Douglass himself pinpointed the exact site of his birth during a visit to his home county in 1878.

He was less successful in answering another question that plagued him throughout his life: In what year had he been born? Working from slender and indirect clues, he eventually came to the conclusion that it probably had been 1817. However, he was by no means certain that this date was correct. He continued to pursue the problem almost to the day he died. And an overwhelming body of evidence indicates that his tentative conclusion was wrong—that he was born in February, 1818, rather than in 1817.

In fact, there is a written record of his birth. It appears in the tables compiled by Aaron Anthony and others that provide genealogical information on the slaves owned by the Anthony family. The notation on Douglass is in these words: "Frederick Augustus son of Harriott Feby 1818."

Taken by itself, this record is persuasive but not conclusive. It is not in Aaron Anthony's handwriting; apparently it was inserted at a later date by a person unknown. But an 1818 birth date is consistent with known

Perry son of Hariott Born Jany 1813
Jerry son of Cate Born apl ... 1813
Sarah daughter Hariott Born augt ... 1814
Tom son of Milly Born sep 21 ... 1814
Cate daughter of Bett Born Jany ... 1815 died 181_
Phill son of Cate Born apl 1815
Eliza daughter of Hariott Born march 1816
Prissey daughter of Bett Born aug 15 1816
Henny daughter of Milly Born sep 2 1816
Mary daughter of Hainny Born feby 1818
Frederick Augustus son of Hariott feby 1818
James son of Cate Born May 29 1819 died
Nancy Daughter of Milly Born July 1819
Isaac son of Jinny Born aug 1819
Henry son of old Bett Born feby 1820
165

From Anthony family papers, Dodge Collection, Maryland Hall of Records, Annapolis

Record of Frederick's birth in February, 1818

facts about Frederick's early life, including the suppositions on which he based his own belief that the year was 1817.

When he wrote his *Narrative of the Life of Frederick Douglass* in 1845, Douglass evidently thought he had been born in 1818. Writing of his unhappiness as a child because "the white children could tell their ages" while he could not, he said: "The nearest estimate I can give makes me now between twenty-seven and twenty-eight years of age. I come to this, from hearing my master say, some time during 1835, I was about seventeen years old."

Ten years later he had changed his mind. In *My Bondage and My Freedom* he said of his birth date: "Like other slaves, I cannot tell how old I am. ... From certain events, however, the dates of which I have since learned, I suppose myself to have been born about the year 1817." He repeated this statement in the 1881 and 1892 versions of his autobiography, amending it only to specify that the month was February. It is on this basis that his birth date is generally given in biographies and reference works as 1817.

The principal event on which he based his supposition was the building of a large frigate at a Fells Point shipyard shortly after he went to live with the Hugh Auld family in that section of Baltimore (see chapter 6). Douglass thought the frigate had been built in 1825, and recalled being told about the same time that he was "eight, going on nine." From that he came to the conclusion that he had been born in 1817.

"I know that it was in the year 1825 that I went to Baltimore, because it was in that year that Mr. James Beacham built a large frigate at the foot of Alliceanna Street [where the Aulds lived] for one of the South American governments," he wrote in 1881.[1] Unfortunately, he erred on this key date in his childhood by a full year. The frigate was built, not in 1825, but in the spring of 1826. The *Baltimore American,* on May 12, 1826, gave a detailed account of its launching at Mr. Beacham's yard, and of the huge crowd that had witnessed the event. If Douglass was right about having gone to Baltimore the year it was built, he made the move in 1826, not 1825; and if he was then "eight, going on nine," it follows that he was born in 1818.

Nor was he as positive as would appear from his 1881 statement that the frigate had been built in 1825. Although it apparently never occurred to him to look it up in newspaper files, he made repeated efforts to find out if his memory was accurate. Writing to Hugh Auld about 1859, he said: "Now my dear Sir, will you favor me by dropping me a line, telling me in what year I came to live with you in Aliceanna St., the year the Frigate was built by Mr. Beacham?" Auld did not answer. As late as 1891 Douglass asked the same question of Benjamin F. Auld, Hugh's son, who replied that one old Fells Point resident thought it had been in 1825 while another said 1826. In March, 1894, less than a year before his death, Douglass again sought information from Benjamin Auld to "get some idea of my exact age." He made a similar inquiry of Thomas Auld when they met in 1877, but refused to accept Thomas's reply that he believed Frederick had been born in 1818.[2]

Working from his mistaken premise, Douglass also confused the dates of other significant events of his childhood. He told Benjamin Auld that Aaron Anthony had died in 1825 and that "in 1826 I was sent from Baltimore to Hillsboro where your uncle Thomas lived, to be divided with the other property among the heirs." Actually, Anthony died on November 14, 1826, and the division of slaves to which Douglass referred took place on October 18, 1827. Thus he placed these two events a year too early, just as he had done with the frigate launching and, we can assume, his birth date.[3]

Other indirect evidence supports the date of 1818. For instance, he said in both *My Bondage and My Freedom* and his later *Life and Times* that he lived with the Auld family for seven years before being sent to St. Michaels in 1833. A simple check would have told him that if that was true, he had gone to Baltimore in 1826.[4]

In addition, the time sequence in which Harriet Bailey's other children were born places Frederick's birth logically in 1818, not 1817. According to the Anthony tables, Perry was born in January, 1813; Sarah, in August, 1814; Eliza, in March, 1816; Kitty, in March, 1820; and Arianna, in October, 1822. If Frederick's birth occurred in February, 1817, then he was born just eleven months after Eliza and more than three years before Kitty, which is possible but unlikely. If he was born in February, 1818, the more normal pattern of about two years between the births of the three children is maintained.

The conclusion is inescapable: Douglass was born in February, 1818, just as the only written record of his birth says he was. He based his supposition that the year was 1817 on faulty evidence.

There is a strong hint that Douglass learned of his mistake in his later years, when it was too late to correct it publicly. Harriet Lucretia Anthony, Aaron's great-granddaughter, wrote in the margin of her copy of *My Bondage and My Freedom,* opposite Douglass's statement that he didn't know how old he was: "Several years before Fred's death I sent him from my great grandfather's records the date of his birth." And Helen Pitts Douglass, his second wife, wrote after his death that "receipt (of) accurate testimony made him one year younger than his generally accepted age." Presumably the "accurate testimony" was the information from Miss Anthony.[5]

As for the precise date of February 14 on which his family celebrated his birthday, that was an arbitrarily chosen date, based purely on sentiment. Douglass recalled that his mother, on her last visit to him, had called him her "Valentine" and had given him a heart-shaped ginger cake (see chapter 4). Knowing he had been born in February, he decided it might have been a birthday visit. So he permitted family and friends to do their celebrating on St. Valentine's Day, February 14.

Early Years

Today the Holme Hill setting is one of quiet beauty, calm tidal water and fertile farm land, one of those pockets of unspoiled charm that still grace Maryland's Eastern Shore. Tuckahoe Creek, rising in the flat fields of Delaware, meanders southwestward for thirty miles or so, much of it in a protected state park, until it reaches an artificial lake and dam. Below that point it is a tidal estuary rather than a freshwater stream. South of the twin villages of Hillsboro and Queen Anne, its eastern shoreline spreads out into marshland that is a winter haven for thousands of wild geese, ducks, and muskrats, while its steeper western bank rises abruptly to fields of corn and soy beans. The region is dotted with century-old farm houses, some abandoned, some still occupied, sturdy reminders of an earlier day. But no trace remains at Holme Hill of the events that took place 160 years ago; no marker signifies that this was the birthplace of Frederick Douglass; no sign of Betsey Bailey's cabin or even of the house that Anthony's tenants and overseers occupied can be found. Those who lived and died there have vanished as if they had never been born.[6]

Aaron Anthony must have spent a good deal of time at Holme Hill in the spring of 1817. He had a new tenant, Perry Ward Steuart or Stewart, who had leased the 154 acres for $120 a year, and there were new arrangements to be made. Harriet Bailey was there, too, a dark and comely woman of twenty-five. After 1816 Anthony never again hired her out as a field hand; instead she stayed at Holme Hill, working for Stewart and his successors, until she died. Betsey Bailey was also nearby, living in the rude cabin she and Isaac had built on the Anthony farm.[7]

In May Harriet became pregnant by an unknown white man; sometime in February, 1818, she gave birth to the boy who was named Frederick Augustus Washington Bailey. Tradition says the birth took place in Betsey's cabin, but that is only supposition. It could have been in the slave quarter behind the tenant house, or even in an open field. Also unknown is how the boy came by his resounding name, except that the "Augustus" was in memory of a son of Betsey Bailey who had died two years earlier.[8] Bailey, of course, was his mother's family name.

Young Frederick appeared to be a mulatto, the child of one black and one white parent, although he was denied that legal status because his father was never acknowledged. His color was far lighter than that of either his mother or grandmother; he was of the shade known then as yellow, not much darker than a sun-tanned white man. There was more than a hint of Indian ancestry in his facial structure; Aaron Anthony may not have been the only one who likened him to a little Indian boy.

While her daughters worked, Betsey Bailey served as sitter to their children. So it is likely that Frederick was taken to live with her as soon as he was weaned. At any rate, his first memories were of his grandparents and their cabin in the woods.

Later he wrote that he did not recall ever seeing his mother there, but it is highly probable that she did visit the cabin from time to time, at least during Frederick's infancy. She was living and working on the Anthony farm, and nothing in either law or custom would have prevented her from visiting him if she so desired. Perhaps she came when he was too

35

young to know her as his mother. By the time he was old enough to recognize her, Harriet had two younger children, Kitty and Arianna, to take her attention away from him.[9]

Frederick's memories of the cabin and his life there were idyllic; he recalled it as a wild and free existence, totally unlike anything he would ever experience after he grew old enough to grasp the implications of what it meant to be a slave. As an adult he wrote lyrically of the freedoms enjoyed by a small slave boy in contrast to the restrictions on white children:

He seldom has to listen to lectures on propriety of behavior, or on anything else. He is never chided for handling his little knife and fork improperly or awkwardly, for he uses none. He is never reprimanded for soiling the table-cloth, for he takes his meals on the clay floor. He never has the misfortune, in his games or sports, of soiling or tearing his clothes, for he has almost none to soil or tear. He is never expected to act like a nice little gentleman, for he is only a rude little slave. . . .

He literally runs wild; has no pretty little verses to learn in the nursery; no nice little speeches to make for aunts, uncles, or cousins, to show how smart he is; and if he can only manage to keep out of the way of the heavy feet and fists of the older slave boys, he may trot on, in his joyous and roguish tricks, as happy as any little heathen under the palm trees of Africa. . . .

In a word, he is, for the most part of the first eight years of his life, a spirited, joyous, uproarious, and happy boy.[10]

The cabin seemed like a palace, as perhaps it was when compared with the crowded, decrepit quarters in which many slave children lived: "The old cabin, with its rail floor and rail bedsteads up stairs, and its clay floor down stairs, and its dirt chimney, and windowless sides, and that most curious piece of workmanship of all the rest, the ladder stairway, and the hole curiously dug in front of the fireplace, beneath which grandmammy placed the sweet potatoes to keep them from the frost, was MY HOME— the only home I ever had; and I loved it, and all connected with it."

The well was a miracle of workmanship, "with its stately and skyward-pointing beam, so aptly placed between the limbs of what had once been a tree, and so nicely balanced that I could move it up and down with only one hand, and could get a drink myself without calling for help."[11]

Just north of Holme Hill Farm stood Levi Lee's mill and mill pond, on a site that had been occupied by water mills for more than a century. The stream below it, trickling down to the Tuckahoe, separated Aaron Anthony's two farms. It was a busy place; there little Frederick spent countless care-free hours, watching the wagons come and go as farmers brought corn to be ground into meal, gazing with fascination at the turning of the ponderous wheel, feeling the tug of sunfish as they nibbled at the worms he used as bait on the bent-pin and tow-thread fishing line Grandmamma Betsey rigged up for him.[12]

It was a happy time, one he would remember always as the most golden period of his life. He was as free as a bird; he could do anything he liked: gallop like a horse, grunt back at the pigs, flap his arms in imitation of the barnyard rooster. Except in the cold of winter he spent most of his time outdoors. He had plenty of playmates, for the cabin was always over-flowing with children: his Uncle Henry, who was two years younger than he was, cousins Mary, Isaac, Steve, Henny, and Nancy, who were all about his own age. As for Frederick, he was, in his own words, a "spirited, joyous, uproarious, and happy boy," without a care in the world.

But gradually, as he grew older, the shape of things to come hove into hazy view. He learned that he was something called a *slave*, and that his grandmother and most of the others in the family were slaves also. There was a mysterious being, called "Old Master," who controlled their lives and who could make them all, even his grandmother, do anything he wanted them to do. Betsey Bailey spoke of this godlike being "with every mark of reverence," but some of the others mentioned him with shudder-ing fear. Whether or not Frederick had heard by then the whispers that "Old Master" was his real father, he early came to regard him with awe as "something more than a man, and something worse than an angel." Some of the other children had fathers—the slave Noah, for instance, was father to Mary and Isaac, Aunt Jenny's offspring—but he had none, and like any boy in such circumstances, he hungered deeply for one. He became eager to learn everything he could about "Old Master" and the equally mysterious Lloyd Plantation, twelve miles away, on which "Old Master" lived.

Much of what he learned, however, was not good. When the children under Betsey Bailey's care grew old enough, they were taken away from the cabin and sent to live at "Old Master's" house. Perry, Sarah, and Eliza, Harriet's older children, had made the journey when Frederick was still too young to know them as his brother and sisters; so had his cousin Tom, Aunt Milly's son. There were always younger children coming along, and Betsey did not have room for them all. Inevitably, Frederick came to realize, he would have to go, too. Most of the family considered it a high honor to be chosen to live at "Old Master's," but not so Frederick. He faced the prospect with childish dread. "I wished that it was possible for me to remain small all my life, knowing that the sooner I grew large the shorter would be my time to remain."

His turn came in the late summer of 1824, when he was six years old. One bright morning, probably in August (for he recalled that peaches and pears were ripe), Betsey wrapped a newly ironed bandanna turban around her head, stuffed some cornbread in a pocket, and told the boy they were going on a journey. She didn't tell him where the journey would take them, but Frederick was afraid he knew. His heart sank; he sensed that he was leaving forever the little cabin that was the only place he ever really regarded as home. And he was right; it would be fifty-four years before he saw the site again.

They set off down the dusty, rutted road that led westward across Talbot County to the crossroads village called Thimbletown and beyond it into unknown land. Every detail of the trip was burned into Frederick's memory, so that half a century later he could recall "the whole journey . . . as well as if it were yesterday." The day was hot and humid. When Frederick's six-year-old legs grew tired, Grandmother Betsey picked him up and toted him on her shoulder like a sack of wheat. Betsey was fifty years old, and there were streaks of gray hair under her turban; but to the child she was a never-to-be-forgotten symbol of strength and love. Despite her age, "grandmother was yet a woman of power and spirit. She was remarkably straight in figure, and elastic and muscular in movement. I seemed hardly to be a burden to her." Nevertheless, it was undignified to be carried like a baby; finally he demanded to be put down because "I felt myself too much of a man to allow it." After that he walked beside her, imitating as best he could her long, effortless strides.

As they traveled on, Frederick's vague worries transformed themselves into specific fears. He clung to Betsey's skirts, terrified "lest something should come out of the woods and eat me up." Everything seemed strange and fearsome. Old logs and stumps turned into monsters; he could plainly make out their legs, eyes, ears, and sharp teeth until he got close enough to discover that the legs were only broken limbs, the eyes washed-out knots, the ears and teeth jagged bits of bark.

From the Tuckahoe to the Wye, as Betsey and Frederick traveled it, is a distance of twelve miles. You can make the journey yourself today, over much the same roads they used, in twenty-five minutes or so by car. You will not find the scenery greatly changed, except that the roads now are of blacktop, and corn and soy beans have replaced wheat as major crops. The route runs from Tappers Corner, which faces the old Anthony place, to Cordova, once called Thimbletown, and on to the hamlet of Skipton. Near there it crosses the great slashing scar of U.S. Route 50 and veers through territory, still largely forested, that in those times was called "Lloyd's Long Woods." That was where Frederick's fearsome monsters doubtless lived.

Eventually, after the road swings westward toward Bruff's Island, you will find on your right two long, parallel lanes. The more westerly of these is for the gentry. It has a handsome ornamental gate, and runs for half a mile under magnificent trees to end in a graceful loop before a noble white Georgian mansion that looks almost exactly as it did when

Frederick first beheld it in 1824. This is Wye House, home since the 1780s of the Lloyds of Wye.[13]

The eastward lane is a service road, and it was the one into which Betsey and Frederick turned when they finally reached their destination in the sweltering heat of midafternoon. Then it was called the Long Green Lane; it ran through the heart of the working plantation, past a long, low "quarter" of rough brick that teemed with slaves, to end at the wharf on Lloyd's Cove. The Long Green, from which it took its name, was a grassy expanse of twenty acres or so.

Some of the buildings Frederick saw that day are gone; the slave quarters in particular have been removed as unsightly relics of the dead past. The ancient icehouse, carpenter's shop, blacksmith's shop, and other working structures that stood near the Long Green have been replaced by more modern barns and sheds, or have been remodeled out of recognition. But sufficient buildings remain to give the modern visitor a sense of how the great plantation must have appeared to the wondering eyes of a six-year-old boy. Off to the left he caught a glimpse of the stately white mansion, ringed with magnificent trees; then his grandmother led him to a neat house of red brick, plain but substantial, that faced the lane. That, she told him, was where "Old Master" lived; the separate kitchen beside it was the domain of his slaves.[14]

Almost at once Frederick was surrounded by more children than he had ever seen before, "children of all sizes and of many colors—black, brown, copper-colored, and nearly white . . . laughing and yelling around me and playing all sorts of wild tricks."

"Be a good boy and go play with them," Betsey said. "They are kin to you. There—that's your brother Perry, and your sisters, Sarah and Liza. They won't hurt you."

Frederick had heard of these three, but didn't remember ever seeing them. They were as strange as all the others, as strange and frightening as this whole place was to him. Reluctantly he joined them in the yard behind the house, but he refused to play. He stood with his back to the brick wall, looking on, like a wild young animal at bay.

His grandmother had disappeared into the kitchen to visit with Kate, the Anthony cook, whom she had known since childhood. Suddenly one of the children came running out, shouting, "Fed, Fed, grandmamma gone!"

"I could not believe it," he recalled. "And yet, fearing the worst, I ran into the kitchen, and lo! she was indeed gone, and was now far away."

The boy burst into tears, and for a long time refused to be consoled. When Perry, a big boy of ten, brought him ripe peaches and pears to comfort him, Frederick angrily threw them on the ground. He was as much indignant as grief-stricken; mingled with his sorrow was resentment that his grandmother, whom he loved and trusted above all others, could have left him without a good-by kiss or even a word.

That night he cried himself to sleep, a bitterly unhappy, betrayed child. At the age of six, he was alone in the world.

Chapter Four

The Colonel and the Slave Boy

The Lloyds of Wye

The Lloyds of Wye, whose fortunes were to be so intricately linked with those of Douglass in the next half-century, were the proudest and perhaps the richest family in Maryland. They formed a unique American dynasty. Today twelve generations of them lie buried in the family grave-yard on the site where Lloyds have lived since the 1660s. For more than two hundred years their affairs were ruled by a succession of Edward Lloyds, men of power in the colony and state of Maryland who lived like English lords on estates as large as dukedoms and owned so many slaves they could scarcely count them.

The first Edward Lloyd was a shrewd opportunist of Welsh ancestry who used religion, the dominant passion of his time, to establish the family fortune. He came into Maryland as one of the leaders of a Puritan band that had been driven out of Cavalier Virginia and to whom Lord Baltimore obligingly opened his colony's doors. Then Lord Baltimore signed the famous 1649 Act of Religious Toleration. The Puritans promptly showed their gratitude by overthrowing Lord Baltimore's pro-Catholic government and seizing the colony in the name of Oliver Cromwell. In the settlement that followed Edward Lloyd was one of the prime movers and winners. He received large grants of fertile land on Maryland's Eastern Shore as a reward for giving Lord Baltimore back his colony. Lloyd set up his family on the Wye East River in Talbot County and went home to England to enjoy his prosperity.

The second Edward Lloyd, a grandson, consolidated the family holdings, dabbled in the African slave trade, cultivated tobacco, and served for five years as de facto Maryland governor. The third inherited much more land plus ships, slaves, and an assortment of business enterprises from his half-uncle, Richard Bennett III, called "poor Dick o' Wye, the richest man in North America." The fourth helped run Maryland during the Revolution, acquired a library of one thousand books, and built Wye House, the present family seat. He was the one of whom it was said: "God Almighty never intended that any man should own a thousand niggers, but Colonel Lloyd has nine hundred and ninety nine."[1] By the time young Frederick came to live on the Lloyd plantation in 1824, the incumbent was Edward Lloyd the fifth, sometime Maryland governor and United States senator, and Edward the sixth was waiting in the wings.

Almost from the beginning, the Lloyds had built their wealth on advantageous marriages, hardheaded plantation management, and black labor. Henrietta Maria Lloyd, first of a succession of strong-minded women to rule the household, had a dozen children by two husbands, and so many well-born descendants that she has been labeled "the great ancestress of the Eastern Shore."[2] She was the forebear of the seemingly endless generations of Lloyds, Tilghmans, Goldsboroughs, Chamberlaines, and Hollydays who married their cousins in a tight ring-around-the-rosy of aristocratic inbreeding. By the time of the Revolution almost everybody in Maryland who mattered was related by birth or marriage to the Lloyds.

The family's slave empire grew more slowly; it required a century or more to mature. Philemon Lloyd, the only non-Edward to control the family estates until recent times, owned only 35 black slaves at his death in 1685; his son, Edward II, died in possession of only 30 in 1719.[3] Edward II had tried his hand at the newly developing African slave trade, but he had been warned that his brigantine was "no Extraordinary sailor" and might lose as much as half her cargo by death from disease before she could tack her way out of the Bight of Biafra, off the coast of modern Nigeria.[4] Edward III, besides his inheritance from Richard Bennett, gained additional slaves by natural increase. By the time of Edward IV, the numbers were becoming impressive; in 1790 he acknowledged owner-ship of 305 blacks in Talbot County alone, not counting those on his estates in Dorchester and Queen Anne's counties. Under Edward V the total soared past 550; and on the eve of the Civil War, Edward VI, who had moved many of his slaves to cotton plantations in the Deep South where ownership of them was more profitable, was said to possess more than 700 blacks in Maryland, Louisiana, Arkansas, and Mississippi.[5] It came as no surprise that he supported the Confederacy.

As slaveholders the Lloyds enjoyed three distinctions: they seldom sold slaves, preferring to keep them in the family; they never granted manumissions; and they were regarded by at least some of their contemporaries as harsh masters. They consistently employed overseers noted for severe discipline, even by Eastern Shore standards. Long before Frederick came on the scene—and long after he left—they were accused of being cruel owners who allotted their blacks the bare minimum of food, clothing, and shelter.

In 1794 these charges reached a climax when the Reverend John Bowie, an Episcopal clergyman and schoolmaster, accosted Edward Lloyd IV on an Easton street. Before numerous witnesses, Bowie denounced Lloyd as "a Tyrant in his Family, a cruel hard Task Master who neither feeds nor cloathes sufficiently his Black Family of People." The resulting furor had comic aspects. Lloyd thought he had been accused of mistreating his wife and children, and produced half a dozen witnesses to testify that he was "a kind and affectionate husband and father." Bowie insisted that he had used the word *family* only in the sense of *black family*, a euphemism for slaves then common on the Eastern Shore. But he stuck to his basic charge of cruelty.

Friends and employees who rose to Lloyd's defense did not deny that discipline was extremely severe on the Lloyd plantations. They said it was necessary in order to "bind his slaves to a sense of their duty," and blamed excesses, not on Colonel Lloyd, but on certain of his overseers. "He has discharged Overseers from his service good in every other respect but [who] could not be restrained from Inhumanity to the slaves," chief overseer Arthur Bryan testified. Richard Grason, who had been in charge during Lloyd's frequent journeys on Revolutionary War business, conceded that in the master's absence he had been "more severe than I would wish to have been," but defended himself by stating his belief that the slaves were being encouraged to revolt by the Eastern Shore's strong Tory faction—which incidentally included some of Colonel Lloyd's close relatives. Several Lloyd employees testified that in their opinion the slaves were not basically mistreated. "His People were well Cloathed and fed," Grason said. "... I thought Colo. Lloyd's Negroes was happy. ... When ever a Negroe was chastised for a fault the Matter was always enquired into, and the Person found guilty before he was punished."

Such "kangaroo courts," with the master and his overseers sitting as prosecutors, judges, and jury, formed the basic legal system that governed Maryland slaves. Nor was any attempt made to take testimony from the blacks themselves, since Colonel Lloyd was a "Christian white person" against whom no black or Indian could give evidence.

Reverend Bowie dismissed the affidavits gathered by Lloyd as mere "panegyrics" issued by "flatterers," but general opinion appeared to be that a master should not be blamed for the excesses of the overseers he hired. Although there was talk of a suit for slander, Lloyd eventually thought better of this, perhaps not wanting the situation on his plantations looked into too closely.[6]

Well into the nineteenth century the opinion persisted among whites that Lloyd slaves were more cruelly treated than other blacks on the Eastern Shore. Writing of Edward Lloyd VI after the Civil War, Samuel A. Harrison, Talbot County's historian, took note of this "current impression" and conceded that it undoubtedly had been in part justified. But he too blamed the cruelties on the "rude men" employed as overseers rather than on the master who hired them. Harrison wrote:

Slavery on his estate differed from the slavery that existed almost everywhere else in the county, in this, that it was plantation rather than domestic slavery. . . . Owing to the great extent of that estate and the great number of slaves upon it, it was necessary to divide them by placing gangs or groups made up mostly of families upon each farm. These gangs were under overseers, and lived in *quarters*, a kind of barracks, or where there were families in separate cabins. The greater portion of those thus situated seldom came in communication with their master or his family, indeed many of them were as unknown to him as he was to them. There was therefore small opportunity for him to become acquainted with their grievances or unusual wants, and an impression became current that these grievances were unredressed and those wants unsupplied. That much hardship was silently endured is probable and there may have been even instances of cruelty at the hands of the rude men over them, but not with the consent . . . of the master. For the maintenance of due discipline a rigid regimen was absolutely necessary, and often without doubt the rules which were proper and mild in themselves were enforced by the overseers in so harsh a manner as to give grounds for a belief that the burdens of slavery, never and nowhere lightly to be borne, on those portions of Col. Lloyd's estate which were not immediately and constantly under his eye, were rendered more heavy and galling than he wished them to be or than they were elsewhere in the county.[7]

The basic facts in Harrison's description will be familiar to any reader of Douglass. In essence he was confirming what the one-time slave boy had written in his controversial autobiographies: the Lloyd estate was so vast and isolated, the master so far removed from his slaves, and the discipline so harsh, that cruelties were common there that would not have been tolerated elsewhere in Maryland.[8]

Harrison expressed the opinion that the Lloyd slaves "were reasonably well housed, well clothed, well fed, not over worked, and cared for in sickness and in old age [but] enjoyed few luxuries." A different view was supplied by Emory Roberts, a Lloyd slave who ran away in June, 1855, and reached Philadelphia via the Underground Railroad. Roberts told the Vigilance Committee of the Pennsylvania Anti-Slavery Society this story: "As a slave, he had served Edward Lloyd. He gave his master the character of treating his slaves with great severity. The lash was freely used on women as well as men, old and young. In this kind of property Lloyd had invested to the extent of about five hundred head, so Emory thought. Food and clothing for this large number were dealt out very stintedly, and daily suffering was the common lot of slaves under Lloyd." [9]

Thus when Douglass wrote of conditions he had observed on the Lloyd estate, he was reporting nothing that was new or that was not already known to Talbot County whites as well as blacks. What gave his account its special sting was that he named names and recounted specific incidents, including an unpunished murder and beatings administered personally by Colonel Lloyd. He told the whole world of things Talbot Countians would rather have kept to themselves; that in itself was an unforgiveable sin.

The Colonel Lloyd whom Frederick knew—Edward V, known as "the Governor"—was probably the grandest and most ostentatious of them all. His lavish entertainment, both at his Wye estate and his Annapolis town house, was famous; in his obituary a Baltimore paper commented that he "was as remarkable for the munificence of his private hospitality as for his public spirit." [10] Whenever the family was in residence at Wye House, as many as two dozen guests at a time enjoyed his bounteous table, sipped his fine imported wines, nibbled at exotic fruits from his gigantic orangerie, strolled through his magnificent gardens, and savored the constant attention of his well-trained, handsomely dressed house servants.

In appearance he was the consummate southern gentleman: tall, handsome, well-fleshed, ruddy-faced, he had vivid blue eyes and prematurely white hair. He was, says Harrison, "eminently a man of the world . . . so dignified in bearing as to repel familiarity, but . . . without a trace of pomposity. . . . His voice, pitched in a low tone . . . was full and sonorous, and was sometimes, upon convivial occasions, attuned in song." He enjoyed the pleasures of the table as much as any of his guests, consuming large quantities of food and drink until the agonies of gout, a congenital affliction of the male Lloyds, forced him to give them up.

His family background, good looks, wealth, and ability as a public speaker all combined to make him a natural in the aristocracy-oriented Maryland politics of the day. He was three times chosen governor by his peers in the Maryland legislature, and twice sent to the United States

Governor Edward Lloyd V, the "Colonel Lloyd" of Frederick's boyhood

Senate, where he voted consistently with southern and proslavery interests. He also served in the United States House of Representatives and in both houses of the Maryland General Assembly.

But his political career was only an avocation; his real occupation was managing the affairs of his huge estate. This he keenly enjoyed. Each morning he would leave his guests to their own devices while he rode out on an inspection tour, conferring with the overseers who ran each of the thirteen farms, comprising nearly ten thousand acres, that clustered around the home plantation. Usually his chief lieutenant, Aaron Anthony, rode along.

By Edward V's time tobacco cultivation, on which the family fortune had been built, had almost entirely ceased; the last commercial crop, which turned out to be mostly trash, was recorded in the Lloyd account books in 1825.[11] Lloyd replaced it with wheat and became the greatest wheat farmer in Maryland and one of the largest producers in the United States at that time. His farms also turned out prodigious quantities of corn, sold off ten thousand pounds of pork a year (and produced, in addition, double that, kept for slave and family consumption). Hundreds

46

of spring lambs and large amounts of wool came annually from flocks of sheep totaling more than seven hundred.

The Lloyd stable of racing and saddle horses, built on imported English stock, was one of the finest in Maryland. Like his father, whose imported bay mare, Nancy Bywell, had been the most celebrated racer of her day, Edward V was a mainstay of the Annapolis Jockey Club. He also introduced English Durham cattle and Merino sheep to the Eastern Shore. He was so fond of cockfighting that in a published satire on the state's politicians he was lampooned as "Lord-Cock-de-doodle-do." He loved blood sports, especially waterfowl gunning and deer stalking. For a time he maintained a private deer park on the estate, but finally had to give this up because the deer were forever breaking through the fences and eating the wheat.

His outside business interests were also extensive. He co-owned a coal mine in western Maryland with John Paca, son of the signer of the Declaration of Independence; was a director and one of the largest stockholders of the Easton bank; owned the Easton Hotel, finest on the Shore; and had other investments.

Socially his standing was the highest in Maryland. His mother had been Elizabeth Tayloe, of the wealthy Tayloes of Mount Airy, Virginia; his wife was Sally Scott Murray, daughter of a prominent Annapolis physician; his brother-in-law was Francis Scott Key; his cousins were the Pacas, Bordleys, Tilghmans, Goldsboroughs, and other Maryland gentry; his close friends included all the political and social leaders of the state as well as such national figures as Virginia's John Randolph.

His children all married well, and Colonel Lloyd settled most of them in gracious mansions near his own. For Edward VI, whose wife was the former Alicia McBlair, he built Wye Heights Plantation, upriver from Wye House and even more ostentatious. For James Murray Lloyd he built the house now known as Presqu'ile, still a Talbot County showplace; for Sally, who married Commodore Charles Lowndes of the navy, he bought an eighteenth-century house on Miles River called The Anchorage; and for Ann Catherine, whose husband, Franklin Buchanan, was later a famous Confederate admiral, he purchased The Rest, which faced The Anchorage across the Miles.

One of his proudest possessions was the massive hoard of silver accumulated by the Lloyds over the centuries. Even though much had been lost when a gang of Chesapeake Bay pirates claiming to be British looted Wye House during the Revolution, Colonel Lloyd paid taxes on more than 110 pounds of plate in 1832.[12] Few in Maryland could match the richness and elegance of the display that greeted guests entering the dining room for midafternoon dinner: French crystal, the finest Irish linen, gleaming English silver, uniformed servants, tables laden with fish, fowl, mutton, beef, and a wide array of vegetables, fresh fruits from the orangerie, Eastern Shore cakes and pies.

The farming enterprise that supported all this luxury was organized on a strictly business basis. No army could have been more tightly structured; it was a system, unique on the Eastern Shore, that had been evolved over a century and a half to serve the special needs of the Lloyds.

At the top was Colonel Lloyd or, in his absence, his designated representative, Aaron Anthony. Headquarters was the central farm, where the mansion was located and the main business of the estate was conducted. This was a small city in itself, with its own blacksmith, carpenter, shoemaker, wheelwright, and other skilled workers; its own dock on Lloyd's Creek; a large windmill where grist was ground; a smokehouse; a milkhouse; an icehouse; and various storage sheds. In 1824, the year Frederick went to live there, its slave population was 181, including the 15 blacks owned by Aaron Anthony who lived there. [13]

At that time there were a dozen outlying farms (Lloyd bought up eight more before his death in 1834 for a total of twenty-one) totaling about nine thousand acres. Each was run by a hired overseer paid $120 to $135 a year and stocked, depending on size and productive acreage, with from eighteen to forty-seven slaves, including old people and young children. The overseers, those "rude men" so often accused of committing evil deeds behind their master's back, were judged by their employer strictly on the basis of their efficiency in cutting costs and increasing farm production, so they had every incentive to drive the slaves under them as hard as possible.

Basic food and clothing for the field blacks on all the farms was doled out monthly, with Anthony in personal charge of measuring out the supplies, which were kept on the central farm. According to Douglass, the food allowance per person consisted of eight pounds of pickled pork or the equivalent in fish, usually herring; a bushel of corn meal, and a pint of salt. He said the pork was often tainted, the fish of the poorest quality, and as much as 15 percent of the meal fit only for pigs. Whether this was an accurate accounting cannot now be checked, but the Lloyd slaves had other food sources that Douglass neglected to mention. For instance, Anthony's return book for 1824 shows that ninety-nine pigs had been given to the blacks to raise for themselves. They also had garden plots, kept chickens, and could help themselves to fish, oysters, crabs, and clams from the waters adjoining the Lloyd properties. The Lloyd slaves may not have been well fed, but Douglass undoubtedly exaggerated the skimpiness of their fare. [14]

Douglass, the only source of information now available, described the clothing allowance for adult males as: "Two tow-linen shirts—such linen as the coarsest crash towels are made of; one pair of trowsers of the same material, for summer, and a pair of trowsers and a jacket of woolen, most slazily put together, for winter; one pair of yarn stockings, and one pair of shoes of the coarsest description. The slave's entire apparel could not have cost more than eight dollars a year." [15] He said bed clothing for the adults was a single coarse blanket, while the little children got none. They were allotted only two tow linen shirts a year, and no shoes, stockings, or other garments. When these wore out they went naked; it was common, Douglass said, even in chilly March to see flocks of boys and girls "as destitute of clothing as any little heathen on the west coast of Africa." Again, no independent evidence has been found to check on the accuracy of this account.

Visitors to the Lloyd estate seldom, if ever, went to the outlying farms where the field hands lived and worked. They saw only the well-trained house slaves, about fifteen in number, who were handpicked for their intelligence, physical attractiveness, and good manners. These enjoyed a special status and responded with a fawning devotion to their master and his family, which many outsiders accepted as proof that Colonel Lloyd's slaves loved him and were happy. Harrison describes a "touching scene" when the colonel, aging and very ill, was carried down to the sloop to make his final journey to Baltimore in 1834: "His servants, standing on the banks of Wye, when he embarked bade him good-bye with sobs and groans more expressive than words, and watched with tearful eyes the receding vessel as it bore him away to return no more." The story is probably based on fact. Edward Lloyd V was a man who attracted respect and affection easily. Even Douglass, many years later, recalled him almost with veneration as "a gentleman of the olden time, elegant in his apparel, dignified in his deportment, a man of few words and of weighty presence. . . . No governor of the State of Maryland ever commanded a larger measure of respect." [16]

Perhaps the most favored of all the slaves was the coach driver, William Wilks. Slave gossip had it that he was Colonel Lloyd's son by a slave woman, Sally Wilks, who had been for many years a household servant. The story is doubtful—according to Lloyd records he was born when Edward V was only twelve years old—but Douglass said he looked every inch a Lloyd. "He was about as white as anybody on the plantation; and in manliness of form, and comeliness of features, he bore a striking resemblence to Mr. Murray Lloyd," one of the colonel's sons, who hated him intensely. [17]

Accounts preserved among the Lloyd papers give several specific instances of favored treatment accorded Wilks. Alone among all the slaves he had his boots and shoes made by the same shoemaker, William White, who fashioned shoes for Mrs. Lloyd and the children—and at the same price. His coats and pantaloons were made by Colonel Lloyd's own tailor, C. Eckhoff, at four times the cost of similar garments Eckhoff made for other house servants.

According to Douglass, however, his privileged status did not save him from corporal punishment—but after giving him a severe whipping at the insistence of Murray, "the heart-sickened colonel atoned to William for the abuse, by giving him a gold watch and chain." Later, Douglass said, Lloyd arranged to sell Wilks to Austin Woolfolk, the Baltimore slave trader. However, by some mysterious means Wilks produced enough money to buy his own freedom. According to the census of 1840, "W. Wilks, free colored," was living in Baltimore in that year.

An idea of the size of the Lloyd operation is shown by random statistics taken from the Lloyd papers: In January, 1824, according to Aaron Anthony's accounting, Lloyd owned 135 work horses (not counting the racers, hunters, and saddle and carriage horses in his private stable); 12 mules; 65 oxen; 573 beef and dairy cattle; 760 sheep; and 439 hogs. The hog population had been far higher; on butchering days in December, 1823, nearly 38,000 pounds of dressed pork had been realized. His 1823 harvest had produced 5,822 barrels of corn and 46 hogsheads of tobacco. Wheat production was not itemized, but 1,991½ bushels of wheat had been set aside for seeding alone.

As for Wye House itself, where the Lloyds lived and did their entertaining, it was unquestionably one of the most handsome houses in America, with the austere grace of the late Georgian period. It still is; Wye House has undergone remarkably little change in a century and a half. Its carriage facade has hardly changed at all, and it retains the magnificent gardens (though on a somewhat reduced scale) that the Scottish gardener, Mr. McDermott, maintained with the help of a black crew of four during Colonel Lloyd's time. The classic "ha-ha," a sunken brick wall, still sets off its inner grounds from the enclosure where until a few years ago prize sheep grazed just as they did in 1824. On the front facade, which faces the bowling green, an enclosed veranda has replaced the open porch lined with Grecian columns that excited Frederick's admiration. Inside, its stately rooms are filled with furniture gathered over the centuries by the Lloyds, and on the walls of the rooms hang ancestral portraits (though now copies; the originals have gone to museums) by Benjamin West and Charles Willson Peale.

Some of its outbuildings are gone, such as the twin "necessaries"—one for men and one for women. The orangerie, a handsome French Provincial

Wye House, the Lloyd mansion, is little changed today from the "Great House" Frederick knew in 1825.

structure eighty-five feet long, with a billiard room in its second story, no longer produces exotic fruits; they can be bought at the supermarket. But it is easy to imagine what Frederick saw: the Great House, overflowing with handsome men and laughing women in broadcloth and silks; the Long Green, a grassy thoroughfare dotted with shops and dwellings; the graveyard, a ghostly city of tombstones, where the Lloyd children played by day but which the superstitious blacks endowed with terrifying spectors by night; the gardens with their flowers of every hue; the meadows filled with sheep and cattle; the deer park; the fields of wheat, corn, tobacco, flax, and rye; and the hundreds of blacks whose strong backs and unpaid skills supported the Lloyds and their chosen guests in the luxury they accepted as their due.

There may have been Marylanders wealthier than Colonel Lloyd: for instance, old Charles Carroll of Carrollton, the last surviving signer of the

Declaration, with his railroad and his banks and his fifty thousand acres of land in Western Maryland. But none flaunted his riches more ostentatiously; none provided a more visible contrast between the opulence of his Great House and the poverty of the slave quarter only a few score yards away.

For a bright six-year-old ready for his first lessons in the realities of slavery, there could not have been a better school.

Frederick's Story

Frederick's first task was to sort out who were members of his own "family"—the Anthonys and the blacks belonging to them—and who were affiliated with the Lloyds. It wasn't easy, since all were strangers, but soon he had it straight. In the brick house lived "Old Master," Captain Anthony, along with his daughter, Lucretia, and Lucretia's husband, Captain Auld, who was often away on Colonel Lloyd's business. Sometimes Anthony's sons, Andrew and Richard, stayed there also. These people had only a business relationship with the Lloyds; they were never admitted to the Great House socially.

The Anthony kitchen, headquarters for the slaves, was presided over by a woman he had been told to call "Aunt Katy," although she was not his true aunt but only a distant cousin of his mother. Two of his real aunts, Milly and fourteen-year-old Hester, were her helpers.

Connected with the household, sleeping where they could, eating the slop Aunt Katy doled out to them, were even more children than Frederick had been used to at his grandmother's: Aunt Katy's brood, Jerry, Phil, Billy, and a nursing baby called Caroline; Frederick's brother and sisters, Perry, Sarah, and Eliza; and Aunt Milly's family, his first cousins Betty, Tom, Henny, and Nancy.

Katy had complete charge of the kitchen and of all the Anthony blacks. She was an industrious worker, but a bad-tempered woman who ruled the children like a drill sergeant with her quick blows and sharp tongue. For reasons he never understood—probably animosity toward his mother—she seemed to dislike Frederick particularly, and took special pleasure in mistreating him. Her favorite means of punishment was to withhold his food, which she then gave to her own children, so that he was often hungry. She also had a habit of giving him a sudden cuff on the head, accompanied by a vicious scolding, and she whipped him often for what seemed to him no reason at all. In fact, most of his personal sufferings during the year and a half he spent on the Lloyd estate stemmed not from any of the whites there but from Aunt Katy, herself a slave woman connected with the Bailey clan. Even Aaron Anthony, indifferent as he was to the welfare of the children, "did not sanction the meanness, injustice, partiality and oppressions enacted by Aunt Katy in the kitchen," and on occasion threatened to flog her if she did not improve her ways. [18]

However, at the time Frederick arrived, Anthony trusted Katy completely and left everything having to do with the slaves and the kitchen up to her. She even collected and distributed the food and clothing, just as Anthony did for the Lloyd field hands. In effect she served as Anthony's overseer, in much the same capacity as he served Colonel Lloyd, and she was just as cruel as any white overseer. In addition to the beatings she administered, Douglass recalled, she "was often guilty of starving myself and the other children, while she was literally cramming her own." Her method of serving the midday dinner, usually mush, reflected her cold attitude:

Our corn-meal mush, when sufficiently cooled, was placed in a large wooden tray, or trough. ... This tray was set down, either on the floor of the kitchen, or out of doors on the ground; and the children were called, like so many pigs; and like so many pigs they would come, and literally devour the mush—some with oyster shells, some with pieces of shingles, and none with spoons. He that eat [*sic*] fastest got most, and he that was strongest got the best place; and few left the trough really satisfied. [19]

Douglass cited this episode often—and with powerful shock effect—as an example of how he had suffered under slavery. He seldom bothered to add that it was not some cruel white overseer who made the children eat like pigs, but a black woman from his own family. Nor did he make clear that this was not the only daily meal the children received; by his own later testimony, they got the usual three meals a day: breakfast, noonday dinner, and a supper consisting of thick slabs of corn bread.

As the newest and one of the youngest children under Aunt Katy's charge, Frederick was usually the first to be elbowed out of the way at the feeding trough. During that first summer, before he learned the technique of fighting for his full share, he was sometimes so hungry that he contended with the dog, Old Nep, for crumbs that fell from the kitchen table or followed the serving girl when she took the Anthony family's tablecloth outside to shake it, so that he could snatch up the crusts, small bones, and other morsels intended for the cats. Broth in which meat had been boiled became a treat, and "the skin taken from rusty bacon, was a positive luxury." He soon learned to forage in the creek for clams, oysters, crabs, and fish, but even those were not an adequate diet without sufficient corn bread. From time to time other slaves, knowing of Katy's unfair treatment, would take him into their cabins, give him a full meal, and console him with words of a "better day comin'."

Aunt Katy distributed clothing and shelter with an equal lack of feeling. In common with the other small children, Frederick received no shoes, stockings, jacket, or trousers; his only garment, summer and winter, was a shirt made of coarse tow linen that reached his knees. He had two of these, and changed them weekly. His bed was the floor of a storage closet, shut off from the kitchen by a door of rough boards. In coldest weather he got a gunny sack used for carrying corn meal and crawled headfirst into it, leaving his feet exposed. This, plus the fact that he went barefoot at all times, made his feet so frostbitten that he sometimes suffered from wide, raw cracks between his toes.

Soon, however, he learned that, if he had an enemy in the kitchen, he had a friend in the parlor. Lucretia Anthony Auld, a gentle and pretty twenty-year-old bride, was captivated by his natural charm. From the first she evidently considered him a special child. He quickly discovered that if he stood outside her window and sang, she would smile out at him and, like as not, give him a piece of real bread and butter, a rare treat for a slave child. So he sang often and loudly, and just as often got his reward.

One day he came home bloody and howling after a fight with young Ike Copper, who had gashed his head severely with a heavy piece of cinder laced with iron from the blacksmith's forge. Aunt Katy merely snapped that it served him right for having anything to do with "dem Lloyd niggers"; but Miss Lucretia took him into the parlor, wiped away the blood, put balsam on the wound, and bound up his head. It was an act of kindness he would remember as long as he lived. [20]

Frederick made an equally good impression on the haughty Lloyds themselves. Out of some eighty black children on the central farm, and ahead of the scores of eligible boys who belonged to Colonel Lloyd, he was chosen to be the companion of twelve-year-old Daniel Lloyd, the colonel's youngest son. Considering all the circumstances, it is remarkable evidence that even at the age of six or seven Frederick was recognized by his white superiors as an altogether exceptional child.

The assignment was a mixed one, combining duties as servant with those of playmate. As it developed, the two became close friends. They played together, hunted birds and rabbits together—Daniel as the gunner, Frederick in the role of "picker-up"—and explored the vast estate together. They talked, as boys will, of many things on a free take-and-give basis. "Mas' Dan'l" divided his cakes and biscuits with Frederick, protected him from bullying by the older boys, informed him of doings in the Great

House. Frederick, a natural mimic, soon began to pick up ''white'' habits of speech from Daniel, just as Daniel fell into the slurred slang of the blacks. Later, when northerners expressed astonishment at his good diction, Douglass would reply that it stemmed from his boyhood association with Daniel Lloyd. [21]

Daniel loved to gossip about the comings and goings at the mansion. This was a fertile topic since, especially during the summer months, the Lloyd estate was as crowded as any hotel. Guests came and stayed for weeks; it was a saying around the county that Colonel Lloyd entertained more visitors at his house than Solomon Lowe, Easton's leading innkeeper, did at his.

On such occasions Frederick would station himself outside the kitchen door where he could sniff the rich fumes of baking, boiling, roasting, and broiling. He watched as the produce of Mr. McDermott's garden was carried in: asparagus, celery, cauliflower, egg plant, beets, lettuce, parsnips, peas, French beans, radishes, cantelopes, apples, and peaches from the orchards, grapes from the arbor, citrus fruits from the orangerie. From Chesapeake Bay and the Wye River came a vast array of seafood—rockfish, perch, drums, croakers, sea trout, oysters, crabs, clams, terrapins—and, in season, wild ducks, geese, and the great graceful swans brought down by gunners. From the poultry pens came chickens, ducks, geese, turkeys, guinea fowl, capons, pigeons; from the nearby fields, pheasants, bobwhite quail (called ''pa'tridges'' by Eastern Shoremen), rabbits, venison; from the colonel's imported herds and flocks, choice beef, veal, pork, mutton; from the smokehouses, great hickory-cured hams and bacon, so unlike the pickled fatback allotted the slaves; from the dairy, finest on the Shore, milk, cream, butter, home-cured cheeses. Daniel told him of more exotic delicacies: almonds, raisins, figs from Spain; wines and brandies from France and Madeira; teas from China, coffee from Java. Frederick had no idea where these places were or what the things Daniel spoke of tasted like; but the very thought of them filled him with an inexpressible longing for the unknown world outside the Eastern Shore.

His only share of all this was the fragrant smell of cooking and an occasional piece of cake or other bite of food that Daniel divided with him. The kitchen of the Great House, unlike that of the brick house, was out of bounds to a slave boy unless he was assigned there. But with Daniel as his mentor he could enter the Great House in his imagination, see the sideboards groaning with food, the gleaming silver, the damask tablecloths, the goblets of wine, the handsome portraits of Lloyd ancestors, the polished furniture, the well-dressed servants creating artificial breezes with fans and shooing flies from their relaxed and smiling masters and mistresses. It was an intoxicating prospect, and in the back of his mind the idea formed that someday, somehow, he would be there in reality as he was at that time in his imagination.

His contact with Daniel gave him an additional insight uncommon to a slave boy, for Frederick formed a clear realization of the contrast between such opulence and the daily life of the field hands whose labor made it possible. These he saw every day, although he no more shared their harsh existence than he did the luxuries of the Great House. Toward both, by virtue of his peculiar position, Frederick was an outside observer and an unusually keen one. His precocious mind absorbed impressions, facts, details, names, and events with amazing sharpness for a child his age. Later he would make use of them with great effectiveness.

As Frederick told it, the Lloyd field hands worked from sunrise to sunset, six days a week, and did their cooking, washing, mending, and other chores after the day's work was done. At dawn they were awakened by a blast from the overseer's horn; he stood at the door of the slave quarter as they filed out, ready to speed with a blow from his whip any who lagged behind. Then came the long walk to the fields—sometimes as far as two or three miles—and long hours of toil under the watchful eye of the overseer, who was mounted on horseback and armed with a cowskin or stout hickory stick.

Their principal food was an ashcake, baked the night before and carried along to the fields. This was prepared by mixing corn meal with water, making a paste so thick a spoon would stand in it, adding a little salt, wrapping the dough in oak leaves, and covering it with hot coals and ashes. The resulting loaf had a crust of ashes, giving it a gritty taste, but, Frederick noted, the blacks didn't seem to mind. They wolfed it down as though it were the finest white bread. Breakfast, eaten in the field, was a slab of ashcake washed down with water; dinner was the same, with a sliver of pickled pork or a couple of herrings. The noon meal was followed by a brief rest period during which some slept, some talked or sang, some performed personal chores such as repairing garments with needle and thread. Nursing mothers were usually given an hour or so off in mid-morning to go home and feed their infants, but sometimes, if the distance was great, were required to bring their babies with them and perch them in a fence corner for the day.

As a child, Frederick was puzzled by the field hands' constant singing. He could not understand how they could sound so happy when their lives were clearly so miserable. Not until years afterward did he come to realize that the songs, far from expressing joy, reflected an underlying emotion of ineffable pain and sorrow. Wild and incoherent, often improvised, they "told a tale which was then altogether beyond my feeble comprehension; they were tones, loud, long and deep, breathing the prayer and complaint of souls boiling over with the bitterest anguish. Every tone was a testimony against slavery, and a prayer to God for deliverance from chains.'' [22]

Food and clothing allowances for the outlying farms were distributed on the last two days of each month. A favored slave was given the honor of driving an ox team to the Great House farm to collect them, usually as a reward by his overseer for diligent labor. The trip was eagerly sought; it not only provided a two-day break in the monotony of field work, but also, at the Great House farm one could pick up the latest gossip, see old friends, perhaps buy a few trinkets the *Sally Lloyd*'s crew had brought back from Baltimore. So the chosen slave would make the woods ring with song as he rode along, perched on the wagon tongue behind his ox team; and he would make sure that, just in case somebody was listening, the words he improvised included a bit of praise for his owner. One song Douglass recalled went like this:

> I am going away to the great house farm,
> O yea! O yea! O yea!
> My old master is a good old master,
> O yea! O yea! O yea!

Sometimes, however, a black would forget himself and express his true feelings, usually with dire consequences. Frederick heard the story of how Colonel Lloyd, traveling alone on horseback, had met a slave walking along the road. Neither had ever seen the other before.

"Well, boy, whom do you belong to?" the colonel asked.
"To Colonel Lloyd."
"Does the colonel treat you well?"
"No, sir."
"Does he work you too hard?"
"Yes, sir."
"Doesn't he give you enough to eat?"
"Yes, sir, he gives me enough, such as it is."

Lloyd asked the slave's name and where he lived, and then rode on. Shortly afterward, according to the story, the slave was sold to a Georgia trader for having found fault with his master. Apocryphal though this tale may be, it illustrates two salient points: Colonel Lloyd's remoteness from his slaves, and the common opinion among his blacks as to how much good it would do to complain to him about their lot.

That Colonel Lloyd sold slaves to southern traders in punishment for alleged crimes is suggested by this story; the extent to which he carried out this practice is something of a puzzle. Douglass thought the practice was common: "Scarcely a month passed without the sale of one or more lots to the Georgia traders," he wrote. Harrison, on the other hand, said the Lloyds "rarely or never" sold blacks, and contended that many of their disciplinary problems arose because they refused to use this method of getting rid of problem blacks.

The truth appears to have been somewhere in between. Records examined by this writer have turned up the names of twelve slaves sold by Colonel Lloyd during the years 1825 to 1827, more than indicated by Harrison but fewer than suggested by Douglass's phrasing. Some of the sales were certainly for disciplinary reasons: a note in the Lloyd papers beside the name of Joseph Copper, for instance, reads: "Run [away] and sold." There may have been other sales not shown in extant records; slave sale records in Baltimore, where Lloyd may well have dealt directly with Austin Woolfolk or other traders, have been destroyed. [23]

As Frederick adjusted to his new life and found ways to scrounge for food to supplement Aunt Katy's spartan rations, he began to enjoy himself. His own duties were light: driving up the Anthony cows at night, picking up trash in the yard, shooing the chickens and ducks out of the garden, doing errands for Miss Lucretia. Except by Aunt Katy, he was not mistreated; in fact his white family, especially Aaron Anthony, for the most part ignored him completely. In company with Daniel, or with other black youngsters, he spent much time exploring the vast "slave city" with its fascinating array of artisans' shops and sheds. He visited the great windmill on Long Point, a mile or so northwestward, where Mr. Kinney, a genial old Englishman, delighted in showing off the workings of the big sails and how they turned the heavy stones that ground corn into meal. From its top he could see sailing craft of all types, some far larger than the *Sally Lloyd*, heading down the Miles River toward the place called Baltimore. He learned to swim and fish in Lloyd's Cove, where fat white perch could be caught with hook and line and delicious crabs, clams, and oysters could be taken by wading, digging, and raking. He took shivery pleasure in listening to the tales told by older blacks about the strange sights and sounds in the ancient Lloyd burying ground: how shrouded ghosts, riding on great black horses, had been seen to enter, and balls of fire to fly among the trees at midnight; and of how horrid groans could be heard there. The blacks said the specters were Lloyd ancestors, forbidden to enter heaven for their crimes on earth as slaveholders.

There was no school as such on the Lloyd estate. Most overseers with children sent them off somewhere for the few years deemed necessary to teach them reading, writing, and arithmetic; the younger Lloyds, Daniel among them, had a private tutor who lived with the family. This was a New Englander named Joel Page, "a tall, gaunt sapling of a man, remarkably dignified, thoughtful, and reticent, and who did not speak a dozen words to a slave in a whole year." Mr. Page spent much of his time pacing silently up and down the garden walks, and seldom spoke even to his fellow whites. Frederick was deeply impressed; half a century later, seeing his tombstone in the Lloyd graveyard, Douglass would vividly recall watching him and wondering what on earth he could be thinking about. [24]

Frederick's own schooling, such as it was, took place under the wrathful gaze of "Uncle" Isaac Copper, an irascible old cripple who had once been in charge of breeding fighting cocks for Colonel Lloyd, and who had been a liveried house servant in the days of the colonel's flamboyant father. Isaac was the head of the Copper clan, the largest family grouping among the Lloyd slaves and the one that would, after freedom, perpetuate its name in a substantial black community. [25] Now nearly sixty years old and "past labor," he had been relegated to the job of presiding over the spiritual and medical needs of the young blacks on the Lloyd plantation. Soon after Frederick's arrival, he was sent, along with a troop of other boys, to take his first lesson at what might be called "Doctor Copper's School of Prayin' and Floggin'."

It was a salutary if not exactly inspiring performance. In his role of "doctor," Frederick quickly discovered, Copper had four standard remedies: "For diseases of the body, Epsom salts and castor oil, for diseases of the soul, the Lord's Prayer and hickory switches."

I found the old gentleman seated on a huge three-legged oaken stool, armed with several large hickory switches; and, from his position, he could reach—lame as he was—any boy in the room. . . . The old gentleman, in any other than a devotional tone, commanded us to kneel down. This done, he commenced telling us to say everything he said. "Our Father"—this we repeated after him with promptness and uniformity; "Who art in heaven"—was less promptly and uniformly repeated; and the old gentleman paused in the prayer, to give us a short lecture upon the consequences of inattention, both immediate and future, and especially those more immediate. . . . On he proceeded with the prayer, and we with our thick tongues and unskilled ears, followed him to the best of our ability. This, however, was not sufficient to please the old gentleman. . . . "Say everything I say;" and bang would come the switch on some poor boy's undevotional head. "What you looking at there"—"Stop that pushing"—and down again would come the lash. [26]

After a time or two, Frederick began to find that he had something urgent to do elsewhere when it came time to attend a session of Doctor

Copper's school. Nobody seemed to notice his truancy, and thus ended Frederick's first group educational experience.

Isaac Copper's fondness for the hickory switch led Frederick to make the trenchant observation that in a society which lives by the lash, its use becomes a universal passion. "Everybody, in the South, wants the privilege of whipping somebody else," he wrote in 1855. ". . . The whip is all in all. . . . Slaves, as well as slaveholders, use it with an unsparing hand." [27]

Nor was that the only similarity he noted between the white culture at the Great House and the black subculture that coexisted with it. In both cases caste distinctions were rigidly observed. Among the whites, the Lloyds and their well-bred guests did not associate with the Anthonys; the Anthonys did not associate with the overseers; and the overseers, with nobody else to look down on, bolstered their egos by lording it over the slaves.

Among the blacks, caste lines were just as firm. The house servants, carefully selected for comeliness of form and feature, were the "black aristocracy. . . . They resembled the field hands in nothing, except in color, and . . . the distance between these favored few, and the sorrow and hunger-smitten multitudes of the quarter and the field . . . is seldom passed over." Just as whites fancied such honorary titles as "captain," "colonel," "master," and "mistress," so older blacks, especially those in skilled positions, insisted that the younger ones call them "uncle" and "aunt" as a token of respect. "Uncle Tony" was the blacksmith, "Uncle Harry" the cartwright, "Uncle Abel" the shoemaker, and so on. Every cook was "Aunt Katy" or "Aunt Liza." Later these titles were adopted by whites with faintly derisive connotations, but according to Douglass their origin was in strictly observed black African traditions. "There is no better material in the world for making a gentleman, than is furnished in the African," he wrote. "He shows to others, and exacts for himself, all the tokens of respect which he is compelled to manifest toward his master. A young slave must approach the company of the older with hat in hand, and woe betide him, if he fails to acknowledge a favor."

In carrying out the caste system, slaves on the central plantation looked down on those from outlying farms. And even the most miserable Lloyd field hands held themselves superior to those belonging to such neighbors as Jacob Gibson, simply because their master, Colonel Lloyd, was richer than Gibson. "To be a slave was thought to be bad enough," Douglass wrote, "but to be a poor man's slave, was deemed a disgrace, indeed." [28]

As for Frederick's own family, proud members of the Bailey clan, they looked down on all the Lloyd slaves as members of the lower classes. Aunt Katy warned Frederick to keep away from the "Lloyd niggers," a term used just as derisively among upper-caste blacks as among whites. The

Lloyd slaves were not "old settlers" like Frederick's grandparents; among them were slaves who had been brought from Africa and others whose parents had been born there, the first such people Frederick had ever encountered. The common speech on the plantation was a strange dialect that Frederick found almost impossible to understand, a mixture of Guinea, slurred English, and a patois indigenous to the inbred Lloyd blacks. The singular possessive was never used, nor was the letter "r" pronounced. Frederick became "Cap'n Ant'ney Fed," his brother Perry "Cap'n Ant'ney Pey," and so on. "Oo dem got any peachy?" meant "Have you got any peaches?" "Oo you dem long to?" was "Who do you belong to?" Even those Lloyd slaves who, like the Baileys, were descendants of slaves who had been on the Eastern Shore for a century had fallen into these speech habits from constant association with those with recent African ties. To Frederick it was another world, and one of which he was never really a part. In his eighteen months on the Lloyd plantation he made no lasting friends among the Lloyd blacks; his playmates were his Anthony-owned cousins, Phil, Tom, Steve, Jerry, Nancy, and Betty, and Daniel Lloyd.

He especially admired Cousin Tom, Milly's son, who was four years older and served as cabin boy aboard the *Sally Lloyd*. Tom had been to Baltimore; he brought home a toy trumpet he had bought there and let Frederick toot on it. In his stuttering voice he told of the wonders he had seen and heard in the great city: shooting crackers that exploded with a bang; marching soldiers; a steamboat; church bells ringing; ships from foreign ports that could hold four of the *Sally Lloyd*; the great markethouse where wares from all over the world were bought and sold; shop windows crammed with goods; buildings that made even the Lloyd's Great House look tiny. Frederick listened shyly, not sure Tom wasn't making it all up; but his imagination was fired by the notion that, just maybe, such an exciting place existed. [29]

Captain Thomas Auld, master of the *Sally Lloyd* and Miss Lucretia's husband, was a puzzling individual. In his thin-lipped way, he seemed almost as aloof as Mr. Page, the gaunt Massachusetts schoolmaster. Auld was often away on trips to Baltimore, Annapolis, and Washington, and when he was at home he ignored the blacks as though they did not exist. Frederick developed a warm affection for Lucretia, but no corresponding feeling for her husband. To him Captain Auld, then and later, was an outsider.

It is perhaps a pity that the two did not learn to understand each other better during Frederick's early childhood. Through circumstances that neither of them could then imagine, their lives would be intimately intertwined. Captain Auld would be forced to make decisions profoundly affecting Frederick's destiny, and Frederick in turn would make the name of Thomas Auld an object of scorn throughout the world. If they had loved and trusted each other from the beginning, much of this could have been avoided—but by the same token, the man the world knows as Frederick Douglass might never have existed.

One of Thomas Auld's failings, as Douglass would note later, was that he had no experience with slaves and slavery. Although his family had been in Talbot County almost as long as the Lloyds, he was not a product of the slaveholding planter class. His training had been in shipbuilding and seamanship, which employed free labor, rather than in agriculture, where slaveholding was concentrated. His father, Lieutenant Colonel Hugh Auld, Sr., had owned a few slaves, but he had freed them all in 1809, when Thomas was still a boy. Incidentally, the senior Auld was not one of those "courtesy colonels" like so many others; he had earned his title against the British, as second in command to Brigadier General Perry Benson at the Battle of St. Michaels in 1813.

Thomas was born in 1795, the oldest boy of the thirteen children of Hugh and Zipporah Auld, and he grew up at the family seat called Wade's Point, a smallish estate on the Bay Shore west of St. Michaels. He trained in shipbuilding at St. Michaels, then a center of the art, and learned his skills at the hands of some of America's most capable masters of the craft of designing and building swift sailing vessels.

When Colonel Lloyd, in 1819, decided to replace the aging schooner, *Elizabeth & Ann*, with a new sloop to be called the *Sally Lloyd*, in honor of his daughter, he hired Thomas Auld to supervise all details of her construction at Joseph Kemp's St. Michaels shipyard. It was a big assignment for the twenty-four-year-old Auld; the *Sally Lloyd*, a luxury vessel like her predecessor, cost a total of $5,608.78, including imported china, hardwood cabinets, a buttery, rigging, and so on. That was ten times as much as the cost of an ordinary sloop. [30]

The *Sally Lloyd* was completed in 1820, and Thomas Auld stayed on as her first master at a salary of twenty dollars per month, plus room and board. Whenever he was on the Lloyd estate between sailings he boarded at Captain Anthony's house. There romance bloomed, and on January 16, 1823, he and Lucretia Anthony were married. He was still boarding there when Frederick arrived in the summer of 1824, but was less a member of the household than a paying guest at the expense of Colonel Lloyd.

Frederick had only sketchy recollections of his mother. As an adult he could recall seeing her only four or five times in his life, and even these visits were at night and of short duration. When he went to live at the Lloyd plantation she was still working as a field hand on Holme Hill Farm.

62

On rare occasions she would come to pay her children a visit, usually walking the entire twelve miles after a day of labor. The fact that she was able to come at all was something of a miracle, an indication, as Douglass fondly pointed out, that "a true mother's heart was hers."

The visit he remembered most poignantly was, as events turned out, the last one she ever made. It may have been in honor of his seventh birthday; circumstances hint that it occurred on or about St. Valentine's Day in February, 1825. Frederick had managed to offend Aunt Katy in some fashion, no very difficult task, and she, with a fierce scowl, told him she "meant to starve the life out of me." There would be no more food for him that day. Frederick had already had his usual breakfast, and managed to get past dinner time at noon without too much difficulty. But by sundown he was ravenous, and when he saw her cutting large slices of bread for the other children's supper, with none for him, it was too much. He went outside and wept, then came back into the kitchen and sat brooding by the fire.

Eventually Frederick spotted an ear of corn sitting on an upper kitchen shelf; when Katy was busy elsewhere, he quickly climbed up and fetched it down. He shelled off some grains, put them into the ashes to roast, and hastily shoved the partly denuded cob back onto the shelf with its telltale bare section turned to the rear. Parched corn was not exactly his favorite food, but it was something; he had just pulled the roasted kernels from the ashes and was starting to munch on them, when who should walk in but his mother.

Frederick rushed sobbing into her arms and poured out his story of the long miserable day and of Aunt Katy's threat to starve him. The jealousy between the two women flared into flame as Harriet Bailey turned to face the tormentor of her child.

I shall never forget the indescribable expression of her countenance. . . . There was pity in her glance at me, and a fiery indignation at Aunt Katy at the same time; and while she took the corn from me, and gave me a large ginger cake, in its stead, she read Aunt Katy a lecture which she never forgot. My mother threatened her with complaining to old master in my behalf; for the latter, though harsh and cruel himself at times, did not sanction the meanness, injustice, partiality and oppressions enacted by Aunt Katy in the kitchen. That night I learned the fact, that I was not only a child, but *somebody's* child. [31]

Afterward he remembered that the cake she had given him was in the shape of a heart, and that she had called him her "Valentine" as she hugged him to her breast. So he surmised that the occasion might have been St. Valentine's Day—when else would the Anthonys be having heart-shaped cakes?—and that his mother might have called him "Valentine'' because his birthday was on February 14. Of such straws did the mature Douglass try to reconstruct the basic data of his youth.

Fed and contented, "prouder, on my mother's knee, than a king upon his throne," Frederick dropped off to sleep; but when he awoke next morning she was gone as mysteriously as she had come. He never saw her again.

Sometime later that year, or early in 1826, Harriet Bailey died on the Tuckahoe Creek farm where she had spent most of her life. Like all the others, black and white, connected with that farm, she was buried in an unmarked grave. Frederick learned only a little about her life and death: that she had suffered a "long illness"; that she could read, "the *only* one of all the slaves and colored people in Tuckahoe who enjoyed that advantage"; and that she had died without telling him, or presumably anyone else, who his father was.

Another event that affected Frederick deeply—and in fact helped change the course of his life—occurred a few months after his mother's last visit. His Aunt Jenny and Uncle Noah—his mother's sister and Aunt Katy's brother—ran away and reached freedom in the North.

Flight to the North in the 1820s was an even riskier business than later, when the Underground Railroad was fully organized and escaping slaves could be moved from "station" to "station" along a well-established course. Nevertheless, under pressure of suddenly increased sales of Maryland slaves to the Deep South, hundreds of Eastern Shore blacks tried it, and many were successful. They fled at the risk of their lives; under Maryland statutes any lawful pursuer could shoot dead a slave caught trying to escape. But the alternative of being "sold down to Georgia" to die hundreds of miles from home and loved ones on a cotton plantation was considered even worse. Every issue of local newspapers carried advertisements offering liberal rewards for the recapture of runaways; two of those so advertised, in the late summer of 1825, were Frederick's aunt and uncle.

Jenny and Noah were a settled couple, both twenty-six years old, with two small children, Mary, seven, and Isaac, six, named for his grandfather, Isaac Bailey. They represented the two separate family strains among the Anthony slaves: Jenny, as noted earlier, was Harriet Bailey's younger sister, a daughter of old Betsey and granddaughter of the original Jenny of 1746, while Noah was a grandson of Emblem and Phil. They lived and worked on Aaron Anthony's Tuckahoe Creek property.

What triggered their flight is unknown. Possibly they had learned that Anthony was planning to sell them to southern traders. At any rate, on Saturday evening, August 27, 1825, Jenny and Noah slipped away from the Tuckahoe farm and were seen no more. They left their children behind, undoubtedly from necessity.

When the news reached the Lloyd plantation, Douglass reported, "a great noise was made about it. Old master was furious. He said he would follow them and catch them and bring them back, but he never did." Instead Anthony scribbled off an advertisement that appeared in the September 6 issue of the weekly *Republican Star* (see illustration). The statement that he had "intended to give them their freedom" was, on the face of it, a self-serving lie. Aaron Anthony never freed a slave in his life, and there is no reason to suppose that he was planning to make an exception of these two.

On the contrary, his next act hints that his intention had been to sell them, not free them. On September 7, the day after the ad appeared, four Anthony slaves, including the couple's two little children, were sold to a firm of Alabama slave traders, Lynch & Robinson. The older two were also close relatives of Frederick—his nineteen-year-old Aunt Maryann, and his first cousin Betsey, a fourteen-year-old daughter of Milly. [32]

Whether Anthony had intended to include Jenny and Noah in this sale, or whether their children were added at the last moment in reprisal, cannot now be determined. In either case, he got quick revenge for the blow to his pride and pocketbook by condemning a six-year-old boy and seven-year-old girl to Alabama slavery for a "crime" committed by their parents.

Gradually the hubbub over the escape died down. Anthony continued to offer his $150 reward in the *Star* for five more months, but he did not carry out his threat to chase after the fugitives in person. Finally word filtered back through the grapevine that Jenny and Noah "had gone to the free states and were free."

This was indeed a revelation. Until the furor over the escape of his relatives, Frederick had not even realized there were free states. He had only known that he hated being a slave, and could not understand why some black people, like Grandpa Isaac, were free, while others, like Grandma and himself, were slaves for life.

Now a new element was added: A slave who went north was no longer a slave. Very well; some day he too would go north, and become free. "The success of Aunt Jennie and Uncle Noah in getting away from slavery was, I think, the first fact that made me seriously think of escape for myself," he wrote later. ". . . Young as I was, I was already, in spirit and purpose, a fugitive from slavery." [33]

He had good reason to loathe slavery. Even at that age Frederick was a sensitive and intelligent observer, precocious far beyond his years, and the

$150 REWARD.

RANAWAY from the Subscriber, living in Talbot county, Maryland, on Saturday the twenty-seventh instant, negro man Noah, 26 years old, about 5 feet 10 or 11 inches high, stout and black, has very full ill shaped feet and is clumsy in his walk : negro Jenny, 26 years old, of a chesnut colour, middling size, and a well shaped woman. These negroes I raised myself; and intended to give them their freedom.

I will give one hundred dollars for the man and fifty for the woman if delivered to me, or so secured that I shall get them.

sep 6   w   AARON ANTHONY.

Advertisement posted by Aaron Anthony after Frederick's Aunt Jenny and Uncle Noah escaped north in 1825

evidence of evil was all around him. Although he personally suffered little or no ill treatment, he saw clearly what living in a whip-dominated world did to the human spirit. Without doubt his own noninvolvement only served to heighten his awareness. It was precisely because he was a privileged child rather than an abused one, because he was spared slavery's burdens rather than being crushed by them, that he remained sensitive to the damning effect of abuse on others.

If Frederick had been less intelligent, the events he witnessed during his eighteen months on the Lloyd plantation might have slipped by unnoticed; if he had personally been more brutalized by slavery, he might have taken hunger, hard labor, and daily beatings for granted. But he was neither stupid nor mistreated; he was an outside observer, and what he saw filled him with a rage against man's inhumanity to man that would not die until he did.

❧ Chapter Five ❧

Rule by Terror

Cowskin and Gun

In the little storage closet off the kitchen, the boy slept fitfully. He was comfortable enough; he needed no cover on this warm spring night, and he was used to the feel of the dirt floor beneath him. But there were noises in the kitchen that disturbed him. Voices, one raised in anger, the other beseeching. Then muffled thumpings. A whimpering cry. And suddenly, ringing out in the night, a high-pitched shriek of pure agony that brought him fully awake.

He crawled to the door and peeked out through a wide crack between the rough boards. A candle burned on the kitchen table, and by its light he could make out two figures. His Aunt Hester stood on a low bench, her arms stretched above her, her wrists tied by a twisted rope to the big iron staple by which hams were sometimes hung from a ceiling beam. She was naked to the waist, and blood trickled from a thin red welt between her shoulder blades.

Old Master stood behind her, his back to Frederick. In one hand was the implement called a cowskin that the boy, without really understanding its purpose, had often seen him carrying. It was a heavy, three-foot long sticklike object, and was made of strips of dried oxhide bound together, tapering to a point. It was painted a ghastly blue. As Old Master raised it, the tip quivered; it was as springy as a hickory stick. With a shock of horror, the boy realized its exact function.

Then Old Master brought it down as hard as he could across the girl's naked back. More blood dripped from a fresh gash in Hester's skin. She screamed and cried out a promise to do it no more. Old Master wiped blood off the cowskin with his free hand. He struck her a third time, choosing a fresh spot so as to form a new cut in her exposed skin. He continued to hit her, again and again. His face grew almost purple as he shouted at her, emphasizing each word with a blow. As the bloody welts crisscrossed her back, her voice rose from a scream to a thin, high wail that was piercing, almost inhuman.

Finally Old Master slumped, exhausted. With a weary gesture he lowered his arm, put the bloodstained cowskin on the table, wiped sweat from his forehead, and walked over to untie the rope that held her.

In the closet, the boy scarcely dared breathe. His whole body was trembling as he watched Old Master lead Hester out the door. He could not comprehend what had happened, what Hester had done, why Old Master had beaten her so savagely; but he was terrified that he might be the next target. What if Old Master suddenly remembered that this was where Frederick slept, and came back in and grabbed him? For what seemed hours he watched the door intently; but it did not open, and at last he fell asleep.

Such was the story Douglass wrote in his autobiographies and recited in detail before countless horrified audiences. As he explained the background, Hester, a fifteen-year-old girl of unusual beauty, had gone out with a boy her own age, Colonel Lloyd's Ned Roberts, after Aaron Anthony had forbidden her to do so. Frederick had watched in horror as some strange passion turned his master in an instant from a kindly old man into a monster. The sexual connotations were obvious, and Douglass did not ignore them. For Victorian audiences, he did not have to go into detail; they understood what he meant when he said Anthony's "motives were . . . abhorrent." The point Douglass drove across was that it was the absolute power conferred by slavery to one human being over another that was the root cause of the evil. Aaron Anthony, he wrote, "was not by nature worse than other men. . . . The slaveholder, as well as the slave, is the victim of the slave system."[1]

The tale of Hester's beating was not, and is not, one to be held at arm's length and examined critically. It either happened or it did not. Douglass said that he was an eyewitness, and most of his biographers, as well as his readers, have taken him at his word. Others, especially Eastern Shore whites, continue to believe that he invented it, or extrapolated the incident from something he had heard. All that can be said on the basis of external evidence is that Douglass did have an aunt named Hester, that Colonel Lloyd owned a slave named Ned Roberts, and that both were fifteen years old in 1825, when the incident allegedly occurred.[2]

The same is true of numerous other episodes that Douglass said he witnessed. For purposes of this account, they will be recited just about as Douglass told them; this writer sees no reason to believe he was not telling the truth, at least as he recalled it. But readers who choose to think they are exaggerations or outright lies, that such things could not have occurred on the estate of the wealthy and cultured Edward Lloyd, suave Southern gentleman and three times governor of Maryland, are welcome to their opinion.

According to Douglass, Colonel Lloyd himself on occasion administered beatings. At the insistence of his son Murray, he whipped William Wilks, a nearly white slave said to be his blood relative, but then gave him a gold watch and chain by way of recompense. And the lashing of "Old Barney," as Douglass related it, could scarcely be blamed on the excesses of some "rude overseer."

"Old Barney" was Barnett Sampson, fifty-five years of age, a dignified and portly man of moderately brown color, gentle in manner, who had charge of the colonel's private stable of English-bred carriage and riding horses. His son, "Young Barney" (Barnett Bentley), was his assistant. Old Barney took his job seriously; he was rated an excellent horse doctor as well as a skilled groom and horseshoer. But Colonel Lloyd was a perfectionist about his horses; he could see faults where none existed— flecks of dust, a twist in the reins, an improperly combed foretop. If he was quick to reward Barney for saving the life of a sick horse, he was just as quick to punish him for a fault, real or imagined. Douglass said he was present on one of these occasions:

One of the most heart-saddening and humiliating scenes I ever witnessed, was the whipping of Old Barney, by Col. Lloyd himself. Here were two men, both advanced in years; there were the silvery locks of Col. L., and there was the bald and toil-worn brow of Old Barney; master and slave; superior and inferior here, but *equals* at the bar of God; and, in the common course of events, they must both meet in another world. . . . "Uncover your head!" said the imperious master; he was obeyed. "Take off your jacket, you old rascal!" and off came Barney's jacket. "Down on your knees!" down knelt the old man, his shoulders bare, his bald head glistening in the sun, and his aged knees on the cold, damp ground. In this humble and debasing attitude, the master—that master to whom he had given the best years and the best strength of his life—came forward, and laid on thirty lashes, with his horse whip. The old man bore it patiently, to the last, answering each blow with a slight shrug of the shoulders, and a groan. I cannot think that Col. Lloyd succeeded in marring the flesh of Old Barney very seriously, for the whip was a light, riding whip; but the spectacle of an aged man—a husband and a father—humbly kneeling before a worm of the dust, surprised and shocked me at the time; and since I have grown old enough to think on the wickedness of slavery, few facts have been of more value to me than this, to which I was a witness. It reveals slavery in its true color, and in its maturity of repulsive hatefulness.[3]

Frederick said he also saw whippings administered personally by Lloyd's grown sons, Edward (VI) and Murray; by his sons-in-law Edward Winder and Charles Lowndes and by his nephew Joseph Nicholson. These, he reported, "enjoyed the luxury of whipping the servants when they pleased. ... I have seen Winder make one of the house servants stand off from him a suitable distance to be touched with the end of his whip, and at every stroke raise great ridges upon his back."[4]

William Sevier (pronounced, with some justice, *severe*) was Colonel Lloyd's overseer for the central farm. Under Aaron Anthony's general supervision, he had charge of the one hundred and sixty five or so blacks who were quartered there. He lived in a little red-painted frame house on the east side of the Long Green. Frederick found him remarkable, not only for his ugliness, but for his skill at cursing. "Nature, or his cruel habits, had given his face an expression of unusual savageness, even for a slave driver. ... Tobacco and rage had worn his teeth short, and nearly every sentence that escaped their compressed grating, was commenced or concluded with some outburst of profanity. ... It was enough to chill the blood, and to stiffen the hair of an ordinary man."[5]

One day, Douglass related, his attention was attracted by the sound of curses and screams. When he rushed to the scene, he saw Sevier struggling with a slave woman named Nelly, whom he was attempting to whip.

Nelly, whose full name was Nelly Kellem, had been accused of "impudence"—talking back, or shrugging her shoulders disdainfully, or giving Sevier a scornful look, or indicating by the tone of her voice what she thought of him, or any of a dozen other actions defined as impudence when performed by a slave. She was a proud and spirited woman who put on airs even with the other slaves, a "bright mulatto" who was the wife of Harry, a favored deckhand aboard the *Sally Lloyd*. Frederick thought her about as likely as anyone on the place to be genuinely guilty of impudence.

She was also almost as big and strong as Sevier was. When Frederick arrived, the overseer was trying to drag her to a tree so that he could tie her up and give her a proper whipping. Nelly was fighting back vigorously, and her three children were pelting Sevier with stones and yelling, "Let my mammy go! Let my mammy go!" One of the youngsters rushed up and bit him on the leg, but Sevier paid no attention. He had his hands full with Nelly, who was repeatedly raking his face with her fingernails and matching his profanity curse for curse.

Eventually Sevier succeeded in overpowering Nelly and lashing her to the tree. He proceeded to give her such a whipping that her back was covered with blood and red stripes laced her shoulders. Through it all she was not subdued; she never ceased to shout back at him, calling him every vile name her imagination could muster.[6]

After that, Sevier let Nelly strictly alone. Nor did he seek to have her publicly punished for her defiance; it would never do to let it be known he had almost been bested by a woman. But the slaves all knew it, and they hated him even more for his cowardice than for his cruelty. He died shortly afterward; according to slave gossip, even on his deathbed "he was uttering horrid oaths, and flourishing the cowskin, as though he was tearing the flesh off some helpless slave."

Brutal attacks on women, Douglass said, were not confined to the Lloyd overseers. He told of an occasion when his cousin Betsey, daughter of Milly, was so savagely beaten and "abused" by a drunken overseer named Plummer who managed one of Anthony's Tuckahoe farms that she fled twelve miles on foot to seek the protection of "Old Master." She arrived in a pitiable state—barefoot, bareheaded, her neck and shoulders a mass of angry wales, her face covered with blood caused by a blow from a club. Frederick looked on, a small boy to whom nobody paid any attention, as Betsey poured out her tale of woe and implored Anthony not to send her back to the vicious Plummer.

Frederick expected to see the old man "boil over with rage at the revolting deed, and to hear him fill the air with curses upon the brutal Plummer." But instead of sympathizing with her, Anthony sternly told her she deserved every bit of it and that if she did not go home at once, he would take the rest of the hide off her neck and shoulders with his own cowskin.

Not until much later did Frederick understand Anthony's heartlessness. It was not, he finally concluded, that Anthony was "dead to all sense of humanity," but that he had to uphold the system. If the master did not support his overseer against a complaining slave, no matter what the circumstances, the whole structure would collapse. The overseer would have no authority, and absentee slave ownership would be unworkable. Anthony may have warned Plummer privately to go easier in the future, but the slaves were not to know about it.

In Betsey's case, there was a tragic aftermath. By daring to complain, she had branded herself as a troublemaker; a few months later, at the age of fourteen, she was sold to a firm of Alabama slave dealers.[7]

All these were events that Douglass said he witnessed. Perhaps his

71

most famous case history, however, is of an episode he could not have seen, since the incident he related must have occurred before he went to live on the Lloyd estate. This is the alleged unpunished murder of a slave named Bill Denby or Demby (Douglass spelled the name both ways) by his overseer, Orson Gore.

As Douglass told the story, Gore had started to give Denby a whipping for some unknown offense when the powerful young slave broke away and plunged into a nearby creek, covering himself up to his neck in water. Douglass continued:

It is said that Gore gave Denby three calls, telling him that if he did not obey the last call he would shoot him. When the third call was given, Denby stood his ground firmly; and this raised the question, in the minds of the by-standing slaves—"will he dare to shoot?" Mr. Gore, without further parley, and without making any further effort to induce Denby to come out of the water, raised his gun deliberately to his face, took deadly aim at his standing victim, and, in an instant, poor Denby was numbered with the dead. His mangled body sank out of sight, and only his warm, red blood marked the place where he had stood.[8]

This coldblooded shooting, Douglass said, horrified everyone on the estate, including even Colonel Lloyd and Aaron Anthony. They called in Gore to account for his action. The overseer coolly replied that it had been a necessary killing, that Denby had become unmanageable, and had set a dangerous example for the other slaves. If he had not been shot after being duly warned, Douglass quoted Gore as saying, the other blacks on the estate would soon rise up and "take the place."

The explanation was said to have satisfied Lloyd, if not Anthony; nagging fear of a black revolt had haunted Eastern Shore whites since early in the eighteenth century. Gore not only went unpunished, Douglass claimed, he was continued as an overseer and even promoted. No official investigation was ever made; Colonel Lloyd's word that the killing was "necessary" was good enough for the authorities. "I speak advisedly when I say this," Douglass wrote, "that killing a slave, or any colored person, in Talbot County, Maryland, is not treated as a crime, either by the courts or the community."[9]

Shocked denials were issued when Douglass wrote the story in substantially the form my telling has taken in his first autobiography, the 1845 *Narrative*. Friends of Gore rose to his defense; he was a good man and a churchgoer, they said, who could never have committed a murder. They also insisted that the late Colonel Lloyd, a pillar of society, would never have permitted a coldblooded killer to go unpunished.[10]

But the Lloyd records themselves offer powerful circumstantial evidence that something tragic happened to Bill Denby during the year 1823, just before Frederick went to live with Captain Anthony. In the return book signed by Anthony that was dated January 1, 1822, Bill Demby (Denby) was listed as a field hand at the Lloyd-owned farm known as Davises or Davis's. He was described as being twenty years old and a first quality worker. In the book for January 1, 1823, his name was again recorded, but a later notation, apparently made during the year 1823, added the word *dead*. He did not appear on the return for January, 1824.[11]

Thus whatever caused Bill Denby's death undoubtedly occurred during 1823, when Frederick was five years old and still living with his grandmother at Tuckahoe. Indications are that it occurred on the Davis's Farm, not the Lloyd home plantation. Frederick could not have witnessed it— nor did he claim he had. The wording of his account as quoted here makes it clear that he was telling the story as it had been told to him by others—which does not necessarily make it any less factual.[12]

Despite all the denials, it seems probable that Bill Denby died of violence, and that the story as Frederick heard it from older slaves, although it may have been embellished in the retelling, was substantially correct. It is worth noting that Gore, although he was still living in Talbot County when Douglass's charge was published, never publicly denied having shot Denby, but let others do it for him.

Gore's name first appears in the Lloyd account books in 1826, which is probably the year he was moved from Davis's Farm to the post of overseer at the central farm. This was indeed a promotion; at Davis's he had had charge of only twenty-three slaves, compared with the nearly one hundred and seventy he oversaw at the main plantation. Frederick thought him the archetype of southern overseer: brutal, malign, vulgar, artful, and ambitious, with the stern and imperious will of a born slave driver and the cutthroat morality of an old-time pirate. Older slaves said that under his rule there was more suffering from violence and bloodshed than had ever before been experienced on the Lloyd plantation.

Where William Sevier had whipped from cowardice, and James Hopkins (who succeeded Sevier briefly) with reluctance, Gore seemed to whip from a sense of duty, without regard for the guilt or innocence of his victims. He lived by the maxim, Douglass said, "that it is better that a dozen slaves suffer under the lash, without fault, than that the master or overseer should *seem* to have been wrong." As for Frederick, who, luckily, was not under his command: "I shunned him as I would have shunned a rattlesnake. His piercing black eyes, and sharp, shrill voice, ever awakened sensations of terror among the slaves. . . . Other overseers, how brutal soever they might be, were, at times, inclined to gain favor with the slaves, by indulging a little pleasantry; but Gore was never known to be guilty of any such weakness. He was always the cold, distant, unapproachable *overseer* of Col. Edward Lloyd's plantation."[13]

In a section of *My Bondage and My Freedom* that he labeled "A Chapter of Horrors," Douglass lumped together several other alleged atrocities to buttress his portrayal of the evil nature of slavery. These were admittedly based on hearsay, and are not now susceptible of proof, one way or the other, on the basis of external evidence.

Douglass reported as a "notorious fact" that a Mrs. Giles Hicks had murdered a cousin of his wife Anna by beating her to death for the "crime" of going to sleep while babysitting. According to Douglass, Mrs. Hicks had the body buried, but it was disinterred by court order, and a coroner's jury brought in a verdict of death by beating. He said a warrant was issued for Mrs. Hicks's arrest, but that it was never served.

No record of this case has been found, but the records do show a Mr. Giles Hicks, who lived in Caroline County. Since that is where Anna Murray Douglass was born and raised, it is probable that Douglass heard the story from her.

Douglass also said a ship's carpenter of his acquaintance, Thomas Lanman (actually Thomas Lambdin), boasted of killing two slaves, "one of whom he butchered with a hatchet, by knocking his brains out." He quoted the carpenter as saying that when "others would do as much as he had done, we should be relieved of the d——d niggers." The possibility that this was merely an ugly joke said in Douglass's presence to frighten him does not appear to have occurred to Douglass.

A third case involved a nonfatal shooting for alleged trespass. Douglass said a "Mr. Beal Bondley"—identifiable as John Beale Bordley, Jr., who lived on Wye Island, across the river from the Lloyd plantation—shot a slave belonging to Colonel Lloyd for poaching on oyster grounds that Bordley considered his private reserve. The slave recovered and the matter was hushed up, according to Douglass.

Douglass cited these cases as examples of the truth of the Eastern Shore proverb that "it was worth but half a cent to kill a nigger, and a half a cent to bury him." He added: "While I heard of numerous murders committed by slaveholders on the Eastern Shore of Maryland, I never knew a solitary instance in which a slaveholder was either hung or imprisoned for having murdered a slave."[14]

"Sold Down to Georgia"

Life under the threat of cowskin and gun was bad, but the alternative was worse. What Maryland slaves of Frederick's generation dreaded more than being whipped or even shot was being "sold down to Georgia" to end their lives far from their families and their native soil on a cotton or rice plantation. This was the ultimate terror from which there was no appeal, the final judgment after which there was no hope.

Perhaps the tales that filtered back north of the horrors awaiting slaves condemned to the Deep South were wild exaggerations; perhaps, as an Eastern Shore newspaper assured its slave-owning readers, blacks who were "sold south" really were better fed and better treated and led more useful lives than those who remained in Maryland.[15] It did not matter; to blacks whose roots were deep in Eastern Shore soil, whose ancestors had lived there for many generations, being transported hundreds of miles away, never to be heard from again, would be worse than death itself.

This was the fear that haunted Frederick's youthful dreams, that gave him nightmares: as a boy in Baltimore, he was aroused from sleep by "the dead, heavy footsteps and the piteous cries" of chain gangs being marched to slave ships waiting at the Fells Point docks. It was dread of being sold, he told Hugh Auld, that impelled him to escape north from Baltimore in 1838, just as the same fear had driven hundreds of his fellow slaves to flee north during the previous decade.[16]

The phenomenon that changed the predictable, and therefore bearable, misery of Eastern Shore slave life into a far more fearsome uncertainty arose during Frederick's early childhood. Spurred by the South's insatiable appetite for black bodies to fuel its explosively expanding new cotton kingdom, slave buyers by the score pushed into Virginia and Maryland offering "Cash! Cash! Cash! for Negroes." On the Eastern Shore especially, they arrived just at a time when slave owners were learning to their economic sorrow that blacks who had been so valuable in a tobacco-dominated agriculture were now a fiscal liability. The buyers had money, and the sellers had surplus blacks. As Frederic Bancroft has said, the Eastern Shore counties "demonstrated what slave-trading became under the most favorable circumstances. . . . Slaves in large numbers were nowhere else so cheap."[17]

Some blacks were sold south during the 1820s and 1830s for disciplinary reasons, but the vast majority of those sold were simply loyal, humble workers. Many were young girls, or small children sold with or without their mothers. Some sellers made efforts to keep families together, but others did not. With few exceptions, the slave traders wanted only young, strong blacks. Older men and women, the parents and grandparents, were a drag on the market.

For those who were victims of this new and profitable commerce, or who feared they might be next, it was as if an earthquake had begun underneath their feet. The only security they had ever known, the security of familiar land and family loyalty, had suddenly vanished. Not since their ancestors were torn from their African villages and thrust into the unknown terrors of a slave environment had there been such a frightening upheaval.

The experience of Frederick's immediate family was typical. In the century before his birth, no member of his family had ever been sold off the Eastern Shore; it was their homeland. In the first fourteen years of Frederick's life, his sister, two aunts, seven first cousins, at least five other near relatives, and dozens of others whom he knew well disappeared without trace into the Deep South. His aunt and uncle, among others, fled north to escape a similar fate. Through no doing of its members, the family circle saw its solidity smashed beyond recognition.

The economics that had created this doleful condition were simple and compelling. The Eastern Shore was in the grips of a fifty-year depression, its agriculture far less profitable than it once had been, its shipbuilding in decline, its economic opportunities few. Without a railroad, it could develop little or no manufacturing. Wheat growing, its principal source of cash, required slave labor in large quantities only during the brief midsummer harvest. And yet the black population, stimulated by mild climate and relatively good living conditions, kept increasing.

Some wealthy slaveholders, including the Lloyds, met the problem by buying up cotton plantations in the South and moving their slaves wholesale to Mississippi, Louisiana, and Arkansas. Others granted their slaves freedom and left them to shift for themselves—particularly the older males and unproductive females. But to many, the fortuitous arrival of slave traders with well-filled moneybags seemed a heaven-sent answer to their problems.

Just as the phrase "sold down to Georgia" became the symbol to blacks of any sale to any part of the Deep South, a man the slaves called "Austin Woldfolk" became the symbol of all slave traders. To Frederick, being "sold to Woldfolk" was synonymous with banishment to the nether ends of the earth. Any trader who came into Talbot County was "Woldfolk" to the illiterate blacks. Any black placed in a cart and hauled down to the county seat of Easton, to return no more, had been "sold to Wold-folk." Any slave who got out of line could be terrorized into submission merely by mention of "Woldfolk."

In truth the name was Austin Woolfolk, and he was only one of many active slave buyers of the period, and one of several related men with the same surname who operated as a group. But Austin headed the family business, and he was the biggest and most successful of all the Maryland slave traders, best known to the white owners as well as most feared by the blacks. He was also the most "respectable" of the lot, with an impeccable reputation for fair dealing. Aristocratic planters who shrank from contact with some of the sleazy specimens whose cash they coveted felt no qualms about dealing with Woolfolk.

Woolfolk appears to have been a native Georgian, but other information about his origins is obscure. Shortly after the end of the War of 1812 he was engaged, with his father, Austin Woolfolk, Sr., in supplying slaves from a headquarters in Augusta, Georgia, for the new cotton lands opening up in Alabama and Mississippi. About 1819 he shifted his base to Baltimore, which offered not only easy water transport to the South but proximity to a rich potential supply source. At first, confining his operations to the Baltimore area, he had small success; but beginning in 1823, when he started concentrating on the Eastern Shore, his business volume climbed spectacularly. He was the right man in the right place at the right time.[18]

Eventually Austin brought at least five of his relatives into the expanding business. Samuel Woolfolk handled the New Orleans end, selling slaves shipped to him from Baltimore on what then was probably the world's largest open slave market. Joseph B. became the principal Eastern Shore representative, setting up residence in Talbot County in 1825. John, William W., and Richard scoured nearby counties for likely prospects, and local agents were hired from time to time on a temporary basis.

Austin made occasional field trips, but for the most part he operated from his headquarters on Pratt Street in Baltimore, where he had built a slave pen discreetly screened behind a neat white house with a tree-lined drive. There he did perhaps half his total business; sellers with job lots to dispose of could strike bargains at his office above the Three Tuns Tavern. The squeamish who wanted to preserve their local image as kindly masters who would not do business with slave traders could consummate their deals in Baltimore, where the sales would be recorded out of the sight of nosy Eastern Shore neighbors. This was an important consideration, since Eastern Shore tradition held strongly that slaves should not be sold to go outside of Maryland. But times were hard and money talked.[19]

Woolfolk advertising, both in the Baltimore daily papers and the county weeklies, showed a curious mixture of shrewd moderation and unabashed boastfulness. The firm never advertised for slaves by the hundreds, as some buyers did; rather it tried to convey the impression that its blacks were destined to go to a private owner, presumably a kindly southern gentleman who would treat them well. In one ad John Woolfolk claimed be was seeking slaves "for his own cotton plantation on the Chattahoochee River." But Austin had a flair for personal publicity; he boasted that his checks, unlike others, were "such as usually pass," and invited slaveholders, when in Baltimore, to call at his residence and "see the justly celebrated AUSTIN WOOLFOLK, free of charge." At one point he assured customers ''that he is not dead, as has been artfully represented by opponents, but that he still lives, to give them CASH and the highest prices for their negroes.''[20]

In Talbot County the Woolfolks set up their field headquarters at Solomon Lowe's Tavern in Easton, owned by Colonel Lloyd. It was handy to the site of the annual slave auction established in 1818, as well as to the offices of the *Republican Star* and the *Gazette*, in which their enticing ads were inserted. Just across Federal Street were the courthouse, where bills of sale had to be recorded, and the local jail, where obliging sheriffs would board slaves for twenty-five cents a day while transportation to Baltimore was being arranged.[21]

The response to their advertising was gratifying. Old Eastern Shore families might claim—as many still do—that they ''never dealt with slave traders,'' but the record proves otherwise. A roster of those who sold slaves to the Woolfolks and other buyers from the Deep South during the 1820s reads like a ''Who's Who'' of Eastern Shore aristocracy. Among them were Edward Lloyd, Henry Hollyday, Nicholas and Charles Goldsborough, Peregrine Tilghman, Edward N. Hambleton, William H. D'Courcy, James Lloyd Chamberlaine, and William Hayward.[22]

At their peak the Woolfolks were pumping as much as $1,000 a week into the faltering Eastern Shore economy. In 1825, with Joseph B. as resident agent, the family paid out $22,702 for 93 blacks in Talbot County alone; added to this were Austin's Baltimore purchases and extensive buying in Queen Anne's and other Eastern Shore counties. From 100 slaves sent south in 1823, the firm's annual shipments climbed to 200 in 1824, and reached a height of 460 a year during the remainder of the decade. Nearly all of them went to brother Samuel in New Orleans.[23]

Nor did the Woolfolks have a monopoly on the business. There were many other traders, some of them large operators, some small. In addition, individual planters came up from Louisiana, Mississippi, and elsewhere on buying trips to stock their own plantations. Frederick's sister Sarah, his Aunt Betty, and several cousins were sold to such a visitor, Perry Cohee, who spent several weeks in Talbot County during the summer of 1832 and bought a total of sixteen slaves for $2,720 before returning to his home in Lawrence County, Mississippi. One estimate is that as many as eighty traders, full or part time, operated on the Eastern Shore during the lush years of the market.[24]

At times several buyers would be in Easton at the same time and would bid against each other, a happy condition for local people with slaves to sell. In the *Gazette* of August 13, 1825, Joseph B. Woolfolk announced that he had just received ''a fresh supply of that much wished for article, CASH!'' that he was anxious to pay out, while John B. Ory of Acadia

Parish, Louisiana, insisted that he would give "from $20 to $25 more than any other purchaser on the Shore." Both found plenty of customers; Ory picked up eighteen slaves for $4,430 before returning to Louisiana, while Woolfolk bought eleven during the same period, and sixty-four during the year, spending a total of $15,202.

To soothe those whose consciences were bothered by the thought of selling their slaves out of state, the Woolfolks and other traders paid a premium of $50 to $100 per slave over the prices paid by local buyers. But local buyers were scarce; most Eastern Shore slaveholders were already overstocked.

Newspaper editors, enjoying the revenue from slave trade advertising, assured their readers editorially that no stigma would be attached to out-of-state sales. On Christmas Day, 1830, the *Cambridge* (Maryland) *Chronicle* published a rosy picture of the life that awaited those blacks fortunate enough to be bought up by Woolfolk or some other dealer. "In many respects the condition of the slave is *bettered* by being sent South. . . . They are well clothed and housed, properly attended to in sickness, and not overworked. They are also well fed and sometimes live sumptuously." The blacks concerned might have disagreed; but few of them could read the *Chronicle's* Christmas editorial.

Slave trade profits were good, but not as exhorbitant as might be supposed. In 1825 a prime young male could be bought for $400 in Talbot County and sold for twice that in New Orleans, but expenses were high, and the net proceeds from such a transaction probably did not exceed $60 to $100. Profit on an eight-year-old child bought for $150 might be as little as $25. In 1828, its best year, the Woolfolk firm netted only about $28,000.[25]

Austin Woolfolk in particular was scrupulous in seeing that the blacks he handled received adequate food and health care. It was part of his public image. Ethan Allen Andrews, a New Englander who visited Woolfolk's Pratt Street slave pen in 1835, wrote that one would expect a slave trader to "be in all respects a monster," but that Woolfolk "is reported, upon the best authority, to be a most mild and indulgent master. . . . When he makes his appearance among his slaves, they gather around him with every demonstration of affection, and even the little children manifest the most eager solicitude to share in his attentions." Andrews also reported Woolfolk had the reputation of being "an upright and scrupulously honest man. His recommendation of a slave will instantly raise his value in the market, for his word is implicitly relied upon by all who know him."[26]

However, Benjamin Lundy, youthful Baltimore abolitionist editor, thought otherwise. He called Woolfolk a "monster in human shape" in

79

his monthly publication, *Genius of Universal Emancipation,* which devoted much space to Woolfolk's operations. He went on to say that Woolfolk was a "soul seller . . . equally guilty in the sight of God with the man who was engaged in the African slave trade."[27]

When they later met on the street, Woolfolk attacked Lundy, threw him to the pavement, and beat him severely. Arrested on a charge of battery, Woolfolk cheerfully pleaded guilty, offering as his only defense the articles Lundy had written about him. Judge Nicholas Brice, after hearing extracts from the articles, fined Woolfolk one dollar and costs, but commented that he had never seen a case in which the provocation for a battery was greater. He added that in his opinion Woolfolk's trade was valuable to Maryland because "it removed a great many rogues and vagabonds who were a nuisance."[28]

Frederick knew Austin Woolfolk well by reputation, although along with the other blacks he called him "Woldfolk." He heard the name spoken often, in tones of fear, at night around the cooking fires, and he grew more and more uneasy about his own future as he watched members of his family and others disappear into the hands of "Woldfolk" and his fellow traders. By the early months of 1826, after he learned of the successful flight of Jenny and Noah, he brooded perhaps more than was good for him about the things he had seen on the Lloyd plantation and his condition as a lifelong slave who was subject to the whims of his master. He was by then "eight, going on nine"—or so Lucretia Auld told him—big for his age, surprisingly mature, an intelligent, sensitive boy who thought the long thoughts of youth about such things as the relationship of God and man, and the nature of slavery.

The logic of what he had heard escaped him. Older children of whom he asked questions explained that "God, up in the sky" made everybody, and that He had made white people to be masters, and black people to be slaves. This made no sense to Frederick. He knew black people, like Isaac Bailey, who were not slaves; and he knew black people who had been born free, like those from Africa, but had been forced into slavery. He also knew white people who refused to be masters and would not own slaves; and he knew white people, or those nearly so, like William Wilks, who were slaves. Besides, he wasn't exactly black himself, and his father had been a white man, and yet he was a slave. Soon he decided that neither color nor God had anything to do with slavery, that it was men who made slaves. And what men could do, other men could undo. He did not yet know how this could be accomplished, but by the time he was eight years old, he wrote later, he was convinced he would be a free man someday.[29]

Others were also concerned about his future. Anyone who knew Frederick could see that he was much too bright a boy to end up as a field hand, but no one was sure what to do with him.

The Anthony household faced a crisis as 1826 began. Old Aaron, his health broken, was retired from his job at the start of the year; his place as Colonel Lloyd's chief overseer was taken by James McKeel. Thomas Auld had resigned in October as captain of the *Sally Lloyd* and was preparing to move to Hillsboro in Caroline County, where he planned to open a store. The brick house facing the Long Green in which the family had lived so long would now become the home of some other Lloyd employee, and for the slaves who occupied its kitchen, new arrangements would have to be made. Katy was rented out for the year, and most of the others were sent back to Anthony's Tuckahoe farms. That left the problem of Frederick.

Fortunately for all concerned, a solution was soon found. Hugh Auld, Thomas's younger brother who lived at Fells Point in Baltimore, wanted a black boy to serve as companion to his little son, Tommy. Frederick already had experience in this role as companion to Daniel Lloyd. He seemed a perfect choice, and so the arrangement was made. Lucretia Auld was clearly delighted as she told Frederick of the decision on a springlike morning in early March; she had dreaded the thought that this charming boy might suffer the coarsening and brutalizing effects common to field slaves.

Douglass later described as a "miracle" the fact that he had been chosen out of all the slave children on the Lloyd plantation to be sent to Baltimore, and attributed it to "a special interposition of Divine Providence in my favor." However, this view seems to give the Anthonys too little credit; all the evidence indicates that they regarded him as a very special child and that this and other decisions affecting his future were made with his best interests in mind.[30]

Lucretia told Frederick that he would be leaving in three days, but first, she warned, he must scrub himself thoroughly. It would never do for him to present himself in Baltimore, a great city where everyone was extremely clean, with the "scurf" of the plantation all over him. Besides, she was going to give him a real pair of trousers to replace the tow linen shirt that had been his only garment. Before he could wear trousers properly, he would have to get all the ground-in dirt and dead skin off his feet, legs, and knees.

Frederick was ecstatic. Baltimore! After all he had heard from stuttering Tom, he was sure it must be the grandest place in the world. He would not be sorry to leave the Lloyd plantation; he had grown to hate its air of casual cruelty, and he had never considered the Anthony kitchen, under Aunt Katy's sadistic rule, to be his home. His mother was dead;

81

his brother and sisters were almost strangers; and aside from Miss Lucretia and Daniel he did not have a real friend. He could leave this phase of his life without a pang.

For the remaining three days he spent most of his time soaking and scrubbing himself in the creek. At night he scarcely dared sleep for fear he would wake up to find the *Sally Lloyd* had sailed without him. But she did not; on a Saturday morning, probably March 18, 1826, proudly wearing his stiff new trousers, he joined a large flock of sheep aboard the sloop and sailed off on the first great adventure of his life.

As the *Sally Lloyd* headed into the Miles River, he walked aft and took one last, unregretful look at the great plantation he was leaving behind. At that moment he fervently hoped he would never see the place again; and in truth it would be fifty-five years before he did.

Assuming Colonel Lloyd was touring his estates as usual that morning, he may well have noticed his sloop as she rounded Long Point and started her tack across the Miles. His glance might even have taken in the small figure of a slave boy standing in her stern. But if anyone had told him that with that sailing a chain of events was being set in motion which someday would help destroy his world, he would merely have smiled in polite disbelief. After all, what could one "nigger" do to disturb the powers and privileges of an Edward Lloyd?

❧ Chapter Six ❧

Fells Point

The *Sally Lloyd* docked briefly late that afternoon in Annapolis harbor, and Frederick caught a breathtaking glimpse of the Maryland capitol's great dome gleaming in the sunlight. Then the captain set the sloop's course northward for Baltimore, which they reached Sunday morning, tying up at Smith's Wharf near Pratt Street in the heart of the city's commercial shipping district. Frederick helped drive the sheep up through the muddy streets to Curtis's slaughterhouse on Loudon Slater's Hill. Next his turn came; the captain instructed a deckhand who knew Baltimore well to deliver Frederick to his new home in the shipbuilding district called Fells Point.

As they walked through the city streets, Frederick's senses were alert to every sight, sound, and smell. It was all new, and all unbelievable; even Tom's excited descriptions, which he had thought exaggerated, hadn't prepared him for anything like this. Houses by the hundreds, in seemingly endless rows, many of them hitched together with a common wall; church bells pealing; carriages and gigs carrying well-dressed people to Sunday worship; strolling families, mama and papa in front, the children lagging behind; couples walking arm in arm. From time to time he saw black men or women going about their business as if they had as much right on the streets as the whites. Even these appeared well dressed to Frederick; nearly all of them wore shoes, a fact quite outside his experience.

At a narrow cross street that he later learned was called Aliceanna they stopped in front of a small frame house, two stories high and badly in need of paint, at the corner of an even narrower lane with the unlikely name of Happy Alley. His companion knocked on the door. It opened, and there, smiling in welcome, were all three members of his new family: Master Hugh, younger, broader shouldered, and rather shorter than Master Thomas; Mistress Sophia, beaming with delight at the sight of him; and little Tommy, a rosy-cheeked, bright-eyed two-year-old who peered out at him from behind his mother's skirts.

He was ushered inside, and Mistress Sophia quickly took charge. "Tommy," she said, "this is your Freddy. He is going to take care of you." To Frederick she said, in gentle warning, "You must be kind to little Tommy." It was a needless admonition; he had already resolved to do that. To ease his feelings of strangeness, she asked small questions: How had the trip been? How were Miss Lucretia and Master Thomas? What did he think of Baltimore? Then she showed him the little loft room above the kitchen, with a straw bed neatly made up and covered with a quilt, where he would sleep. He looked around in wonder. Could those really be blankets underneath the quilt?

That night, for the first time in his life, he sat at a table and had a proper supper of meat, cornbread, and milk; and later he slept in his own bed, under the rafters, luxuriating in its privacy as well as in its warmth and softness. The bad time was over. He had entered a new world.

For her part, Sophia Auld could scarcely believe her good luck. She had been told to expect a black child rather superior to most; but what she had seen already was a boy who exceeded her fondest hopes: light-skinned, broad-cheeked, with an engaging smile and intelligent dark eyes, surprisingly well spoken and with instinctive good manners; in short, she felt immediately, a boy she could not help taking to her heart.

For the first few days Frederick stayed close to the little house on Aliceanna Street,[1] getting to know his family, the first one he had ever had all to himself. It was a warm sensation, being a part of something, a special person and not just another of the scores of ragged little black children running around the Lloyd estate.

His new mistress he adored at once. She was much like Miss Lucretia—a kind and gentle woman who treated him as a child, not as a slave. Tommy, too, was easy to love. He was a cheerful toddler, into everything, talking a blue streak in a language all his own. He accepted Frederick immediately, and instinctively put him in the place of companion and older brother rather than servant. Hugh Auld was another matter—gruff and distant, rather stern in his manner toward Frederick. He was working as a ship's carpenter, and when he came home at night, smelling of brandy and sweat, the household took on a different and chillier aspect.

Almost at once there was the matter of names to straighten out. Mrs. Auld quickly became "Miss Sopha," the *i* lost in Frederick's childish lisp. Tommy was Tommy from the start. Master Hugh he shied away from calling anything but that, even in his mind. As for himself, he was no longer "Cap'n Ant'ney Fed," as he had been on the plantation, or even "Frederick." Somehow it seemed more natural to call him "Freddy."

Soon he began to explore his new environment—first, down to the corner of Washington Street, where one of his daily duties was to fetch pails of water from the town pump, and then farther, into the maze of Fells Point's twisted streets. He found the place exciting and frightening, confusing and sometimes hostile. Wagons clattered through the cobblestone streets, their drivers shouting angrily at him to "look sharp!" Troops of strange boys pounced on him at corners, chasing him and calling him "Eastern Shore man," until sometimes he almost wished himself back on the Lloyd plantation.

Fells Point in 1826 was less a section of Baltimore than a separate entity, a town within a city with its own peculiar ways and its own throbbing life. It existed entirely by, of, and for shipping and ships. Every street ended in a shipyard, and nearly every house sheltered the family of a master carpenter, ship's calker, fitter, chandler, sail maker or sailor. The swift, graceful sailing vessels it produced, known as Baltimore clippers, were world famous.

Alongside the shipyards were wharves whose commerce had helped boost Baltimore in a few decades from a sleepy village to the third largest city in the United States. By day the docks were piled high with wheat from the interior; sugar, rum, and molasses from the West Indies; coffee from Brazil; finished goods from Britain and Europe. By night sailors from many ports roamed the streets looking for sinful pleasures—and finding them in the taverns and bordellos of "the Hook," which jutted into Baltimore's inner harbor at the tip of Fells Point.

A source of wondrous sights and sounds to Frederick was James Beacham's shipyard, at the foot of Lancaster Street and only a short distance from the Auld house. Hugh Auld was working there that spring, although he hoped soon to go into business as a master builder himself. Beacham had need for much skilled help; he was building a sixty-four-gun frigate for the Brazilian government, at 1,800 tons the largest ship ever constructed in Baltimore up to that date. Launching-time was near, and the neighborhood rang with the clang of hammers and the shouts of workmen from morning to night.

A few weeks after Frederick's arrival came a morning he would never forget. He was awakened at dawn by the sound of voices and laughter outside the house. The frigate was to be launched at 10.30 A.M., and all of booming, bustling, seagoing Baltimore wanted to witness the event; already people were streaming down Aliceanna Street and Happy Alley to secure the best viewing points.

By midmorning spectators were packed solidly around the scaffolding that supported the ship, and additional thousands jammed every nearby yard and wharf. The harbor was crowded with boatloads of viewers; others looked on from the hills facing Beacham's yard from the north and east. By one estimate forty thousand persons—half the population of Baltimore— were assembled for the launch.

At 10:15 workmen began removing the outer supports that shored up the ship. Then they knocked out the great blocks that held the keel and, on a signal from Beacham, sawed away the final stays. According to the *Baltimore American*: "The ship moved toward her destined element with an easy and gradually accelerated motion, and having made one plunge of obeisance to old Neptune, rose majestically upon the water, amidst the shouts in admiration of the assembled thousands. We believe that a more beautiful and better managed launch has never been made. There was not the least hesitation or check in her movement, and not an inch of copper was removed in her passage to the water." [2] Most amazing of all, the *American* reported that nobody got hurt; that was truly remarkable in view of the packed crowds that pressed in close to get a better look.

Afterward there were celebrations everywhere. The Fifth Regiment Band from Fort McHenry provided music that could be heard throughout Fells Point. Families spread picnic lunches; ship's captains and yard owners broke out kegs of rum, brandy, and wine to refresh their guests; taverns did a booming business. Beacham, bursting with pride, led a party of high officials to the Shite Hall Tavern to drink to the success of the ship. Then they sat down to a dinner of ham, turkey, terrapin, and oysters, topped off, in honor of their Brazilian guests, with goblets of sangaree. [3]

The noise and excitement made a lasting impression on Frederick, who had never before seen or heard anything even remotely like it. Forever afterward he dated key events in his own life from the launching of that frigate. Unfortunately, he dated them wrongly—for the launch took place, not in 1825, as he believed, but on May 11, 1826. [4]

As summer came on, Frederick was sometimes homesick, but he found balm in the creature comforts of his new situation: a real bed instead of a cold floor; good bread and mush instead of coarse corn meal; clean clothes instead of a tow-linen shirt. Best of all, in place of Aunt Katy's scoldings and cuffs on the head, he basked in "Miss Sopha's" loving warmth.

"I . . . soon came to regard her as something more akin to a mother than a slaveholding mistress," he wrote. "So far from deeming it impudent in a slave to look her straight in the face, she seemed ever to say, 'Look up, child;

don't be afraid.' . . . If little Thomas was her son, and her most dearly loved child, she made me something like his half-brother in her affections. If dear Tommy was exalted to a place on his mother's knee, 'Freddy' was honored by a place at the mother's side. Nor did the slave-boy lack the caressing strokes of her gentle hand, soothing him into the consciousness that, though motherless, he was not friendless.'' [5]

Some of Douglass's later comments have tended to obscure the importance of Sophia Auld as the dominant mother figure in his early life. This is unfortunate; as the quoted passage indicates, she filled an aching void for a boy whose real mother had never been more than a distant, almost ghostly figure. For most of the years they spent together, they had a warm if sometimes strained relationship. Undoubtedly Mrs. Auld implanted in Frederick the sturdy moral standards and sense of self-reliance she had learned from her strictly religious, working-class parents.

Although she was a native of the St. Michaels area of Talbot County, Sophia (and her parents) had not been associated with the slave-owning aristocracy. Richard and Hester Keithley were simple country people, strict Methodists who held with Francis Asbury that slavery was a crime against the laws of God, man, and nature, and their daughter had been brought up to echo that belief. Before her marriage Sophia had worked as a weaver, performing a servant's job more akin to the duties of a slave than the authority of a mistress. So she had acquired none of the haughtiness traditional in "genteel" Eastern Shore ladies trained from birth to believe they were superior to almost everyone, especially blacks. Frederick was the only black with whom Sophia Auld was ever closely associated, and she could no more treat him as an inferior than she could her own children. "Look up," she told him. "Don't be afraid." And Frederick never would look down again. Those words became the dominating credo of his life.

A threatened disaster and a return visit to the Eastern Shore only served to strengthen Frederick's sense of belonging, in the deepest meaning of the word, to Sophia Auld and to his Fells Point family.

Aaron Anthony, still his legal owner, died in November, 1826. Perhaps he had intended to give Frederick to Lucretia, or even to little Tommy Auld; but he left no will, and therefore under the law his property was required to be divided equally among his heirs. So, in due time, Frederick was sent for, to be returned with the other slaves to the Tuckahoe Creek farm of his birth, and there to be allotted to a new owner. [6]

The heirs at the time of Anthony's death had been his three children, Andrew and Richard Anthony and Lucretia Auld. But, although Frederick had not been aware of it, Lucretia had died during the summer of 1827. Her portion of the estate fell to her husband, Thomas Auld. Thus, when he was called home in October, 1827, for the official dividing of the slaves, the boy saw that his fate lay with three men, none of whom he knew well and none of whom he trusted.[7]

There was an unhappy scene when the time came for Master Hugh to take him down to the wharf and put him aboard the schooner *Wildcat*, Captain Rowe commanding, for the voyage to the Eastern Shore. "Miss Sopha" burst into tears and hugged him close to her. Frederick cried, too, and even little Tommy howled, not sure what was happening but aware that it must be something bad involving his Freddy.

Sophia Auld and Frederick understood only too well. The standard practice in Maryland was that, on a prenamed day, all the slaves who belonged to a person who had died intestate should be lined up, and a value placed on each. The valuation would be done by outside appraisers appointed by the Orphans Court. Then the blacks would be divided into lots of approximately equal value, and each lot assigned to one of the heirs. In theory, at least, no one could predict under whose ownership a black might fall.

If Frederick were allotted to Richard or Andrew Anthony, there was little chance he would ever see his Baltimore family again. The young Anthony men, no kin to the Aulds except by marriage, were unlikely to do them any favors where a property as valuable as a nine-year-old slave boy was concerned.

The trip by schooner took twenty-four hours; *Wildcat* was a slow tub of a boat, stubby and broad of beam, with shallow draft and a centerboard rather than a keel, so that she could creep up the Eastern Shore's many tidal creeks. Frederick spent much of the time brooding, or dozing on tarpaulins piled on the open deck. When he awoke next morning, the schooner was far up the Choptank, near the mouth of Tuckahoe Creek and the old Anthony farm where his fate would be decided.

Nothing he found when he was put ashore made his mood any more cheerful. The farm itself was even more run down than he remembered it, and everything somehow seemed to have grown smaller in the three years since he had last seen it. His grandmother greeted him with a hug and a kiss, and there was much talk of how he had grown, but all the rest of the assembled blacks seemed like strangers. With his town clothes and "white folks" way of talking, Frederick, young as he was, already stood out in sharp contrast to the others. He was not as they; and even then most of his black family must have known it. They were the product of Eastern Shore field slavery, he of a Baltimore white family where he was treated more as a son than as a servant.

Altogether, twenty-nine slaves were on hand to await the distribution. Mean Aunt Katy was among them, bad tempered as ever, with her brood of three sons and a daughter. Most of the others were descendants of Betsey Bailey—five daughters and a son, and fourteen grandchildren.

Some of these Frederick had known well on the Lloyd plantation: Cousin Tom, the stutterer; Nancy and Steve, his playmates; Henny, the cripple, burned so dreadfully as a baby that she could scarcely use her hands; Aunt Prissy, his mother's plump and genial sister; Aunt Hester, the beautiful one whom Old Master had whipped so savagely. Hester was now nursing a baby; looking at it, Frederick may have wondered fleetingly if the father was Ned Roberts—or Aaron Anthony.

His brother, Perry, now nearly fifteen, was a full-fledged field hand, a grown man by slavery's standards. The girls were growing up, too; Sarah was thirteen, Eliza eleven. There were also two little ones, Kitty and Arianna, who he was told were his younger sisters. And how about the child named Harriet, who didn't seem to belong to anyone? Could she have been his mother's last baby, perhaps the cause of her fatal illness? [8]

The attitude of the other slaves bothered Frederick from the beginning. They seemed resigned to their fate—or at least prepared to accept it without question. Frederick was not. He cared desperately what happened to him. His life in recent months had been so different from theirs, so atypical of slavery, that already he and his black family had little in common.

Of this trying period he wrote:

I probably suffered more than most of my fellow servants. I had known what it was to experience kind, and even tender treatment; they had known nothing of the sort. Life, to them, had been rough and thorny, as well as dark. . . . The overseer had written his character on the living parchment of most of their backs, and left them callous; my back (thanks to my early removal from the plantation to Baltimore,) was yet tender. I had left a kind mistress at Baltimore, who was almost a mother to me. She was in tears when we parted, and the probabilities of ever seeing her again, trembling in the balance as they did, could not be viewed without alarm and anxiety. [9]

One possibility did cause alarm among even the oldest and most hardened of the group. Whichever ones became the property of Andrew Anthony were surely in for trouble. At thirty, he was already considered "almost a confirmed sot" who was rapidly wasting his share of his father's property by "reckless mismanagement and profligate dissipation." To fall into his hands was considered merely the first step toward being sold away to the Deep South. [10]

For seemingly endless weeks, while the last of the adult slaves were being assembled, Frederick waited to learn his fate. He soon was given a taste of what might be in store for him if he were awarded to Andrew. A few days after Frederick's arrival, Anthony, in a fit of rage, "seized my brother Perry by the throat, dashed him on the ground, and with the heel of his boot stamped him on the head until the blood gushed from his nose and ears." Then he turned to Frederick and said, "*That* is the way I will serve you, one of these days."

For a city boy who never in his life had been brutally treated, it was a terrifying prospect.

When he looked back on it later, the legal process of valuation and distribution seemed to Frederick the ultimate in human degradation. It took place on October 18, 1827, a Thursday. The court-appointed appraisers were James Chambers and William A. Leonard, old friends of Aaron Anthony. They were not, by the standards of the times, brutal men; they simply carried out their role as it had always been done in Maryland, where black slaves were regarded in the same light as hogs, horses, and cattle.

The twenty-nine blacks who had belonged to Aaron Anthony at his death were lined up in a row in front of the log quarter at the Holme Hill farm. Chambers and Leonard moved slowly down the line, looking closely at each slave, asking for names, occasionally stopping for a physical inspection. From time to time they consulted a list, checking off names against it. The blacks stood silently, heads down; even the children, clustered near their mothers, were quiet. Douglass eloquently recalled his impressions of the spectacle:

What an assemblage! Men and women, young and old, married and single; moral and intellectual beings, in open contempt of their humanity, leveled at a blow with horses, sheep, horned cattle, and swine! Horses and men—cattle and women— pigs and children—all holding the same rank in the scale of social existence; and all subjected to the same narrow inspection, to ascertain their value in gold and silver—the only standard of worth applied by slaveholders to slaves! How vividly, at that moment, did the brutalizing power of slavery flash before me! Personality swallowed up in the sordid idea of property! Manhood lost in chattelhood!

. . . Our destiny was now to be *fixed for life,* and we had no more voice in the decision of the question, than the oxen and cows that stood chewing at the hay-mow. One word from the appraisers, against all preferences or prayers, was enough to sunder all the ties of friendship and affection, and even to separate husbands and wives, parents and children. We were all appalled before that power, which, to human seeming, could bless or blast us in a moment.[11]

To give them their due, Chambers and Leonard demonstrated in their decision that they were not entirely heartless. They had a distasteful job to do—dividing twenty-nine human beings into three lots of approximately equal monetary value—and they did it with as much consideration as was practical for the feelings and desires of the slaves involved.

Totting up their estimated valuations, they came to the conclusion that the twenty-nine Negroes, including infants, were worth $2,800. By law, therefore, they were to be divided into three lots, each valued at approximately $935. This could have been done arbitrarily—nothing in the law said family relationships had to be considered. But it was not; the result showed that Chambers and Leonard made a serious effort to keep families together.

To Andrew Anthony, they assigned grandmother Betsey and four of the six children of her deceased daughter, Harriet. All these would stay at Holme Hill, which Andrew had inherited and where Betsey had her cabin. For the motherless youngsters, the decision to keep them near their grandmother was as humane a solution as could be worked out under the circumstances. Another of Betsey's daughters, young Betty, also was allotted to Andrew, along with her two small children, Stephen and Angelina.

Richard Anthony was awarded Aunt Katy and her two youngest children, along with an adult slave named Harry, who may have been her husband (there is, of course, no way of telling from the record). Frederick's Aunt Milly and her four children—his cousins Tom, Henny, Nancy, and an infant—all went to Thomas Auld in what was obviously a family grouping.

As for Frederick himself, the news, when it came, was the best that he could possibly have imagined. All his fears subsided in an instant. Instead of being allotted to the dreaded Andrew, as were his brother, sisters, and grandmother, he was given to Thomas Auld, who promptly sent him back to Baltimore to live with the Hugh Auld family. This can scarcely have been an accident; the fact that in this one instance the pattern of keeping family groups together was broken suggests that it was done by prior arrangement. Once more Frederick's interests were given special consideration. [12]

By November Frederick was back in the warm circle of his "family" and the loving arms of Miss Sopha. "It was a glad day for me," he wrote of his return to the house on Aliceanna Street. "I had escaped a [fate] worse than lion's jaws. I was absent from Baltimore . . . just about one month, and it seemed to have been six."

The other members of the Bailey family soon faced yet more disruption. Richard Anthony died within a year, and there was another slave distribution. Andrew, as predicted, wasted his inheritance on gambling and drink, and he sold off several slaves, including Frederick's sister Sarah, before dying in 1833. Soon the clan that had held together for a century was scattered among strangers from Maryland to Mississippi.

But none of that was of direct concern to Frederick. Home to him was now Fells Point, and there he found much new activity. Hugh Auld, in partnership with Edward Harrison, was beginning his own business as a shipbuilder. The pair already had their first contract, to build a sloop for Valentine Wareham of Queen Anne's County, and had acquired a location on the strip known as the "City Block," on the north side of the Fells Point hook. In order that Hugh live near his work, the family soon moved to a rented house on Philpot Street. It was an eventful move for Frederick, for there he would spend the next five years, the most important formative period of his youth. [13]

The friends he made on Philpot Street were white boys, sons of the master carpenters and shipfitters whose yards and shops bordered the street. Among them he later remembered Gustavus Dorgan, Joseph Bailey, Charles Farity, and the Cordery boys, Jim, Bill, and George. Frederick had about as much freedom as any of them, and in the rough democracy of boyhood he was accepted as an equal. When the Philpot Street gang met on Sundays to pitch pennies, keeping a sharp lookout for constables North and Bangs, Frederick's supply of coppers was as good as anyone's; and when the "town boys" came down from Baltimore city and crossed the drawbridge onto Fells Point looking for a fight, he was among the best at repelling their attack. Already growing tall and strong, he was a natural leader as well as a tough opponent.

At this stage Frederick seems to have had little or no feeling of being the object of color prejudice, either at home or among his playmates. He was probably the only black boy in the neighborhood, and he was accepted by his friends, as he was by "Miss Sopha," as a human being, without regard to his color. Thinking this over later, he decided it demonstrated what became another of his cardinal principles: color prejudice is not a natural human emotion, but must be learned from others.

"Prejudice is not the creature of birth, but of education," he wrote in 1848 in justification of his controversial stand against separate black churches.

When a boy in the streets of Baltimore, we were never objected to by our white playmates on account of our color. When the hat was tossed up for a choice of partners in the play, we were selected as readily as any other boy, and were esteemed as highly as any. No one ever objected to our complexion. We could run as fast, jump as far, throw the ball as direct and true, and catch it with as much dexterity and skill as the white boys; and were esteemed for what we could do. And such, in our judgment, would be the case here at the North, but for the many influences tending to a separation of white from colored children. [14]

Exciting as his street adventures were, they were nothing compared with the adventure unfolding in his mind. Frederick had discovered the world of letters on a printed page, which would fascinate him all his life. And it was the Book of Job, one of the masterpieces of the human spirit, that was responsible for the discovery.

As he later told the story, Frederick had gone to sleep one Sunday night under the parlor table, where "Miss Sopha" kept her Bible. He was awakened by the sound of her voice, "mellow, loud and sweet," reading verses to herself from the book of Job:

Wherefore then hast thou brought me forth out of the womb? Oh that I had given up the ghost, and no eye had seen me!

I should have been as though I had not been; I should have been carried from the womb to the grave.

Are not my days few? Cease then, and let me alone, that I may take comfort a little,

Before I go whence I shall not return, even to the land of darkness and the shadow of death. . . .

Job's magnificent lament was more than any child of eight could understand, but there was magic in the way the words expressed beauty and melancholy, both at once—and magic, too, in the way Miss Sopha's rich voice had made them come alive from the printed page. It was a magic he must possess for himself.

"From that night I date my thirst for knowledge," he often recalled later. "The next day, I asked Mrs. Auld to teach me to read. She consented, and soon taught me the alphabet and to read words of three or four letters."

It was only a little knowledge, but no less dangerous for that. When Mrs. Auld, with naive pride, told her husband what she had done, he exploded in anger. She must stop at once, or her misguided action would ruin her Freddy for life.

"If you give a nigger an inch he will take an ell," Douglass quoted him as saying. "Learning will spoil the best nigger in the world. If he learns to read the Bible it will forever unfit him to be a slave. He should know nothing but the will of his master, and learn to obey it. As to himself, learning will do him no good, but a great deal of harm, making him disconsolate and unhappy. If you teach him how to read, he'll want to know how to write, and this accomplished, he'll be running away with himself." [15] Douglass also quoted Auld as saying that what his wife was doing was against the law. If Auld said this, he was mistaken; there was no law in Maryland forbidding masters, if they so chose, from teaching slaves to read, and in fact many did so. [16]

Granting the conditions of the time, Auld's logic was dead on the mark. Learning would indeed spoil the best slave in the world, as far as being happy in his slave status was concerned. Neither Mrs. Auld nor

Photo courtesy of Carl G. Auld

Hugh Auld

young Frederick could find fault with his edict—but their reactions were opposite to each other.

"Miss Sopha" took her husband's command at face value. Freddy was a slave, and as far as she knew he always would be one. She loved him and wanted him to be happy. But he would not be happy if he learned to read; he would be yearning for things that were beyond his reach. Therefore it was her duty, in fairness to him, to discontinue her teaching immediately and to discourage any further efforts at learning on his part.

Frederick, on the other hand, found "a new and special revelation" in Hugh Auld's words. If knowledge made a person unfit to be a slave, then knowledge was what he wanted; for he had long ago made up his mind that he was not going to be a slave for life. From that moment on, he was more determined than ever to pursue an education any way he could.

But learning to write and spell, without a teacher to guide him, was much more difficult than learning to read. It was several years before he mastered these arts, and with them a smattering of arithmetic.

His first chance came when Hugh Auld, with his wife's approval, decided to put Frederick to work at the Auld & Harrison shipyard. The business was not prospering, but orders did come in from time to time, and meanwhile there were refittings and overhauls, so that the partners were able to keep a crew of half a dozen or so workmen busy most months. A boy could be useful in many ways, and Frederick had a good deal of free time once little Tommy started taking lessons at a public school, the first in Baltimore's history, which opened in 1829.

Frederick, now about eleven years old, was assigned simple duties: doing errands, beating and spinning oakum, keeping the fire going under the steam box of the pitch boiler, turning the grindstone on which adzes and other cutting tools were sharpened. When the workmen went to noontime dinner he was often left alone to keep an eye on things, and he soon had an idea of what to do with the time.

He had noticed that the carpenters, after dressing a ship's timber, chalk-marked it with initials in script to indicate its intended placement: *s* for starboard, *l* for larboard, *sa* for starboard aft, *sf* for starboard forward, and so on. He learned the names of these letters from the workmen, and when no one else was around he practiced making them with a bit of chalk or a stick in the dirt until he could fashion half a dozen acceptable letters. He was careful not to let Master Hugh find out what he was doing; the result would have been a raging tirade.

Armed with this accomplishment, Frederick next employed a sly trick on his young friends. He would scrawl an *s* or *f* with chalk on a fence board, step back proudly, and say, "Let's see you beat that." The other boy would scornfully top him by writing *b* or *q* or *r*—and Frederick would have another letter to add to his store of knowledge.

At home, working by candlelight in his attic room, he copied out the italic letters from a worn copy of Webster's spelling book until he could make all the symbols from memory. Then he found a better source: Tommy, a good student, had brought home a number of copy books to show his progress in writing, and his mother, after proudly displaying them to the neighbors, had stored them away in a cupboard. Frederick soon discovered this treasure trove, and whenever Mrs. Auld left him alone to take care of the younger children, he would get out Tommy's books and recopy each letter as precisely as he could in the spaces between the lines, or on clean pieces of pine plank filched from the shipyard. One day when he was busy at this and not watching the children, little Benjamin (born at Christmastide in 1828) fell down stairs and cut a fearful gash in his forehead. Frederick hastily hid away the copy books before rushing to a neighbor for help. [17]

In his room, where he had fashioned a rude writing desk out of a flour barrel, Frederick continued his practice in writing by copying from a

Methodist hymn book and other volumes that he had accumulated without the knowledge of the Aulds. It was a long, slow process, but by the time he was about fourteen he could write as well as he could read. In later life he regretted, half jokingly, that his handwriting followed no particular school, since it had come from a variety of models, and he envied the neat script of his school-trained friends. Nevertheless, it was a remarkable achievement. He had also learned basic arithmetic, including the multiplication tables, so that he was as well educated as most working-class white boys of his time, and far better than many.

But he was still a slave, and circumstances would not let him forget it. Most of the blacks with whom he came into contact were free—in Baltimore at that time they outnumbered slaves four to one—and although less than full citizens, they suffered few restrictions, and worked alongside whites at such skilled jobs as shipyard calking and carpentry. Their wages belonged to themselves; whatever he earned, except for a few coppers, went to Master Hugh.

And there were fearful reminders, late at night, of what happened to many slaves and could, at any time, happen to him. Often his sleep would be disturbed by the thud of heavy footsteps, the clank of chains, and the piteous cries of slaves being marched past the door of the house on Philpot Street. These were blacks being taken from Austin Woolfolk's Pratt Street pen to ships that waited off Fells Point to transport them to New Orleans. They were moved under cover of darkness because Baltimoreans preferred not to be reminded of this evil side of slavery. Frederick would listen in terror: "The anguish of my boyish heart was intense." But he would be consoled, in the morning, by hearing "Miss Sopha" say that the slave traffic "was very wicked; that she hated to hear the rattle of chains and the heart-rending cries" as much as he did. More than ever, at these times, he clung to her as his shield against the world. [18]

Two other experiences at about this same time affected Frederick deeply. He underwent a religious conversion, and he stumbled on a book, *The Columbian Orator,* that would exert a profound influence on his life and thinking.

From earliest childhood, Frederick's introspective mind had led him into deep ponderings about the meaning of religion. Now, with an adolescent's thirst for answers to fundamental questions, he began to listen seriously to the Christian teachings of Fells Point preachers, black and white. One of the first was the Reverend Beverly Waugh, afterward a bishop but at that time presiding elder of the East Baltimore station of the Methodist Episcopal church. Reverend Waugh preached often at Sophia Auld's church, Wilk Street Methodist, and took a special interest in her; whenever she felt her faith slipping, which appears to have been fairly often, he would come to the house on Philpot Street to exhort and pray with her. Frederick thus was exposed to a good deal of Reverend Waugh's eloquence, but he found it somehow unsatisfying. To the boy's critical taste, he seemed much too complacent about things as they were.

More to Frederick's liking was the preaching of another white Methodist minister, the Reverend Mr. Hanson. He taught that "all men, great and small, bond and free, were sinners in the sight of God; that they were, by nature, rebels against His government; and that they must repent of their sins, and be reconciled to God through Christ." This made more sense to Frederick. He could perceive that, according to Reverend Hanson, white slaveholders were equally guilty of sin with black slaves, and both must repent or be condemned to hell.

For weeks he wrestled with the problem of his own seeming inability to find salvation. He consulted a black lay preacher, Charles Johnson, whom he had met at the Bethel African Methodist Church, and who advised him "in tones of holy affection" to seek the Lord through prayer. He tried this, but suffered agonies of doubt and fear until at last, in a flash of revelation, he gained faith, as he said, "in Jesus Christ, as the Redeemer, Friend and Savior of those who diligently seek him." Although he would have little use for organized religion in later life, his entire career would reflect his respect for basic Christian doctrine as opposed to the hypocrisy of those who professed it.

Once converted, young Frederick became the most eager of apostles. "I saw the world in a new light ... I loved all mankind—slaveholders not excepted; though I abhorred slavery more than ever. My great concern was, now, to have the world converted." He was avid to learn more; when he saw some scattered pages from a Bible lying in the gutter, he gathered them up, washed and dried them, and added them to the precious store of reading matter hidden away in his loft room.

In this mood of spiritual exaltation, he came under the influence of a kindly old black man named Charles Lawson. Lawson, a free black, was a drayman for rope-maker James Ramsey and a devout member of the Bethel Church, which Frederick also joined. His life was one of constant prayer, and when he spoke it was almost always in terms of a better world to come. To Frederick he seemed to live more in the next life than in this one.

This odd pair—the long-legged, eager-eyed boy and the saintly old black drayman—became constant companions. They went to prayer meeting together, and to Sunday church, where Frederick, with his natural skill at mimicry, absorbed the techniques as well as the thunderous messages of such gospel-shouting black preachers as Nathaniel Peck and Father Waters.

Deserting his street friends, Frederick spent most of his leisure time at "Uncle" Lawson's little shack on Happy Alley. They read the Bible aloud to each other for hours at a time; Frederick, the better reader, worked out the "hard words" for his friend.

Lawson had a mystic's vision about Frederick; it had been revealed to him, he said, that the boy was destined to become a mighty preacher and do "a great work" for the Lord. Therefore he must go on reading and studying the scriptures. Frederick argued that this could not happen to a person who was a slave for life; but Lawson's simple reply was: "Trust in the Lord. . . . The Lord can make you free, my dear. All things are possible with him, only have faith in God." The thought gave Frederick new confidence and "fanned [his] already intense love of knowledge into a flame." It was one more bit of evidence that all who knew Frederick as a child considered him remarkable.

When Hugh Auld learned Frederick had been spending so much time with Lawson he forbade it, threatening a whipping if he ever went there again. But as usual with Auld this was mostly bluster; Frederick continued his visits, and Auld, though he must have known of them, never did inflict the promised flogging.

His association with Father Lawson was a stimulant to Frederick's pursuit of knowledge, and his discovery of *The Columbian Orator* was an even stronger one. He came upon the book by accident; one day he overheard some of his white friends reciting passages from it that they had been required to memorize for a school exercise. Frederick's interest was intrigued by such intoxicating words as *freedom, liberty,* and *hatred of tyranny.* With fifty cents he had earned by polishing boots, he bought a second-hand copy at Nathaniel Knight's bookstore at number 28 Thames Street. It was possibly the best investment of his life.

Compiled in 1797 by Caleb Bingham, a Massachusetts pedagogue, *The Columbian Orator* was a collection of patriotic speeches by Cato, Washington, William Pitt the elder (Lord Chatham), Charles James Fox, Napoleon, Socrates, and many others extolling liberty, freedom, democracy, temperance, courage, and industry. Mingled with these were original poems, playlets, and dialogues by Bingham designed to "inspire the pupil with the ardour of eloquence, and the love of virtue." It was not easy reading, but Frederick plowed into it with the aid of Walker's dictionary, reading some sections over and over until he grasped their meaning. In the process he added greatly to his limited vocabulary.

One passage in particular struck him with the force of a blow. Bingham had been an early and uncompromising foe of slavery, and tucked away among the patriotic speeches was a short section, "Dialogue Between a Master and Slave," which would have shocked racist Baltimoreans if they had ever bothered to read it. The master began by scolding the slave for trying to run away, but in the course of their dialogue the slave argued so convincingly against his lot that in the end the master set him free. Frederick soon knew the entire dialogue by heart. It described his own situation so precisely that it brought tears to his eyes, and much of his youthful thinking on slavery was drawn from it almost word for word.

When the master chided his servant for fleeing even though he was well treated, the slave replied: "What can you do for me, that will compensate for the liberty which you have taken away?"

To the argument that "Providence" had decreed one man should be subservient to the other, the slave's answer was: "The robber who puts a pistol to your breast may make the same plea. Providence gives him a power over your life and property. . . . But it has also given me legs to escape with; and what should prevent me from using them?"

The master again appealed for gratitude for his kindness, but the slave told him: "You have done nothing for me more than for your working cattle. . . . Is not the rule of treating both designed only for your own advantage?"

As for the master's promise to provide for him in his old age, the slave responded with a mournful cry: "Alas! is a life like mine, torn from country, friends, and all I held dear, and compelled to toil under the burning sun for a master, worth thinking about for old age? No; the sooner it ends, the sooner I shall obtain that relief for which my soul pants."

At last, convinced that the slave would never willingly remain in bondage, the master set him free, whereupon the slave exclaimed in gratitude: "Now I am indeed your servant, though not your slave." [19]

Today this dialogue may seem naive; but to Frederick, a thirteen-year-old boy who had been steeped all his life in proslavery propaganda, it was a revelation. Clearly and logically, it answered one by one all the childish doubts that bothered him. Should he be grateful to Miss Sopha and Master Hugh for their kind treatment? No, for they were only doing it for their own advantage. Was it wrong to think of running away? No, for the runaway slave was only taking back the liberty that was rightfully his. Had God ordained slavery? No, not any more than He sanctioned the right of a robber to use a gun.

"I had now penetrated to the secret of all slavery and oppression," Frederick wrote of his discovery of this dialogue. ". . . 'Slaveholders,' thought I, 'are only a band of successful robbers, who left their homes and went into Africa for the purpose of stealing and reducing my people to slavery.' "

The book held much more to stir his imagination: an eloquent extract on the evils of the slave trade and the hypocrisy of Christians who engaged in it; a ringing declaration by William Pitt the elder on the fundamental rights of Englishmen; a vow by the great O'Conner, in the Irish House of Commons, to "risk every thing dear to me on earth" for the emancipation of Catholics; a passage on the French revolutionaries who had "sworn that they will live free or die"; and the Roman Cato, faced with death or surrender, declaiming:

> ... in Cato's judgment,
> A day, an hour of virtuous liberty,
> Is worth a whole eternity in bondage.

The message of all this eloquence was clear. If liberty, as Fox and Sheridan, Pitt and Burke and Washington declared, was the fundamental right of every man, then it was the fundamental right of Frederick Bailey also. And yet he had no liberty. He was a lifelong slave.

But Bingham also taught that there was a remedy for injustice. The art of oratory, eloquence in public speaking, was the most powerful weapon for truth yet devised by man. "To instruct, to persuade, to please; these are its objects. To scatter the clouds of ignorance and error ... to remove the film of prejudice from the mental eye; and thus to irradiate the benighted mind with the cheering beams of truth. ... An Alexander and a Caesar could conquer a world; but to overcome the passions, to subdue the wills, and to command at pleasure the inclinations of men, can be effected only by the all-powerful charm of enraptured eloquence." On the practical side, he included a detailed guide to "the ornamental and useful art of eloquence" that contained specific instructions for effective use of such platform devices as gestures and facial expressions, cadence and voice inflexions, the dramatic pause, and much more.

The importance of *The Columbian Orator* in shaping Frederick's future can hardly be overestimated. Not only did it open his eyes to the "moral dungeon" of slavery, but it fixed his course toward two fundamental goals: someday he would be free, and someday he would master the art of oratory. Forever after, he kept the little book he had bought for fifty cents close to him; he modeled his texts on the words of the masters Bingham had quoted; and his early oratorial style, even to gestures and dramatic pauses, was taken from Bingham's instructions almost line for line. When he finally succeeded in becoming "Old Man Eloquent" — the greatest public speaker of his time — he owed much of his success to *The Columbian Orator.*

In August, 1831, the news of Nat Turner's rebellion in nearby Virginia swept through Maryland like a tidal wave. Inspired by what he claimed were voices from God, Turner had sparked a blood bath in which some sixty whites, including many women and children, were murdered, and more than one hundred blacks slain in reprisal.

White Marylanders, fearful that the insurrection might spread to their slaves, reacted with panic and counterterrorism. County militias were called out, black leaders were arrested, and armed vigilante bands patrolled the roads at night. No Maryland uprising occurred; the blacks, in Jeffrey R. Brackett's words, "were no doubt more frightened than the whites" by the furor. [20] Nevertheless the Maryland legislature that met in December, 1831, passed harsh restrictive measures against blacks, both slave and free, that would poison race relations for years to come.

At Hugh Auld's shipyard that fall, there was much talk about the rebellion and its root causes. Reprisals were called for. One carpenter, Thomas Lambdin, boasted that he personally had killed two slaves, and that "when others would do as much as he had done, we should be relieved of the damned niggers." The others may have grinned knowingly, aware that Lambdin was just a bragging windbag, but Frederick took him seriously, and shuddered. [21]

The whites were unanimous in blaming the trouble on people they called "abolitionists" who were riling up the blacks with propaganda for something called "abolition." These were new words to Frederick; he could not comprehend their meaning. He looked up *abolition* in Walker's dictionary, but got little help; it defined the word merely as "the act of abolishing." What was to be abolished remained a mystery. A leaflet he found in the gutter that poked bitter fun at the "Bobolitionists" provided a slight clue; apparently the "Bobolitionists" were abolitionists who wanted to deprive slave owners of their property. [22] But it was not until he chanced upon a news article in the *Baltimore American* in December, 1831, that he fully understood who the abolitionists were and what they were trying to do.

The item reported that former President John Quincy Adams, who had just returned to Washington as a congressman from Massachusetts, had laid before the House a group of petitions from Pennsylvania Quakers calling for the abolition of slavery and of the slave trade in the District of Columbia. The wording of the petitions was clear: "We believe slavery and the slave trade, in the human species, is a great national and moral evil; we therefore ask your body to take the subject into serious consideration, and pass such law or laws as will entirely abolish slavery and the slave trade in the District of Columbia, over which Congress has exclusive jurisdiction." [23]

So it was slavery, his own hated condition, that the abolitionists wanted to abolish! And, judging from the numerous petitions and Marylanders' nervous reaction to them, there must be many thousands of abolitionists in the North. The news struck Frederick like a thunderbolt. It was the first time he realized that he and the other slaves were not alone. "There was HOPE in those words," he wrote of this discovery. "... I had a deep satisfaction in the thought, that the rascality of slaveholders was not concealed from the eyes of the world." God, too, must be on his side; when a cholera epidemic scourged Baltimore in the summer and fall of 1832, he saw in it the angry hand of God punishing "the white people because of their slave-holding wickedness," and thought the day of judgment for slavery surely was at hand. [24]

Henceforth Frederick was as fervent an abolitionist as he was a Christian. He talked abolition to anyone with whom he thought it safe: he tried to convince his fellow slaves they were wrong in their hopeless belief that their bondage was preordained; and several of his young white friends agreed that Frederick "had as good a right to be free as they did," and that they did not believe "God ever made any one to be a slave."

But he shied away from such talk with strangers. When two Irishmen he met on the wharf urged him to run away and go north where he would find friends and be as free as anyone, Frederick pretended not to be interested. It could be a trap; he had heard of men who encouraged slaves to escape and then recaptured them to collect a reward.

Not all the abolitionists were in the North. Scarcely a mile away, in downtown Baltimore, a fiery young revolutionary Frederick later would come to know well was writing about slavery and slaveholders with an acid pen during those same years.

William Lloyd Garrison was twenty-four years old when he came to Baltimore in 1829 from his native New England to assist an acquaintance, Benjamin Lundy, in publishing a struggling antislavery monthly, the *Genius of Universal Emancipation.* The two had sharp philosophical disagreements—Lundy favored gradual emancipation as well as colonization for freed blacks, while the more radical Garrison demanded immediate abolition and full rights as American citizens for the freedmen. But they were united in their scorn for the "fiends in human form" who profited from the slave trade, a business that was then centered in Baltimore. Lundy had already clashed physically and legally with trader Austin Woolfolk, and soon after his arrival Garrison made Woolfolk the target of a fresh editorial barrage.

Then Garrison went further afield, to attack two of his fellow New Englanders who engaged in the "foul commerce." In Lundy's absence, Garrison published an article bitterly condemnatory of Francis Todd, owner, and Nicholas Brown, captain, of the ship *Francis* that had sailed from Baltimore with seventy-five slaves bound for New Orleans. Such men as Todd, he wrote, should be "sentenced to solitary confinement for life; they are the enemies of their own species—highway robbers and murderers." As for Brown, he was guilty of nothing less than "domestic piracy."

As a result Garrison and Lundy were indicted for "gross and malicious libel" against Todd and Brown, who were engaged in what was at the time a perfectly legitimate enterprise. The charge carried both criminal and civil penalties. The criminal count against Lundy was dropped on grounds he had had nothing to do with the article; but Garrison was convicted and fined fifty dollars and costs. When he couldn't raise the money, he was sentenced to six months in jail. He actually served forty-nine days before Arthur Tappan, a New York antislavery leader, bailed him out by sending Lundy a draft for one hundred dollars.

While the civil suit was still in litigation, Garrison decided he had had enough of Baltimore. In October, 1830, a Baltimore County jury awarded damages of $1,000 to the plaintiffs, but it was never paid; by then Garrison was back in the Northeast campaigning for funds to found a newspaper of his own. He succeeded, and the first issue of the *Liberator* was published January 1, 1831—the same year young Frederick Bailey learned the meaning of the word *abolitionist*. [25]

So passed the swift years of childhood for Frederick, a childhood unique in many ways. For a slave boy from the Eastern Shore, he was remarkably fortunate. He was lucky to escape the "feudal darkness" of the Lloyd plantation; he was lucky to be put under the care of Sophia Auld, who taught him his letters and to look up at the world; he was lucky to be in Baltimore, a busy and booming city filled with intellectual ferment; he was lucky to have almost as much freedom of movement as any white child; he was lucky to have friends, white and black, who recognized his talent and helped him on his way; he was lucky, at a crucial moment in his development, to discover *The Columbian Orator*.

In the long run it was his own native talent, his courage and strength of character, that enabled him to educate himself against all odds and to climb out of the cesspool that was slavery. But it is taking nothing away from him to point out that there were helping hands along the way, and that not all of them were black ones.

As Frederick grew into adolescence, the warm climate of his life in the Auld household deteriorated. Hugh Auld's bid to be an independent shipbuilder did not prosper; he became increasingly morose and increasingly addicted to drink. Sophia Auld, worn down by poverty and childbearing,

103

was no longer the gentle and motherly person Frederick had first known. She was guilt-ridden for her failure to halt his quest for knowledge, a "crime" for which she felt she was to blame. If she saw him with a book or newspaper, she would rush at him angrily and snatch it out of his hand; if she noticed that he had been off by himself for any length of time, she would demand to know if he had been "reading again." As for Tommy, as he grew older he had, perhaps unconsciously, adopted the racist outlook of his school chums. He no longer considered Frederick his companion; instead, Frederick was his servant.

Change also had come over Frederick as he grew into his teen-age years. He was, he himself admitted, "no longer the light-hearted, gleesome boy, full of mirth and play, as when I landed first at Baltimore." He had become sullen and discontented, had become obsessed by brooding over slavery, secretive about his activities, seeking his companionship outside the household. In retrospect he admitted that his gradual estrangement from "Miss Sopha" was at least as much his fault as hers. "I have no doubt," he wrote, "that my state of mind had something to do with the change in the treatment adopted, by my once kind mistress toward me. I can easily believe, that my leaden, downcast and discontented look, was very offensive to her." The impasse was by no means a simple matter of her disapproval of his reading. Like many a real parent and a rebellious teenager, they had lost the ability to communicate. [26]

Early in 1833, purely by coincidence, Frederick was removed from the Hugh Auld household. The change had nothing to do with his estrangement from "Miss Sopha" or his growing independence; it resulted from a quarrel between Hugh and Thomas Auld over another slave, Frederick's crippled cousin Henny. According to Douglass, Thomas Auld thought that as long as Hugh had the free services of the valuable Frederick, he should be willing to take care of the useless Henny as well. He sent her to Fells Point, but the Aulds promptly sent her back to St. Michaels, where Thomas, having married again, was now storekeeper and postmaster. Thereupon Thomas, infuriated at what he considered his brother's ingratitude, insisted in reprisal that Hugh give up Frederick.

Since Thomas was the legal owner of both Frederick and Henny, Hugh had no choice. And thus, in March, 1833, Frederick was peremptorily ordered back to the Eastern Shore.

❧ *Chapter Seven* ❧

Teen-Age Rebel

St. Michaels

Frederick was in a bitter mood as he traveled from Baltimore to St. Michaels aboard the sloop *Amanda,* with Captain Ed Dodson at the wheel, on a late March day in 1833.[1] With no choice in the matter, he was being forced to give up everything he loved—the bustle and excitement of Baltimore, the white friends who had been his teachers and the black friends he had recently begun to instruct, dear old Father Lawson and his associates at Bethel Church—for an uncertain future in a sleepy Eastern Shore village with a new master and mistress toward whom he felt an instinctive distrust.

He barely knew Thomas Auld, having seen him but a few times in seven years, and he was prepared to dislike on sight Auld's new wife, the former Rowena Hambleton, if only because she had displaced his beloved "Miss Lucretia" in the household. Being anybody's slave was bad enough; but being a slave to these strangers, in the repressive atmosphere of the Eastern Shore, would be even worse.

What was more, in leaving Baltimore he was giving up his best chance of carrying out his cherished dream of escaping to freedom in the North. In the city this had seemed relatively easy, if once he put his mind to it. He could simply start walking north and, with luck, eventually arrive in Philadelphia, where he would be safe. But St. Michaels was another matter altogether; it was situated on a long, narrow peninsula. Walking to free-

105

dom from there would be almost impossible, and even if he got away from the town somehow, in rural Talbot County he would be easily spotted as a strange—and therefore suspicious—black.

As *Amanda* plied her slow way down the Patapsco and into Chesapeake Bay, she was passed by several steamboats—odd, ungraceful craft, flat decked, with paddle wheels amidships and stacks of cordwood to fire their boilers. Frederick knew they were headed for Philadelphia via the new Chesapeake and Delaware Canal, and as he watched them round North Point and head up the bay, he had an idea. If escape by land from St. Michaels was next to impossible, why not seize a boat and, like the steamers, go north up the Chesapeake? It was a thought that grew and blossomed in his mind until eventually he tried it, with disastrous results.

The village of St. Michaels, when they finally reached it, looked even worse than Frederick had imagined it would. It was a cluster of houses around a small harbor and an almost deserted town square, with a few stores strung along the muddy road that led west to Bayside and east to Easton, the Talbot County seat. There were a few brick or well-kept frame houses, but most of the inhabitants lived in shabby, unpainted hovels that wind and weather had turned almost black.

In former times St. Michaels had enjoyed prosperity as a shipbuilding center, but that industry had virtually died out with the depression that followed the War of 1812. Now most men who were strong enough earned a precarious living fishing for oysters, which were packed in barrels and shipped to the Baltimore and Philadelphia markets. The log canoe fleet sailing out of St. Michaels harbor on a crisp morning headed for the oyster grounds in Miles River was a beautiful sight, but oystering was a hard life, calling for long hours, uncertain rewards, and constant exposure to chilling winds. Every canoe carried a jug of rum "to ward off the cold," and heavy drinking was commonplace. At the time Frederick arrived there, the once-lively town was marked by an air of indolence, unsightliness, and defeat. Along the rivers on both sides were fine old plantation houses where genteel families, surrounded by slaves, still lived much as they always had; but even there the "hard times" that would grip the Eastern Shore for nearly half a century were making themselves felt.

Frederick's fears about Rowena Auld proved only too accurate. He resented her from the start, and she lost no time in showing that she felt the same way about him. She was a thin woman with flushed cheeks and a persistent cough; already, at twenty-one, she showed signs of the "consumption" that would take her life within a few years. She had lost her first child, a boy who died in infancy, and that spring was carrying a second—Sarah Louisa was born in July.[2]

In Frederick's eyes, she could do nothing right. He thought she treated seven-year-old Amanda, Lucretia's daughter, like a despised stepchild. Her manner toward the kitchen servants was overbearing and cold, in contrast with the gentleness of Lucretia as he remembered her. She snapped out orders that were to be obeyed instantly, without a hint of please or thank you. Worst of all, she was stingy. Frederick soon decided that, under her influence, Thomas Auld was half-starving the slaves who served him.

The Auld household consisted of eight people: Thomas and Rowena, Amanda, and Haddaway Auld, Thomas's younger brother, in the main house on Cherry Street behind Captain Auld's store; and Frederick, his sister Eliza, their Aunt Priscilla, and the crippled Henny in the kitchen, a separate building in the rear.[3]

As far as the blacks were concerned, the feeding arrangements were stark and simple. Once a week half a bushel of corn meal was fetched from the mill, and from it a small loaf of corn bread was baked fresh each morning for the white family's breakfast. The rest went to the slaves— just under half a peck per week apiece, according to Frederick's calculations. And they got little else; there was plenty of meat in the larder, but Rowena kept it locked up and carried the key in her pocket. She also kept a sharp eye on the slaves when they were carrying food to and from the kitchen. She'd rather let it spoil, as some of it did, than see it go into the stomachs of these "worthless niggers"—especially Frederick, with his sullen ways.

So for the first time in the seven years since he had escaped from Aunt Katy's harsh rule, Frederick was constantly hungry. At Fells Point, even when relations were strained, "Miss Sopha" had always seen that he got plenty of food. As a rapidly growing boy of fifteen, he undoubtedly suffered more than the others—being hungry is a constitutional affliction of youths that age. He soon translated the gnawing ache in his stomach into an abiding hatred of Rowena, and through her, of her husband. They were a fit pair, he decided; Rowena was as cruel as her husband was mean, and each possessed the ability to drag the other down to the lowest depths.

As for Captain Auld, Frederick had no respect for him whatever. He thought him far worse than his brother Hugh, even though he didn't drink or swear and went to church every Sunday at the little brick Methodist meeting house, called Sardis Chapel, on St. Mary's Square. Douglass wrote of him:

> When I lived with Capt. Auld I thought him incapable of a noble action. His leading characteristic was intense selfishness. I think he was himself fully aware of this fact, and often tried to conceal it. ... He was only a slaveholder by marriage-right, and of all slaveholders these were by far the most exacting. There was in him all the love of domination, the pride of mastery, and the swagger of authority,

but his rule lacked the vital element of consistency. He could be cruel, but his methods of showing it were cowardly. . . . His commands were strong, his enforcements weak.[4]

It was a harsh judgment, and probably not a fair one. What Frederick failed to realize was the extent of the problem he himself presented. He was an angry teen-ager in rebellion against everything in his world. Perhaps he had good reason; but if he was going to continue to be a slave, he had to be brought under control. The inexperienced Captain Auld had no more idea than his sister-in-law Sophia how to handle the boy. There was no excuse for Auld's selfishness, but the "swagger of authority" that Frederick found so offensive was undoubtedly just an inept attempt to assert command.

Frederick soon found an ally in his sister Eliza, who shared his spark of independence, though in a quieter, less aggressive way. At seventeen, she had grown into a woman; she was going out with a young free black man named Peter Mitchell, and they were considered married. Captain Auld had promised to sell her to her husband in lieu of granting her manumission, which had become a difficult and risky business under newly enacted Maryland laws. She and Peter, who worked for Samuel Hambleton at the Perry Cabin farm near St. Michaels, were scraping together every penny they could raise toward the one hundred dollars Auld demanded for his generosity.[5]

Under Eliza's expert tutelage Frederick began to learn the sly ways in which slaves could get even with unkind masters and mistresses. It was better to play dumb than to be defiant, better to "forget" than to disobey. "They think we're animals," Eliza said, "so they're not surprised if we act like animals. What upsets them is when we act like human beings."

Together they worked out schemes to frustrate their mistress's imperious orders. When she demanded that they call her husband "master," which she considered the only proper form of address, they kept "forgetting" to do it; try as they might it would come out "Captain Auld," which she thought was much too familiar. If she wanted something fetched from the store, they would "disremember," and have to be told all over again. If she left a bit of food unguarded, it would disappear. Frederick was forever "forgetting" to tie up Captain Auld's horse; it would immediately gallop off to the farm of Rowena Auld's father, William Hambleton, who had given it to the Aulds. Frederick would be sent after it, and while there would get a meal and an armload of fresh bread from the Hambleton cook, Aunt Mary.[6]

Eliza also helped Frederick convince himself that it was no sin to steal food, a practice that had bothered him in his state of religious conversion.

Photo courtesy of William B. Sears

Captain Thomas Auld, ca. 1870

"Thou shalt not steal" did not apply to slaves and their masters' food, he reasoned, since ownership of the food did not really change hands. A piece of pork had belonged to his master in the meat tub; it still belonged to his master in Frederick's stomach, which was also the master's property. So no theft was involved. In fact, by feeding himself he was improving his master's property—and who could object to that?

Pilfering food from outsiders was more difficult to justify, but he worked it out with the belief that all whites were part of the society that supported slavery. Slavery stole not only Frederick's liberty but also the wages he might have earned, as Peter Mitchell did, by his own labor. Therefore, in taking property up to the limit of his unpaid earnings, he was merely taking back from an unjust society what should have been his in the first place.

On Frederick's visits to Martingham, William Hambleton's estate, he saw Cousin Tom and Uncle Henry, Grandmother Betsey's youngest son. They now belonged to Thomas Auld, as he did, but were farmed out to work for Auld's father-in-law. When he asked about others in the family, however, Eliza shook her head sadly. Their sister Sarah and Aunt Betty, with their children, had been sold south, by Andrew Anthony in the summer of 1832, to a man from Mississippi, Eliza had heard.[7] Frederick felt the familiar sting of fear. What if he should be next? Captain Auld loved nothing more than money, and the word was that young "bucks" Frederick's age were bringing higher prices every year.

Then in June came news that Andrew Anthony had died, at the age of thirty-four, leaving a wife and three-year-old son. Served him right, Frederick thought vindictively; at least he would not be selling any more family members down to Mississippi to satisfy his taste for drink. But it also meant the family might be shuffled around once more. He wondered especially about Grandmother Betsey; she was still living in the little cabin, but alone now since Isaac had died. And she was growing old. Frederick had not seen her in half a dozen years; with a pang of homesickness he wondered if he would ever again visit her at the woods cabin where he had been so happy as a child.[8]

The summer of 1833 passed fitfully. Frederick, with a fifteen-year-old's contrariness, hated everything he saw. Not only Thomas and Rowena Auld, not merely the fact of his status as a slave, but the grubby, sleepy little town of St. Michaels, with its countrified ways, in such sharp contrast to the sophistication and excitement of the city he had known. He scorned the white youths he met on the streets, who grinned at him as they walked by in their straw hats and bare feet. Most were far more ignorant than he was; St. Michaels at that time didn't have a public school. He longed to escape somewhere, anywhere, from this backwater community on the poverty-riddled Eastern Shore. He thought again and again of the steamers disappearing in a smudge of smoke on the northeastern horizon, and of the idea they had given him.

Thomas Auld, for his part, must have been well aware of the seething rebellion in Frederick's eyes. He also was undoubtedly aware that this was no ordinary black boy, but an uncommonly intelligent youth who promised to grow up into a handsome and talented man. There surely were many times that summer when he wondered—if he didn't know for certain—about the question of Frederick's parentage, whether this was Lucretia's half-brother, his first wife's own flesh and blood.

Years later Douglass and Captain Auld traded angry words on the extent to which corporal punishment was inflicted by the master on the slave. Douglass declared that Auld had given him "a number of severe whippings." Auld replied, "I can put my hand upon my Bible, and with a clear conscience swear that I never struck him in my life, nor caused any person else to do so."[9] When that statement appeared in print, Douglass

110

bluntly called Auld a liar. But he offered only one instance in support of his claim.

The whipping, if Douglass's memory was accurate, must have occurred during the summer of 1833. One night, he related, Captain Auld discovered that a lamp from his carriage had been lost or stolen. He accused Frederick of knowing what had happened to it. Frederick, in his aggressive manner, denied hotly that he knew anything about the lamp. Captain Auld, according to Frederick, angrily grabbed a cart whip and lashed Frederick with it on the head and shoulders. Edward Auld, the captain's younger brother, who happened to be a witness, begged him to stop; but as Frederick related the story, Captain Auld continued the flogging "until he wearied himself."[10] The story has the ring of truth; but it should be noted that it was the only specific example Douglass produced to support his charge of "a number of severe whippings" by Auld.

In midsummer, however, a change took place that appeared to give promise of better relations. Captain Auld "got religion"—or so it seemed at the time. Auld had been active for several years in the affairs of the Methodist church. In 1830 he had served on the committee to collect money for the rebuilding of Sardis Chapel, and in 1833, the year Frederick arrived, he was secretary of the board of trustees. He also had a sharp eye out for his own interests; in January, 1833, he presented a claim for damages "done to his carriage by the preacher's Horse." The Methodist Quarterly Conference ordered it paid.[11]

But he had not yet been *saved* in the special sense that word conveyed in evangelical Methodism—or if he had, the ecstacy of his experience had worn off, and he needed to be saved again. The opportunity came at a great Methodist camp meeting held at Haddaway's Woods on the Bayside, as Tilghman peninsula was then called.

This was, for the religiously inclined, the most stirring emotional event of the year. It lasted six days, from August 16 through August 21; hucksters, especially those peddling alcoholic beverages, were warned to stay away. Only bread, baked each morning by a designated (and presumably Methodist) baker, was permitted to be sold. Attendants came from far and near; two boatloads of salvation seekers from Baltimore arrived at Haddaway's Wharf (now Lowe's Wharf), while hundreds of families thronged in from Talbot and neighboring counties by carriage, and cart, on horseback, or afoot. Most stayed through the entire period. They camped out at night in tents, covered wagons, or on the ground. Their physical hunger was appeased by oxen, pigs, sugar corn and sweet potatoes roasted at huge communal fires, and their spiritual hunger by sermons shouted practically nonstop by eloquent preachers who declaimed from the platform in the center of the campground.[12]

Many brought their blacks with them, less for the sake of their spiritual welfare than to cook, chop wood, fetch water, and police the grounds. A narrow space behind the preachers' platform was allotted to the "colored," whether slave or free. Here they could stand, if there was room and they had finished their chores, and listen to the preachers shouting about hellfire, join the cries of "Amen" and "Hallelujah" from the assemblage, sing with the others the simple, moving hymns. It was an affecting scene, even though the preachers ignored them except for an occasional over-the-shoulder remark about God having made "colored" people to be slaves. Many blacks found themselves seized by fits of religious frenzy, moaning and screaming with the whites who were being saved.

Frederick was standing in this section one day when, to his amazement, he saw Captain Auld being led forward by one of the exhorters who had been shouting to repentant sinners to "come up to Jesus, come up to God!" Then his master, unbelieveably, was kneeling before the rude altar that had been erected in front of the preachers' platform.

Having undergone a similar experience, Frederick thought he knew the power of the emotion that must be sweeping through his master at that moment. It was enough, he remembered, to make a person love everybody; he had even loved slaveholders, although that had eroded with the passage of time. "If he has got religion," Frederick thought to himself, "then he will emancipate his slaves—or at least he will treat us more kindly, and feed us more, than he has done before."

He edged forward into a sort of "no man's land" that separated the black and white areas, and from which he could observe his master closely. Captain Auld, he could see, was deeply stirred. His face was red, his hair disheveled. He let out a groan, and a tear rolled down his cheek.

But something seemed to be missing. The groan was not repeated. The tear was not followed by others. Captain Auld did not wave his arms or fall writhing to the ground, as Frederick had seen others do. He simply knelt there, and after a time he got up and moved away. It was as though he had wanted to see a light that did not shine for him, to feel a power that was not there. Or at least so Frederick suspected.

And although he heard people saying afterward, in awed tones, "Captain Auld has come through," Frederick's doubts remained. The proof, he thought, would come in whether there was any change in Master Thomas's treatment of his slaves.

He had not long to wonder. There was, to be sure, a great upsurge of religion in the Auld household. Thomas and Rowena prayed and sang hymns morning, noon, and night. But there was no increase in the corn meal ration, and no sign that Auld intended to set anyone free. Instead he became harsher than ever toward his slaves, at least in Frederick's eyes.

112

He seemed soured rather than mellowed by piety. Frederick, with his one-track view of life, thought Captain Auld was wrestling with his conscience. How could he keep his slaves and go to heaven too?[13]

Poor Henny, perhaps because she was so helpless, suffered worst. The burns she had sustained as a child had left her hands like claws, the fingers bent inward to the palms. She could scarcely pick anything up, and was likely to drop it if she did. On top of this she had acquired the habit, perhaps in imitation of Frederick and Eliza, of "forgetting" to obey orders until they had been repeated several times. According to Douglass the exasperation of having Henny on his hands brought out the worst of his "cruelty and meanness" in Captain Auld. As Douglass told the story in *My Bondage and My Freedom*:

I have seen him tie up the lame and maimed woman, and whip her in a manner most brutal, and shocking; and then, with blood-chilling blasphemy, he would quote the passage of scripture, "That servant which knew his lord's will, and prepared not himself, neither did according to his will, shall be beaten with many stripes." Master would keep this lacerated woman tied up by her wrists, to a bolt in the joist, three, four, and five hours at a time. He would tie her up early in the morning; whip her with a cowskin before breakfast; leave her tied up; go to his store, and, returning to his dinner, repeat the castigation; laying on the rugged lash, on flesh already made raw by repeated blows. He seemed desirous to get the poor girl out of existence, or, at any rate, off his hands.[14]

Douglass did not confine himself merely to describing this horrendous scene in his autobiographies. He told the story hundreds of times, with numerous variations, to audiences throughout Great Britain and America, always emphasizing the hypocrisy of a man who could quote scripture while beating a defenseless cripple. Auld, although he disputed other things Douglass wrote and said about him, never denied having beaten Henny.[15]

Meanwhile the Aulds had turned their Cherry Street home into an open house for the traveling preachers of the Eastern Shore's Methodist circuit. Some stayed overnight whenever they came to St. Michaels; as many as three or four might be there for Sunday dinner. By and large they were an uncouth lot, notable for religious fervor rather than for education or manners. After praying long and loudly, they would pull up chairs, tuck napkins underneath their chins, and help themselves to chicken and dumplings, mashed potatoes and gravy, roasting ears, cole slaw, sweet potato pie, and apple pie. Frederick, who served at table, loathed them as much for the way they shoveled down food while he went hungry as for their casual assumption that only white souls were worth saving.

113

Their names as well as their well-fed faces stuck in his memory. Years later he could still recite the list: Storks, Ewry, Hickey, Humphrey, Cooper. And even his phonetic spelling was close to the mark; church records show that the Reverend Levi Storks was presiding elder of the county conference, the Reverends William Urey and William Hickey were circuit preachers, the Reverend Joshua Humphries was an elder, and the Reverend Ignatius T. Cooper was an ex-attorney from Dover, Delaware, who had abandoned law for the ministry.[16]

"Not often did we get a smile of recognition from these holy men," Frederick wrote of them. "They seemed almost as unconcerned about our getting to heaven, as they were about our getting out of slavery." It was probably true; since Francis Asbury's day the Methodist Church had reversed its posture against slavery. By the 1830s a majority of its bishops supported the institution wherever it existed. Whether it was the preachers' indifference toward his immortal soul or their big appetites that most riled Frederick at that stage, he was building a bitterness against the organized Methodist church that would last a lifetime.

There was one notable exception. When the Reverend George Cookman came for a meal and a night's lodging, he made sure the blacks were called in from the kitchen for family prayer service. Then he would ask probing questions about their spiritual as well as their physical welfare, while Thomas and Rowena Auld listened, alert challenges in their eyes. According to Frederick, the slaves did not quite dare to tell the truth. "I was frequently asked, while a slave, if I had a kind master, and I do not remember ever to have given a negative reply," he noted later. Among slaves the maxim was that "a still tongue makes a wise head." Even so, blacks in the St. Michaels area appreciated the fact that Cookman did not believe, as the other Methodist preachers evidently did, that blacks had second-class souls or even that they should be second-class citizens. On the contrary, Frederick wrote of him, "our souls and our bodies were all alike sacred in his sight. . . . There was not a slave in the neighborhood that did not love, and almost venerate, Mr. Cookman."

George Cookman was an unlikely man to be riding the Methodist circuit on Maryland's Eastern Shore in the 1830s. He was no untutored zealot, like many of his contemporaries, but a well-bred Englishman of wealth and education who had given up a prosperous business career to became a minister. Later he became chaplain to the United States Congress, and still later was lost at sea aboard the steamer *President,* which vanished without a trace on a voyage to England in 1841. But in the summer of 1833 he was preaching sermons noted for their eloquence to farmers and their wives in St. Michaels, Easton, and Trappe, and trying to persuade them that holding blacks in bondage was a mortal sin. Most set their

faces against him, but a few were convinced. For example, he had per-
suaded Samuel Harrison, one of the area's largest slaveholders, to emancipate all his slaves in his will. At Harrison's death in 1837 he not only
freed all his adult male slaves but left a legacy of $1,000 to his good
friend, George Cookman.[17]

Like many sincere whites of his time, Reverend Cookman thought
the solution to slavery's evils was to send the blacks back to colonies in
Africa. This was an approach that Frederick scorned, then and later, since
he considered himself as much an American as any descendant of English,
Irish, Scottish, or German immigrants. Nevertheless Frederick shared the
feeling of all slaves in the area that Reverend Cookman was "a great and
good man" in spite of his colonization views, and joined in their sorrow
when he was removed—perhaps because of his antislavery preaching—
from the Talbot circuit.

Not long after the camp meeting Frederick was approached by a "pious
young man" named Wilson who had heard that he could read and write,
and asked if he would like to help establish a Sabbath school for blacks.
This was not against the law, but it was strictly against local custom.
Especially since the Nat Turner rebellion, Eastern Shore whites had opposed
letting blacks learn to read for fear they would be infected by northern
abolitionist propaganda. Even Bible reading, except under the supervision
of a "responsible" (that is, white) person, was frowned upon. Under an
ancient statute, dating from 1723, local constables were empowered to
break up "tumultuous meetings of slaves" on the "Sabbath and other
Holy-days," using the whip if necessary, and calling on white posses to
help them. Any slave found at such a meeting could be punished by
thirty-nine lashes.

Nevertheless, Frederick was thrilled by the prospect of assisting at a
Sabbath school. He probably was not familiar with the 1723 law. In
Baltimore such schools were encouraged, and Frederick had attended
several of them. Although slaves were supposed to be barred, no one had
questioned his presence. But St. Michaels, as he was soon to learn, was
not Baltimore.

Wilson collected several discarded spelling books and a few testaments,
and on the following Sunday some twenty scholars, young and old, gathered
at the home of James Mitchell, a free black, to begin learning their *ABCs*.
Although Douglass later gave the impression that the sole purpose of the
school was "simply teaching a few colored children how to read the gospel,"
several adult males were among the students.[18]

As word of the school spread through the white community, indignation meetings were held. Wilson was informed that there were strong

objections to his continuing, but he refused to give up what he considered a legal operation. Despite the warnings, he gathered the group together for a second session. Wilson and Frederick had been at their teaching only a short time "when in rushed a mob ... who, armed with sticks and other missiles, drove us off, and commanded us never to meet for such a purpose again. One of this pious crew told me, that as for my part, I wanted to be another Nat Turner; and if I did not look out, I should get as many balls into me, as Nat did into him."[19]

Frederick recognized most of the men as leaders of the Methodist church that he had been attending with Captain Auld every Sunday. One was Garretson West, a huge, hulking oysterman considered a saint by some and a simpleton by others. Completely illiterate, West was a perfect choice to head a school-smashing posse.[20] Another was Wrightson Fairbank, like West an exhorter (a sort of religious cheerleader) at Sardis Chapel. Giving the raid a cloak of legality was Constable Thomas Graham, the Aulds' next-door neighbor. And at the rear, frowning in pious disapproval, was Master Thomas.

That ended the school, and with it the last shred of Frederick's respect for Methodism as practiced by Southern slave holders. These men were pillars of the church, and yet they had used whips and sticks to prevent children from learning to read the word of God. He would never again have anything but contempt for such hypocrisy.

For Thomas Auld the school incident was almost the last straw. Now the whole town was talking about Frederick, calling him a "bad nigger." On the street he walked with his head up, looking people in the eye; it was not the way blacks behaved in St. Michaels. The fact that he could read and write only made things worse; according to Frederick, he was the only slave in the entire area who could do so.[21]

At home he was openly defiant, defending himself boldly against Auld's criticisms and complaints, barely masking his contempt for Rowena. Auld blamed Hugh and Sophia for letting the boy have too much freedom in Baltimore; he told Frederick angrily that city life "had almost ruined me for every good purpose, and had fitted me for everything that was bad." Auld's disciplinary efforts had no visible effect, and by year's end he was growing desperate. If Frederick was going to be of any use on the Eastern Shore, his defiant attitude must somehow be broken.

The solution Auld worked out was to rent Frederick for a year as a field hand, to a tough master who would "knock some sense into him." It was a common enough practice; rebellious white boys were often apprenticed to stern taskmasters who taught them a trade with the aid of a hickory stick (and later many a "bad boy" was given a choice of reform school or the army). In Auld's opinion, a year of hard work and strict discipline would "be the making" of Frederick.

His choice was Edward Covey, a poor and ambitious young man who was farming rented land just south of Wade's Point on Bayside. There is no evidence that Covey was actually a "professional slave breaker," as he has often been presented, but he had a reputation for being able to handle stubborn-spirited slaves. If anyone could break Frederick's rebelliousness, Auld decided, Ed Covey could. Besides, he was a religious man, a fellow member of the Methodist church, which was a recommendation in Auld's eyes if not in Frederick's.

So it was decided; and on New Year's Day, 1834, Frederick was sent off to the Covey farm to begin a year that would indeed be the making of him—though not at all in the way Thomas Auld expected.

Introduction to Covey

Frederick was a city boy, and he was not going to be of much use as a field hand. That was evident almost from the moment he arrived at Edward Covey's farm seven miles from St. Michaels. And Covey, a born tormentor, was quick to take advantage of his new slave's awkwardness and ignorance of country ways.

Frederick had walked the whole distance by himself, a long, lonely journey on a blustery New Year's morning. The rutted dirt road took him past the Hambleton estate of Martingham, which he had visited often, and curved south along Bayside, a narrow spit of land lashed by northwest winds and white-capped waves from the relentless Chesapeake. He had met almost no one, and there was plenty of time for bitter reflection.

Everything he had heard about this Covey filled him with dread. Covey was cruel; he was sly; he took delight in making life miserable for slaves hired out to him. He used the whip often and skillfully.

A friend who had served a year under Covey had told Frederick what it was like—rolling his eyes, shaking his head, perhaps taking secret pleasure in frightening this fifteen-year-old greenhorn with his superior airs and his city style of talking. The blacks called Covey a "nigger-breaker" and believed he got his hired hands virtually rent free for his skill at breaking them, like horses or oxen, to a life of bondage. Whether or not this was exaggerated, it had made a deep and fearful impression on Frederick. He had never known the lash, but he had seen its effects, and he was terrified by the thought of it.[22] Only one good thing could be said for Covey, according to Frederick's informant. He did give the blacks on his place enough to eat. That at least put him one up on Master Thomas and the stingy Rowena.

Covey's house, small, unpainted, weatherbeaten, stood near the bay shoreline at the end of a lane that stretched westward for nearly a mile from the main road down Bayside. Today nothing remains of it; even the site has been eaten away by erosion, which has devoured hundreds of yards of shore land in the century and a half since Frederick first beheld it. But the lane up which he walked on that January morning is still there, although considerably shortened; and the farm Covey worked, called Hatton, is still rented land occupied by tenant farmers. On a bleak winter day one can still stand at the water's edge and see what Frederick saw: "The Chesapeake Bay ... white with foam, raised by the heavy northwest wind; Poplar Island, covered with a thick, black pine forest, standing out amid the half ocean; and Kent Point, stretching its sandy, desertlike shores out into the foam-crested bay." It was, and is, a stark and desolate prospect.

Covey rented his land, about one hundred and fifty acres, from the Kemp family, who lived at Wade's Point, the next farm north. Both Wade's Point and Hatton had once belonged to the Aulds; Thomas and Hugh Auld had been born there, before their father, Colonel Hugh Auld, Sr., sold the place to Thomas Kemp, the famous Fells Point shipbuilder. Adjoining Hatton on the south was a place called Mary's Delight, where Dr. Absalom Thompson practiced medicine and operated a surgery, said to have been the first hospital on the Eastern Shore. It was also said that when Dr. Thompson sawed arms or legs off injured patients, he buried the remains in his cellar. Later Dr. Thompson's son, Absalom Christopher Columbus Thompson, would figure in a celebrated controversy involving Frederick. [23]

Covey was about twenty-eight years old, recently married and the father of an infant son, Edward. Before his marriage he had worked as an overseer, which may have been when he got his reputation for handling rebellious slaves. Incidentally, his name was pronounced "cove-ee," as in *cove*, not "covey," as in a flock of quail.

Physically, he was considerably smaller than Frederick, who described him as about five feet ten, short necked, with round shoulders, "of quick and wiry motion, of thin and wolfish visage; with a pair of small, greenish-gray eyes, set well back under a forehead without dignity, and constantly in motion. .... When he spoke, it was from the corner of his mouth, and in a sort of light growl, like a dog, when an attempt is made to take a bone from him."

Aside from Frederick's unflattering description, two independent but conflicting assessments have been found of Covey's character. Harriet

Lucretia Anthony, who knew him during her childhood, agreed with Douglass that he "was really noted for his cruelty and meanness." But A.C.C. Thompson wrote that Covey was just "a plain, honest farmer . . . a hard-working man [who] makes every one around him work, and treats them well."[24]

In the household when Frederick lived there, in addition to the three Coveys, were Covey's cousin William Hughes and Mrs. Covey's sister Emma Caulk, a hunchbacked woman. Only three blacks were on the place: Caroline, the cook, a big, strong woman of about twenty, whom Covey had bought from Thomas Lowe; Bill Smith, a man of about thirty who had been hired from his owner, Samuel Harrison; and Frederick. According to Frederick, Covey had acquired Caroline "as a breeder" and kept her locked up at night with Smith; before the year ended she gave birth to twins.[25]

Frederick's initiation into life as a farm worker began quickly. On January 3 he spent the day chopping wood in a forest lot two miles from the Covey house, a task at which he had acquired some skill from using an axe at Hugh Auld's shipyard. But on January 4 he faced a new and unfamiliar assignment; at dawn on a bitter cold morning Covey, undoubtedly with gleeful malice, roused him out of bed and informed him he was to take a team of oxen and fetch home the wood. In the barn lot Covey introduced him to the oxen, a pair of huge horned beasts that stared at Frederick sullenly. Frederick stared back at them, appalled; never in his life had he driven a yoke of oxen. He had not the slightest idea how to go about it.

Briefly—much too briefly—Covey explained the technique. Buck was the "in hand" ox, Darby the "off hand" ox, which meant that Buck, in theory at least, did the leading while Darby followed. *Whoa* meant stop; *back* meant back up; and *gee* meant pull to the right, while *hither* meant pull to the left. That was the entire vocabulary, as Covey explained it, between driver and oxen. Covey then tied a heavy, ten-foot rope around Buck's horns, handed it to Frederick, and explained that if the oxen should run away he could pull on it to stop them.

To Covey it must have seemed a hilarious practical joke. Anyone who has handled oxen knows that it is a hard-learned art; they respond, if they respond at all, only to someone in whom they have complete trust. Covey didn't bother to mention that this particular team happened to be only half-trained—nor that, as any experienced driver would have known, they would need a hard workout in the open fields to settle their spirits before they could safely be taken into the woods.

Happily ignorant of all this, Frederick gave Buck a slap on the rump

119

with the rope, and off they went up the lane: 3,000 pounds of oxen running at full speed, and perhaps 180 pounds of long-legged boy racing along behind, hanging onto the rope and thinking how smoothly his first venture as an ox driver was going. Beside him the empty cart bounced neatly along through the ruts of the lane.

But when they reached the road and crossed it, still on the dead run, Frederick began to have misgivings. His tugs on the rope to slow down the oxen had no more effect than if he had been yanking at a brig under sail with a piece of clothesline. And when the oxen plunged into the woods, bouncing the cart against trees and stumps, swinging it wildly from side to side, Frederick suddenly realized that at any moment it might hit him and crush him.

At last the oxen smashed into a big tree and came to a halt in a tangle of saplings and underbrush. The cart flew into pieces, the body going one way, the tongue and wheels another. The beasts stood panting, sides heaving, eyes wild with fear. Frederick, panting as hard as the oxen, surveyed the damage and wondered what to do next. It occurred to him that Covey had deliberately set him up for this mishap and that the end result was likely to be something he would like even less.

After catching his breath, Frederick set to work. With much effort, he succeeded in getting the cart body back on the wheels; then with an axe he cut away the vines and saplings in which the oxen were entangled. The team, wearied by their runaway spree, now moved smoothly and sedately through the woods to the pile of firewood Frederick had cut the day before, and stood quietly while he loaded the cart. As they headed for home, Frederick even felt a surge of pride; he had wasted some time, but he had got the job done. Once more all was going well.

At the lane gate, however, a new disaster struck. The oxen had bypassed it on their mad dash out, and it was still shut. It was a flimsy wooden structure suspended between two huge, rough-hewn oak posts; opening it required a strong push, so Frederick had to let go of the rope. As he swung the gate inward, the oxen saw their chance, and off they dashed again. One of the big cart wheels hooked into the gate and smashed it into splinters. Frederick narrowly missed being crushed himself.

Eventually boy and team reached the barn lot and found Covey waiting impatiently, an angry scowl on his narrow face. He listened in silence while Frederick tried to explain what had happened, then curtly ordered, "Go back to the woods again." This time he followed. To Frederick's chagrin, the oxen behaved as if they had been making the journey all their lives, and even responded to his shouts of "gee" and "hither." He had hoped they would act up again so that Covey could see that they, not Frederick, were responsible for all the trouble.

But Covey wasn't interested in punishing dumb oxen. Frederick was his target. Stopping near a large black gum tree, he looked at the boy ferociously, and said: "I'll teach you how to waste time and break gates." With his jacknife he cut off three wiry young gum shoots of the kind commonly used for ox goads. "Take off your clothes," he ordered.

Frederick refused. If he was going to be beaten, he thought, it would be with his clothes on; but Covey rushed at him, ripped off his shirt and pants, and proceeded to give him the most savage flogging of his life. The switches cut deeply into the skin of Frederick's bare back; blood flowed freely; and wales were raised in his flesh as large as his little finger.[26]

Later Frederick would be proud of those wales and the scars they left. Later they would be indisputable proof that he had suffered under slavery; and when he denounced the system of bondage as a living hell he could whip off his shirt and turn his back to show shocked audiences that he knew what he was talking about from firsthand experience. Later he would answer his critics by saying the scars on his back were his authority for speaking out.

But not that day. That day he was just another miserable black boy who had been whipped until the blood ran and could do nothing about it.

❧ *Chapter Eight* ❧

Rebirth

As winter turned into spring, and spring into summer, the floggings continued. Frederick's undeniable awkwardness was nearly always Covey's excuse. He said the youth was as inept a field hand as ever picked up hoe or sickle, and as a result Frederick was seldom without a sore back.

Covey, to his credit, was a hard worker himself; Frederick had to admit that he "was one of the few slaveholders who could and did work with his hands." But if he drove himself hard, he drove the men under him even harder, keeping them in the fields from dawn to dusk and sometimes, especially at the peak of the wheat harvest, until midnight. And he made sure that he, at least, got plenty of rest; he would take a long afternoon nap and come back in the evening refreshed, ready to drive the others on by his example and, if necessary, his whip.

He took such delight in sly tricks designed to catch the slaves loafing that Frederick and Bill Smith, between themselves, called him "the snake." Even in his absence they dared not slack off for fear he would suddenly pop up out of nowhere.

When we were at work in the cornfield, he would sometimes crawl on his hands and knees to avoid detection, and all at once he would rise nearly in our midst, and scream out, "Ha, ha! Come, come! Dash on, dash on!" This being his mode of attack, it was never safe to stop a single minute. His comings were like a thief in the night. He appeared to us as being ever at hand. He was under every tree, behind every stump, in every bush, and at every window, on the plantation. He

122

Rebirth

would sometimes mount his horse, as if bound to St. Michaels ... and in half
an hour afterwards you would see him coiled up in the corner of the wood-fence,
watching every motion of the slaves. [1]

So he behaved six days a week, but on the seventh he was a changed
man. Everything stopped: work, floggings, even the habitual scowl on
Covey's face. He seemed literally to believe that, while six days belonged
to Edward Covey, the seventh was the Lord's. He and Mrs. Covey, beaming
with smiles, would put on their best clothes and drive off to church,
leaving the blacks to do whatever they wished. Punishments as well as all
but the lightest essential chores were suspended until Monday morning.

Through the week there were morning and evening services—a short one
in the morning, when the Lord was expected to realize that there was
work to be done, and a longer one, accompanied by hymns, at night.
In these exercises, the blacks joined with the whites; Frederick, with his
fine voice, was expected to lead the singing. Sometimes he refused, sulking
because of the repeated floggings; but Covey never punished him for this.
Instead, "he was thrown into much confusion. ... His religion was a
thing altogether apart from his worldly concerns."

By midsummer the repeated beatings, Covey's trickery, and the long,
exhausting hours in the fields had finally gotten to Frederick. Of this
period, he wrote: "I was broken in body, soul, and spirit. My natural
elasticity was crushed, my intellect languished, the disposition to read
departed, the cheerful spark that lingered about my eye died; the dark
night of slavery closed in upon me; and behold a man transformed into
a brute!" [2]

On Sundays he would spend his free hours lying "in a sort of beast-
like stupor" under a tree. At times he seriously considered murdering
Covey and then killing himself. But then hope would rise again; he would
walk to the bay shore and watch the great white sails of the passing ships,
and swear that some day he would be as free as they were. He would
steal a boat, and sail up the bay, and walk into Pennsylvania; and there
he would find freedom at last.

In July the wheat that was Covey's principal crop was cut, shocked
and left to dry out. Early in August came time to thresh it by the primitive
process then common on the Eastern Shore. The grain was spread on the
ground and horses driven over it in an endless circle to trod out the wheat
from the straw. Then it was fanned to separate the kernels from the chaff.

On a hot and humid Friday afternoon, Covey's entire work force was
engaged in this task: Bill Hughes, the white cousin; Bill Smith; a slave
named Eli, who had been taken on temporarily as extra help; and Frederick,
whose job was to carry the wheat from the treading yard to the fan. Covey

123

was at the house, a hundred yards away, but as usual was paying sharp attention to make sure his men kept at their work. Everyone was hurrying; if they finished in time, they had been promised a fishing trip.

At about three o'clock, as nearly as he could remember later, Frederick began to feel a fierce headache and extreme dizziness. Suddenly he collapsed, a victim of sunstroke. Just as he succeeded in crawling into the skimpy shade of a nearby board fence, Covey rushed up. He asked Frederick what the trouble was, and when the boy tried to explain, "gave me a savage kick in the side . . . and commanded me to get up." Frederick staggered to his feet, but fell again. Covey grabbed a heavy hickory slab and struck Frederick on the head with its sharp edge. "If you have got the headache, I'll cure you!" he shouted, and again ordered the boy to stand up.

Frederick didn't move. After glaring at him for a moment, Covey began to reorganize the work force, filling in for Frederick himself so that no time would be lost. In a short time Frederick began to feel better; but he had no intention of returning docilely to work. He waited his chance, and when Covey was looking the other way leaped to his feet and dashed across the fields into a nearby woods. If he could make it, he was determined to go St. Michaels and plead with Master Thomas to take him away from this savage brute. It was a forlorn hope; he had no illusions about why Captain Auld had sent him to Covey in the first place. But it was the only plan he could think of. Maybe, he thought desperately, he could appeal to Auld's selfishness. Surely his master would not like to see his own property bruised and battered like this.

As he ran, he could hear Covey shouting at him to come back, and when he reached the woods he saw a horse being brought out and saddled. Covey was coming after him. If he tried to walk in the road, he would certainly be caught; so he decided to stay in the neighboring wood lots, rough as they were, for the entire seven miles. But after going a short distance, he once more collapsed.

Perhaps forty-five minutes later he staggered to his feet, still feeling faint, his face covered with blood, and plunged ahead through the bogs and briers, barefooted, bareheaded, without a jacket. How he made it he never knew; but sometime that evening he finally reached St. Michaels. He was a pitiable sight, his face blotched with dried blood and the back of his shirt stiff with it, his bare feet and legs torn and scratched by thorns.

Captain Auld was still at his store at the corner of Talbot and Cherry streets. When he first saw Frederick, the boy thought he registered sympathetic shock; but as he listened to the story, Captain Auld's expression hardened into disapproval. At the end Auld took Covey's side, just as Aaron Anthony had taken the side of his overseer against the girl who dared to protest against a brutal beating. He had no doubt Frederick deserved the floggings, and he suspected Frederick was merely playing sick in order to get out of work. In any case, what did Frederick expect him to do about it?

"Find me a new master," Frederick replied. Covey, he argued, would never forgive him for running away. If he went back now he would be killed, or if not killed his spirit would be destroyed and he would be ruined for life.

"Nonsense," was Auld's answer to that. Covey was a good, religious man, a fine influence on Frederick. Besides, if he took Frederick away from Covey now, Auld would lose the whole year's wages, a not inconsiderable sum.

Finally Auld agreed that Frederick could remain at the store overnight, but said he must go back to Hatton Farm early the next morning. Thereupon he forced the boy to swallow a large dose of epsom salts, the universal remedy for all slave ailments, and went home to bed.

After a restless night, Frederick set off on the long trip back to Bayside at sunup on Saturday. By nine o'clock he was at the lane gate; but as he slipped through it, "Covey, true to his snakish habits, darted out at me from a fence corner, in which he had secreted himself." Frederick saw him just in time and dashed through a cornfield into the woods. There he dived into a thicket and stayed hidden, hugging the ground, until Covey, muttering to himself, reluctantly gave up the search and headed back to the house.

For the moment, Frederick was safe; but what next? He really had only two choices. He could stay in the woods and starve, or he could give himself up and submit to the lash. He thought of a saying among the slaves, that God loved those best who prayed with their feet; but he saw no chance of a successful escape. In his battered condition, covered with dried blood and scratches, he would be taken into custody by the first white man who saw him.

For the rest of Saturday and well into the night he lay hidden in the woods, resting and brooding. No one came looking for him; Covey evidently was relying on hunger to drive him back to the house. Near midnight he heard footsteps on the main road. Peering out through the leaves, he saw a black man he recognized in the moonlight: Sandy Jenkins, who worked for Mrs. Covey's father. Sandy's wife, a free woman, had a cabin on Pot Pie Neck, south of the Covey farm, and he was headed there to spend Sunday with her.[3] He had a reputation for kind-heartedness and common sense. Frederick decided to take a chance. He stepped out on the road and hastily identified himself.

Sandy listened without a word as the bloodstained youth poured out his story. Then, motioning for silence, he led the way to his wife's hut. He was taking a chance, and he knew it. Under Maryland law a slave could get thirty-nine lashes for aiding a runaway, and his wife, despite her nominally free status, could go to prison if she helped Frederick.

Neither of them appeared worried by that. At the cabin Sandy built a fire and his wife shaped an ash cake of corn meal mixed with salt and water. While it baked she cleaned up his cuts and put his bloody shirt in a basin of water to soak. When the cake was ready Frederick, who had not eaten for thirty-six hours, wolfed it down. Later he wrote: "Though I have feasted since, with honorables, lord mayors, and aldermen, . . . my supper on ash cake and cold water with Sandy, was the meal, of all my life, most sweet to my taste."

After supper the two held a strategy session. Sandy agreed that escape was impossible; geography, if nothing else, ruled it out. Chesapeake Bay lay to the west, the Pot Pie River and Harris Creek to the east. Northeastward, the town of St. Michaels lay across the narrow neck of land like a cork in a bottle. Therefore Frederick must go back to Covey, and a means must be found to protect him from the beating that Covey undoubtedly had in mind for him.

Sandy, in Frederick's words, "was a genuine African," and he had inherited a belief in "some of the so-called magical powers, said to be possessed by African and eastern nations."[4] Consulting this ancient lore, he came up with what seemed to him to be a perfect answer. There was an herb growing wild in the woods, and its root, he assured Frederick, had a potent magic. All Frederick had to do was carry one of these roots on his right side, and it would be impossible for Covey to so much as strike him a single blow. Sandy knew this was true, he explained earnestly, because he had carried the root for years, and in all that time had never once been struck by a slaveholder.

To Frederick, brought up in a thoroughly American tradition, all this talk of magical roots seemed ridiculous. He had seen the plant Sandy named many times, and considered it just a common weed. But Sandy's faith in it was infectious—and besides, what did he have to lose? As the other pointed out, all his book learning hadn't protected him from Covey's lash. So he took the pieces of root that Sandy dug up for him and put them in his right-hand pocket. Thus protected, fed, washed, and refreshed, he set out for home early Sunday morning. Whatever was coming next, he felt a lot better able to face it.

At the yard gate he met the Coveys, dressed in their Sunday best, setting out in the cart for church. To his astonishment, Covey actually smiled at him, asked him how he was, and in a mild tone told him that the pigs had gotten into the barn lot and he would be obliged if Frederick would shoo them out. Then he drove off down the lane.

For a moment Frederick felt the pieces of root burning in his pocket, and almost believed in their magical powers. But on reflection he decided it was Christian magic, not African, that had brought about the miraculous change. On Sunday, the Lord's day, Covey wished all men well—even Frederick. Monday would be different.

And so it was. Early Monday morning Frederick was ordered to go to the stable and feed, rub, and curry the horses. While he was standing on a ladder fetching fodder from the loft, Covey sneaked into the stable, seized him by one leg, and threw him to the floor. Covey then tried to slip a noose around Frederick's ankles, but Frederick leaped away.

What happened next forms one of the most celebrated scenes in all the annals of slavery; for at that moment young Frederick Bailey ceased to be a mere chattel and became a man. From somewhere within him the spark of independence that had almost died burst into flame; the courage that had sustained his ancestors rose to meet the challenge. He had had enough of this snakish brute. From now on he would fight back, no matter what the consequences. He found himself grappling with Covey and could scarcely believe it; he was as startled at the change in his personality as Covey:

Whence came the daring spirit ... I do not know. ... The fighting madness had come upon me, and I found my strong fingers firmly attached to the throat of my cowardly tormentor; as heedless of consequences, at the moment, as though we stood as equals before the law. The very color of the man was forgotten. I felt as supple as a cat, and was ready for the snakish creature at every turn. Every blow of his was parried, though I dealt no blows in return. I was strictly on the defensive, preventing him from injuring me, rather than trying to injure him. I flung him on the ground several times, when he meant to have hurled me there. I held him so firmly by the throat, that his blood followed my nails. He held me, and I held him.[5]

For nearly two hours they struggled, face to face, locked like strange lovers in each other's arms, neither able to gain an advantage. At one point Covey yelled for Bill Hughes to come and help him; but as Hughes approached with a rope, Frederick gave him a savage kick in the groin. Hughes staggered away, doubled up in agony, and showed no more disposition to join the fight.

Eventually their death-dance moved out of the stable and into the cow yard. Covey tried to drag Frederick toward a heavy stick that he hoped to seize and use as a weapon. As he leaned over to pick it up, Frederick grabbed him by the collar and threw him full length into a pile of cow dung. Covey, his face smeared with the stuff, leaped up and seized Frederick again; like a man with a tiger by the tail, he seemed afraid to let Frederick go, and afraid not to. From time to time Covey would shout, "Do you mean to resist, you scoundrel?" and Frederick would reply, "Yes, sir!" and again they would go at it.

Bill Smith arrived, back from a Sunday visit to his family at the Harrison estate, Rich Neck Manor. Covey called on him for help; but Smith, with a fine display of black solidarity, pretended he could not understand what Covey was talking about.

"What shall I do, Mr. Covey?" he asked, as if mystified.

"Take hold of him! Take hold of him!" Covey shouted.

Smith shook his head in refusal. "Indeed, Mr. Covey, I want to go to work," he said with the utmost politeness.

"*This* is your work!" Covey roared. "Take hold of him!"

But Smith was firm. "My master hired me here to work, and not to help you whip Frederick," he told Covey. And when the boy begged him not to interfere, he replied, "My God! Frederick, I ain't goin' to tech ye," and walked off.

Next came Caroline, on her way to milk. Unlike Smith, who knew his master would never let Covey get away with whipping him, she was Covey's property and he could do what he wanted with her. Yet she, too, refused to help subdue Frederick, even after Covey gave her several sharp blows. Weary as he was, Frederick was proud of his race at that moment.

In the end, it was Covey who gave way. Letting go of Frederick's arms, he said: "Now, you scoundrel, go to your work; I would not have whipped you half as much as I have had you not resisted."

"The fact was," Douglass wrote of that face-saving remark, "he had not whipped me at all. He had not, in all the scuffle, drawn a single drop of blood from me. I had drawn blood from him; and even without this satisfaction, I should have been victorious, because my aim had not been to injure him, but to prevent his injuring me."

So ended the fight, and so ended Covey's efforts to tyrannize Frederick. Though the youth stayed on at Covey's farm for five more months, and even went out of his way several times to try to goad "the snake" into another fight, never again did Covey attempt to whip him. Nor did he invoke the law that prescribed a public lashing for a slave who resisted his master.

Why Covey failed to take revenge remains a mystery. Frederick's explanation that Covey did not want it known around St. Michaels that he, the vaunted "nigger-breaker," had been bested by a sixteen-year-old black boy, seems at best only a partial answer. It leaves open the question of why he no longer vented his fury on Frederick in private—and in any case the story of the fight became common knowledge. One suspects that Thomas Auld, despite his stern official manner toward Frederick, intervened with Covey, warned him he had gone too far, and instructed him to be gentler in future.

For Frederick, the battle with Covey was one of the two or three most important points in his career: "I felt as I had never felt before. It was a glorious resurrection, from the tomb of slavery, to the heaven of freedom. My long-crushed spirit rose, cowardice departed, bold-defiance took its place; and I now resolved that, however long I might remain a slave in form, the day had passed forever when I could be a slave in fact. I did not hesitate to let it be known of me, that the white man who expected to succeed in whipping, must also succeed in killing me."[6]

Frederick's term with Covey ended on Christmas Day, 1834. He had a week, the annual holiday period for all Eastern Shore slaves, to rest and refresh himself; for 1835 he had been hired out to William Freeland, who was an altogether different sort of man and master. Once again Thomas Auld's hand seems to be evident. The experiment in terror had failed; Frederick's spirit was simply too strong to be broken. Now Auld would try another method by placing him under a master whose reputation for gentleness and fair dealing was the exact opposite of Covey's.

Readers may wonder what became of Covey, the sadistic "snake" who so nearly succeeded in crushing Frederick's spirit. Did he, as sentimental nineteenth-century fiction would have demanded, suffer for his crimes, and end his life in poverty and disgrace?

Unfortunately, no. Whatever his moral values, his hard-driving system was a practical success. Within eighteen months after Frederick left him, by June, 1836, he had saved up enough money to buy a farm of his own, 196 acres on Broad Creek, for $2,940. In the 1850 United States census he was listed as one of the district's wealthier farmers, with property valued at $23,000. He also possessed five slaves, presumably Caroline and her children, worth several thousand additional dollars. At his death in 1875, even though he had given away much of his property to his children, his gross estate came to $15,559.91, no small amount for a man who had started life as a tenant farmer.[7]

In his new situation, even the chronically discontented Frederick found little to complain about. He quickly came to respect Freeland as much as he had despised Covey. Freeland neither whipped his slaves nor made excessive demands on them; he had a sense of justice and honor; he "was open, frank, imperative, and practiced no concealments, disdaining to play the spy." All in all, Frederick thought him " a well-bred southern gentleman, . . . the best master I ever had, until I became my own master." The Freelands were not wealthy, but they were "old family," a status that meant much on the Eastern Shore. William's mother, Betsey Freeland, who kept house for him, was sister to William Hambleton and aunt to Rowena Auld (which undoubtedly explains why Frederick was assigned to them). Her other brothers were also men of consequence in the county: Edward N. Hambleton, sometime Talbot sheriff; Samuel, known as "the Purser," who had been a hero of the Battle of Lake Erie; and John, also a United States Navy purser.

Best of all from Frederick's viewpoint, Freeland attended no church and did not profess to be religious. This seemed a virtue to Frederick, who had already decided from bitter experience that "of all slaveholders, . . . religious ones are the worst. I have found them, almost invariably, the vilest, meanest and basest of their class. . . . Religious slaveholders, like religious persecutors, are ever extreme in their malice and violence."

In contrast with the irreligious Freeland were two of his neighbors whom Freeland came to know well: the Reverend Daniel Weeden, a Methodist Protestant preacher, and the Reverend Rigby Hopkins, whose affiliation was Methodist Episcopal. Both were notorious for their use of the lash on slaves in the name of piety. The Reverend Weeden, said Frederick, worked on the theory that "the good slave must be whipped, to be *kept* good, and the bad slave must be whipped, to be *made* good." The Reverend Hopkins worked on a different principle—he believed in whipping slaves in advance of their deserving it. Every Monday morning he managed to have one or two slaves lined up to be lashed for some trivial offense, "by way of preventing the commission of large ones." [8]

Freeland's farm fronted on the Miles River, two or three miles northwest of St. Michaels and next to William Hambleton's home estate of Martingham. [9] It was worn-out soil, exhausted from years of tobacco planting, and much labor was required to make it produce paying crops of wheat and corn. But Frederick did not mind hard work; he was no longer the green and awkward city boy who had reported to Covey, but a powerful youth who could handle a hoe or spread manure with as much skill as most of the older men. His harsh year at Covey's had turned him into a first-rate field hand. This had become a matter of pride with him; but he soon learned better than to race against the others to see who could turn out the best day's labor. If a man did too much in a day, they told him, the master would demand that every slave do as much every day. It was better to appear a little slow and clumsy.

This was one of many ways in which blacks could register a silent protest against slavery. There were others. If a new tool or farm implement was introduced, they managed to break it or seem too stupid to master its use; if an easier way of doing things was suggested, they shook their heads and went back to the old method. Gates were left open and bars down, so that stock escaped and had to be rounded up. Slaves reported themselves "sick" or "injured," or wandered off like irresponsible children and had to be fetched back, grinning and bobbing their heads in apology. While an overseer was checking one end of a line of workers, those at the other end merely went through the motions. Only at night, when they were working on their own gardens or money-making projects, or at times when they were permitted to hire themselves out and keep part of their earnings, did the slaves show signs of skill and diligence.

Slave owners saw in all this, of course, added proof that blacks were "naturally lazy." It was an article of faith among whites that all blacks were childish; they loved to sing and dance but could not be made to work; they had no sense of responsibility and lived only for the present. The fact that they had nothing to work for, and no future to look forward to, was beside the point. But in truth the blacks with whom Frederick worked in the 1830s were employing an effective slowdown tactic that would be employed by white workers in the 1930s to combat the "new slavery" of the assembly line and piece work.

Frederick soon found that he had acquired something of a reputation. Probably through Sandy Jenkins, who had finished his year's stint at the Caulk farm and was now working for Freeland, word had been spread about the showdown fight with Covey. It was said that Frederick was impossible to whip, that he kicked back, that, as he said, "Though generally a good tempered Negro, I sometimes 'got the devil in me.'" This, plus the fact that he could read and write, caused him to be regarded with suspicion by the whites and with something approaching awe by the ignorant blacks of the St. Michaels area. Already, although he was only seventeen, they looked on him as a leader.

He was quick to take advantage of his reputation by organizing a clandestine school among the younger blacks who worked for Freeland and other landowners along the Miles. His first pupils were Henry and John Harris, who belonged to Freeland, along with Sandy and Charles (Handy) Caldwell. Soon other youths joined in, until by midsummer more than twenty at a time were gathering on Sunday afternoons to practice their letters from discarded Webster's spelling books and discuss the dangerous doctrines of liberty and equality that Frederick read to them from his precious copy of *The Columbian Orator*. With the violent end of Frederick's first attempt at teaching fresh in his mind, he was careful to keep the purpose of these meetings secret; to a casual observer they might have appeared just a bunch of "young bucks" wasting their leisure time in idle chatter. Through the summer they met wherever they thought it safe—in the woods, in the shade of a big oak tree, behind Freeland's barn—but when cold weather came on, a free black who knew about the school gave them the use of a room in his house. There Frederick taught reading, writing, and freedom three nights a week as well as on Sundays. Altogether he had more than forty scholars, several of whom told him later that they had fled to the North at least partly because of the spark he had implanted. It was one of the most satisfying experiences of his life.

At Christmastide he had an altogether different kind of experience. He received his first introduction to strong drink, and found he loved it much too well.

The week between Christmas and New Year's Day was an annual holiday for Eastern Shore slaves. All work was suspended except for such necessary chores as tending the stock and looking after fires. By tradition, the holiday lasted as long as the yule log burned in the great house; and it was said the blacks stretched their free time by soaking the big logs in swamp water for months before hauling them in on Christmas Eve.

Older, more settled slaves made good use of the holiday by visiting their families or making such items as corn brooms, mats, horse collars, and baskets, which they could later sell for pocket money. Others went hunting for the small game—opossums, raccoons, squirrels, and rabbits—that abounded on the Eastern Shore. But the majority spent their time in ball playing, wrestling, boxing, foot racing, dancing, singing, and—the most popular sport of all—getting drunk on the free liquor doled out by their masters as a "reward" for having worked hard all year.

William Freeland was a liberal master in this as in other things; he distributed large quantities of applejack, a potent homemade brandy distilled from hard cider. Frederick tried it, modestly in the beginning but then in greater amounts, until he was drinking his entire ration and cadging that of others who liked it less than he. He found its effects marvelous at first acquaintance. A few gulps of applejack "made me feel I was a great man. I used to think I was a president." Later in life he recognized its danger and became a teetotaler, but admitted that as a slave youth without any real hope of bettering his condition, "I found in myself all those characteristics leading to drunkenness." He often told the story of how a certain "old soaker" (probably himself) passed out in a pig sty, woke up to hear the hogs grunting around him, and leaped up shouting "Order! Order!" under the impression that he was presiding at an important meeting. [10]

The dancing and drinking were accompanied by black fiddlers and by "jubilee beating"—usually shortened to "juba beating"—a primitive form of rhythmic music that undoubtedly had African roots. The performer beat out his rhythms on a crude drum made of a barrel top or wooden bucket, and improvised songs as he went along. Most of these were nonsense rhymes, or ditties dealing with local people and happenings, but sometimes ironic digs at slavery were slipped in. One Frederick remembered went:

> We raise de wheat,
> Dey gib us de corn;
> We bake de bread,
> Dey gib us de cruss;
> We sif de meal,
> Dey gib us de huss;
> We peal de meat,
> Dey gib us de skin,
> And dat's de way
> Dey takes us in.
> We skim de pot,
> Dey gib us the liquor,
> And say dat's good enough for nigger.
> Walk over! walk over!
> Tom butter and de fat;
> Poor nigger you can't get over dat;
> Walk over! [11]

As much as he enjoyed the revels, Frederick was acute enough to see these yuletime frolics for what they were: a safety valve provided by the masters to make life bearable for the slaves. In an otherwise bleak existence, they were something to look forward to, and to look back on; without them, Frederick thought, "the south would blaze with insurrections.... The rigors of bondage would become too severe for endurance, and the slave would be forced up to dangerous desperation."

With the New Year came enforced sobriety and, for Frederick, a hard look at his own situation. He was still a slave for life, even though a reasonably well-treated one. If anything, he decided, he was *too* well treated. He was adequately fed and not overworked, he had not been whipped even once during the year, he had warm clothing and sleeping quarters, and he had been let alone to conduct his school and other private affairs as he pleased. All in all, he had no complaints about life under Freeland. And that was exactly the trouble; he was in danger of becoming contented, and therefore of giving up the dream of freedom that had sustained him for so long.

On New Year's Day he made a resolution that 1836 would be his freedom year, and before January was over he was actively working on an escape plan. He had two choices: a land route, which would force him to travel down the long peninsula on which St. Michaels was situated and then across heavily settled Talbot County to the Caroline County marshlands; or a bold strike over water to the head of the bay. The first seemed hopeless; as Sandy had warned him that night when he was hiding out from Covey, few, if any, slaves ever succeeded in escaping that way. The second had the virtue of surprise—until now, no black that he had ever heard of had dared sail north to freedom. Remembering the great ships he had seen as they vanished over the northern horizon, he made up his mind.

But he could not make the long water trip alone. Nor, in his enthusiasm, did he want to leave his close friends behind to suffer in slavery while he went free. So he enlisted five others: the Harris brothers, John and Henry; Sandy Jenkins; Charles Roberts; and Henry Bailey, his youthful uncle who, like Roberts, worked at William Hambleton's farm. Frederick was the youngest but one of this sextet, but from the start there was no doubt he was its leader.

Through February and March they met on Sundays and at night to discuss and polish the scheme Frederick had conceived. It was classically simple. On the Saturday night before Easter, a time when restrictions were relaxed, they would steal a log canoe belonging to William Hambleton, paddle north up the Chesapeake, and then strike overland for Pennsylvania. From that point on their plans were vague. None of them knew how far Pennsylvania was, nor what they would do when they got there. Frederick had heard of Delaware, Pennsylvania, New Jersey, and New York City, but even he was not then aware that there was a New York State beyond the city, nor a Massachusetts, nor a Canada where blacks were welcomed and treated as free men. In their ignorance, they conjured up all sorts of dreadful troubles that might befall them:

Upon either side, we saw grim death assuming a variety of horrid shapes. Now, it was starvation, causing us, in a strange and friendless land, to eat our own flesh. Now, we were contending with the waves, . . . and were drowned. Now, we were hunted by dogs, and overtaken and torn to pieces by their merciless fangs. We were stung by scorpions—chased by wild beasts—sleeping in the woods—suffering hunger, cold, heat and nakedness—we supposed ourselves to be overtaken by hired kidnappers, who, in the name of the law, and for their thrice accursed reward, would, perchance, fire upon us—kill some, wound others, and capture all. [12]

It was a dismal prospect, enough to make even the most stout-hearted give up and accept the known evil of continued slavery; and several times they almost did. But in the end Frederick's zeal and the ringing words of *The Columbian Orator* prevailed. He put down every argument the others raised: that the canoe might be swamped by the rough waters of the bay; that its absence would soon be noticed and swift sailing vessels would set out after them; that if they did reach the head of the bay they would have to set the canoe adrift and its discovery would put the "head hunters" on their trail. To counter the main objection, that they surely would be stopped and questioned en route, Frederick wrote out passes for each of the conspirators along this line:

This is to certify, that I, the undersigned, have given the bearer, my servant, John, full liberty to go to Baltimore, to spend the Easter holidays.

William Hamilton
Near St. Michaels, Talbot County, Maryland[13]

The others remained fearful, but all—or so Frederick thought—were good and trustworthy men. Only Sandy seemed to have serious doubts. He was the oldest and most settled of them all; he had, as Frederick knew, a wife who was free; and he had no history of brutal treatment to make him hate slavery as Frederick did. He was also a "true African" who believed implicitly in signs and portents. One day he came to Frederick, greatly troubled. He had had a dream in which he saw Frederick "in the claws of a huge bird, surrounded by a large number of birds, of all colors and sizes. These were all picking at you, while you, with your arms, seemed to be trying to protect your eyes. Passing over me, the birds flew in a south-westerly direction, and I watched them until they were clean out of sight."

Sandy was sure the dream meant that the plot would fail, and Frederick would be caught and shipped south to be devoured by the "carrion birds" of slavery. "I saw this as plainly as I now see you," he warned. "There is sumpin' in it, sho's you born."[14] Frederick was worried by the dream, but shook it off. However, Sandy did not; much to the regret of the others, he announced he was withdrawing from the plan.

That left five desperate young conspirators, three of them in their early twenties, one a boy of sixteen, even their leader barely turned eighteen. Considered simply as property, they would be stealing a small fortune from their masters by escaping: prime young males their age were worth $1,000 or more in the Talbot slave market.[15]

Through the week preceding Easter, which fell on April 3, the five were in a fever of excitement. They could hardly restrain themselves; they whispered passwords back and forth, smiled knowingly at each other, at times burst spontaneously into hymns commonly used by Eastern Shore slaves to signal an impending escape. "O Canaan, sweet Canaan, I am bound for the land of Canaan!" they sang; they also sang an even more revealing spiritual that had a double meaning known to every slave:

I thought I heard them say,
There were lions in the way,
I don't expect to stay
    Much longer here.
Run to Jesus—shun the danger—
I don't expect to stay
    Much longer here.

At a secret meeting at midweek they all clasped hands and took a solemn pledge to carry through the escape as planned, and to fight and die if need be rather than be brought back into bondage. Only Sandy was absent; but the others firmly believed he was still with them in spirit if not in fact.

On Saturday morning, April 2, Frederick and Sandy went to work as usual, spreading manure on Freeland's fields. All was in readiness for the escape that night—food and clothing were packed, the canoe was beached near Hambleton's wharf and paddles were stashed nearby, the passes were distributed—when suddenly Frederick's high spirits took a dismal plunge. He had a strange presentiment; turning to his companion, he said: "Sandy, we are betrayed." He felt as certain of it, he wrote afterward, as if his long-dead mother had appeared before him and told him so. Sandy, with an odd look, replied, "Man, that is strange; but I feel just as you do."

Shortly afterward they were called back to the house for breakfast. As they neared their destination, Frederick looked down the lane to the main road and saw six men approaching—four whites on horseback and two blacks, whose arms appeared to be tied, walking behind. As he watched, a white man whom he recognized as William Hambleton left the others and came toward the house at a gallop, his horse kicking up a cloud of dust behind him in the lane. This in itself was ominous; Hambleton was an elderly, fat, and dignified man who seldom rode a horse at any speed faster than a walk. Reaching the house, he asked for Freeland, and when Frederick replied that he was at the barn, he sped off in that direction. Then the three other horsemen arrived; they proved to be armed constables, two of whom, Tom Graham and Ned Hambleton, Frederick knew well. They had left their black captives tied to the gatepost at the head of the lane, but Frederick guessed with a dreadful certainty who they were: Charles Roberts and Henry Bailey. "It is all over with us," he said to himself. His premonition had been right; they were surely betrayed.

After that things happened swiftly. Frederick was seized by two of the constables, securely tied, and taken into the kitchen. They told him only that he was accused of being "involved in a scrape" and that he was going to be taken to St. Michaels, where he would be examined by his master, Captain Auld. If the accusation was not true, they assured him, he had nothing to fear.

136

They also tied up John Harris; but when his brother Henry came into the kitchen and Constable Graham ordered him to cross his hands so he could be tied, Henry shook his head defiantly and said: "No, I won't." The other two constables drew their pistols, cocked them, and pressed them against his chest, saying that if he did not cross his hands "they would blow the damned heart out of him."

"You can't kill me but once," Henry replied. "Shoot! Shoot and be damned! I won't be tied." With a swift upward thrust, he knocked the pistols out of both constables' hands. All the whites now rushed at him and, after beating him severely, succeeded in overpowering and tying him.

Frederick watched the struggle with a sense of shame. Henry had been true to their solemn pledge; he had fought, and fought bravely, while Frederick had made no resistance. He consoled himself with the thought that there was really not much point in fighting against hopeless odds; and meanwhile, it occurred to him, there was something much more practical that he *could* do.

Just before the scuffle began William Hambleton had remarked, in his mild drawl: "Perhaps we had now better make a search for those protections, which we understand Frederick has written for himself and the others." So they had been told about the passes—and, from the sound of things, that was the only real information they had. While the whites were subduing Henry, Frederick, despite his bonds, succeeded in flinging his pass into the fire. Now, he thought, just let them try to prove anything on me.

As captors and captives prepared to leave, old Betsey Freeland came to the kitchen door. She was carrying a handful of biscuits, which she divided between her two home-bred boys, Henry and John. They she turned toward Frederick, pointing a long, bony finger at him, and screamed: "You devil! You yellow devil! It was you that put it into the heads of Henry and John to run away. But for you, you long legged yellow devil, Henry and John would never have thought of running away!" Frederick gave her a look in return "which called forth a scream of mingled wrath and terror" as she hastily scuttled through the kitchen door and slammed it behind her.

The five suspects were tied behind two horses and pulled at a forced march the three miles to St. Michaels, where they were to be interrogated by Captain Auld. On the way Henry Harris, who was yoked with Frederick, whispered: "What shall I do with my pass?" "Eat it with your biscuits," Frederick told him. Moving his tied hands clumsily to his mouth, Henry did so, chewing long and swallowing hard. The word was passed along, and soon all the telltale passes were disposed of.

Frederick, who had been thinking about their situation, decided it might not be quite so desperate as it had at first appeared. After all, they had not actually done anything, and without the passes as evidence it would be difficult to prove the existence of a plot unless one of them confessed. "Own nothing! Own nothing!" he whispered to Henry, and that warning also was passed along.

When they came before Captain Auld, Frederick's hunch was strengthened. Auld spoke accusingly, asserting in his most solemn tones that their guilt was known and they might as well admit it; but something in his manner gave Frederick the impression that he was not as certain as he tried to sound. If so there was hope—and the hope was strengthened when all four of his comrades joined him in steadfastly denying any intention of running away. Auld scoffed at this; the evidence that they were in fact plotting an escape, he said, was "strong enough to hang [them] in a case of murder."

Frederick attacked this notion boldly. "The cases are not equal," he replied. "If murder were committed, some one must have committed it—the thing is done! In our case, nothing has been done! We have not run away. We were quietly at our work. Where is the evidence against us?"

With this approach, he thought they might be confronted by their accuser, so that they could at least learn who had betrayed them. But Captain Auld would not do this; even though it became clear in the course of their questioning that there was only one witness against them, he would not say who the witness was. Nor did he decide on their innocence or guilt; when he had finished with them, they were hitched behind the horses again and marched twelve more miles to the county seat of Easton, where they were to be put in jail.

The journey seemed endless. At every hamlet and neighborhood— Spencer's Cove, Royal Oak, Kirkham, Miles Ferry, Ratcliffe—word had gone forward that a gang of slaves had been trying to escape, and people were out in force to jeer as they went by. Everyone seemed to know that Frederick, the "yellow devil," was the ring leader. Some shouted that he "ought to be hanged," others that he "should be burnt," or "have the hide ripped off his back." Only the blacks, peering fearfully from behind rail fences, seemed to have any sympathy for him.

Through the long march, Frederick had only one question in his mind: Who was their betrayer? It had to be Sandy Jenkins—and yet, surely, it couldn't be. All the circumstantial evidence pointed to him: he had known the details of their plan and up to a point had participated; he had known about the passes; he had prudently withdrawn after his dream foretold failure; and he alone of all the conspirators had not been rounded up and questioned. It could be no one else, but neither Frederick nor the others could believe it of him. Sandy was their comrade-in-arms, their elder statesman and advisor. And he was a brave man; a year earlier, in the incident at Covey's, he had boldly helped Frederick at the risk of his own skin. In the end, Frederick decided that someone unknown must have learned about the plot and informed on them; but if he had any suspect other than Sandy Jenkins, he never said who it was.

At the county jail on Easton's public square they were placed under the care of Sheriff Joseph Graham, a basically decent man who made them as comfortable as he could under the circumstances. The room in which Frederick and the Harris boys were placed was neat and spacious, "the best in the jail ... with nothing about it necessarily reminding us of being in prison, but its heavy locks and bolts and the black, iron lattice-work at the windows." The food was coarse and skimpy, but the view was excellent. Through the grated window Frederick could see Solomon Lowe's brick tavern across Federal Street and the black waiters in their white jackets moving from table to table inside. He would have given almost anything to hear the gossip they picked up about what was to be done with the prisoners, but none came close enough to be spoken to.

Despite the comfortable quarters, that day, April 2, 1836—was the lowest of Frederick's life. His hopes of escape were dashed; his dreams destroyed; he had been betrayed by someone—Sandy?—whom he had considered a friend; and here he was, in jail like a common criminal, for the "crime" of wanting to be free. Now he would undoubtedly be "sold down to Georgia" and would end his days in a cotton field.

That fear was strengthened when the jail door opened, and in rushed "a swarm of imps in human shape—the slave-traders, deputy slave-traders, and agents of slave-traders—that gather in every country town of the state, watching for chances to buy human flesh (as buzzards to eat carrion)." They were there to learn if the five were to be sold, and if so what value should be placed on them. After taunting the prisoners with leering remarks about trying to escape, they subjected each to a humiliating physical examination, a practice permitted by Maryland law even though the blacks had been convicted of no crime. Frederick in his turn was forced to stand while the traders went over him thoroughly, feeling his arms and legs, poking him in the stomach, shaking him by the shoulders to see if he was sound and healthy. The look in his eyes evidently told them what he thought of them. One of the group, blowing his whiskey-laden breath in Frederick's face, sneered, "If I had you I would cut the devil out of you pretty quick."

Surprisingly, however, the "human imps" did not get their way. On the Tuesday after Easter, Hambleton and Freeland arrived at the jail, not to sell their slaves to the traders, but to take them home. Roberts, Bailey, and the Harris brothers were released without punishment, leaving Frederick alone in his spacious jail cell. Miserable as he was, he had to admit that this was only fair; after all, the whole affair had been his idea, not theirs.

Captain Auld let Frederick languish in jail for a week, which seemed a month to the unhappy boy. Then he, too, showed up one day, signed Frederick's release papers, and took him back to St. Michaels. On the way he told Frederick he had arranged to sell him to "a friend in Alabama" who, Auld said, would grant Frederick manumission after eight years. Frederick did not know what was up, but he strongly doubted the story. For one thing, he had never heard of Captain Auld having a friend in Alabama; and for another, he could not believe that if there were such a person he would actually emancipate a healthy young male slave.

In truth, although Frederick did not know it then, Auld had been agonized by the dilemma in which he found himself. Even though it had not been proved, neither he nor anyone else in the county doubted that the charge of an escape plot was true, and that Frederick had been the ringleader. Custom, and strong public opinion, dictated that he now be sold south as a warning to other slaves. William Hambleton, Auld's stern old father-in-law, had gone even further; unless Auld got him out of the area immediately, Hambleton said, he would personally shoot the boy.

But Auld could not bring himself to do it. Cousin Tom Bailey told Frederick later that while Frederick was in jail, "Master Thomas was very unhappy; and that the night before his going up to release me, he had walked the floor nearly all night, evincing great distress." The slave buyers had made very enticing offers; but Auld, Tom said, rejected them all, saying "money could not tempt him to sell me to the far south." [16]

From this it seems clear that Auld had no real intention of selling Frederick to Alabama or anywhere else. When he talked about his "friend," he was merely trying to frighten Frederick, to let him worry for awhile about what might happen if he did not mend his ways. After a few days, when he decided the youth had suffered enough, he took him down to the wharf and put him aboard a boat bound for Baltimore, assigned once again to the household of Hugh Auld.

As they parted, Auld told Frederick earnestly that he wished him to learn a trade, and promised that if Frederick behaved himself properly he would be emancipated at the age of twenty-five.

Frederick could scarcely believe his luck. A few days earlier he had thought himself doomed to a deep south cotton plantation; now here he was, headed back to the relatively free and easy life of Baltimore. It all seemed too good to be true—and especially that part about being emancipated at the age of twenty-five. The more he thought about it, the more he became convinced that Auld must be trying to trick him in some way. Not for many years would he come to the realization that, for all his petty meanness, Thomas Auld really had been trying to do what was best for his rebellious young slave. [17]

❧ *Chapter Nine* ❧

Preparation for Freedom

He had left Fells Point in 1833 a rebellious, unhappy boy. He came back a man, both physically and emotionally—powerfully built, well over six feet tall, lean and hard from two years of working in the fields; but, more than that, finished for life with the shameful business of bowing and scraping before men who claimed they were his masters simply because their skin color was lighter than his. While he had to resign himself to the fact that, at least for a time, he must remain legally a slave, he was resolved that his bondage henceforth would be no more than a form.

His new resolution soon found a test in the heightened racial tensions that had developed in Baltimore during his absence. Two relatively new elements were responsible: Irish immigrants by the thousands, attracted by construction jobs on the railroads and canals, were pouring into the city's slums; and newly freed blacks in almost equal numbers were fleeing the poverty and prejudice of rural Maryland to congregate in Baltimore. By 1836 more than fifteen thousand free blacks were living in the city.

Conflict was inevitable. The Irish were an uneducated and violently racist group—Frederick thought them the most bigoted element in American society[1]—and their economic status placed them in direct competition with the blacks they despised. They rapidly moved in on jobs traditionally performed by blacks: heavy labor, shipyard work, carting and draying, even domestic service. In building the railroads that were stretching out like fingers to the west, north, and south of the booming city, they were

142

employed almost exclusively. One observer from Connecticut, Ethan Allen Andrews, who rode the first train out of Baltimore in the direction of Washington in 1835, noted that the road bed "has been constructed [entirely] by the labor of Irish immigrants, although the country which it traverses is teeming with colored men, who stand greatly in need of more profitable employment." He had been told by Maryland whites that this had nothing to do with skin color, that it was because of the "idle habits of the free blacks, who, in general, will not labor regularly. . . . Foreigners . . . are far more industrious than the negroes. On the whole, the Irish are fast encroaching upon the territory of the blacks, and threaten ultimately to supplant them wherever slavery may cease." [2]

Most whites with whom Andrews conversed considered the condition of the free blacks "much worse than that of the slaves," and cited this as their reason for opposing general emancipation. "The proportion of deaths among them is much greater than in any other class of society," he reported. ". . . They are addicted to sloth, with all its attendant evils. . . . Their imperfect moral discipline, and indolent habits, lead them also to the commission of petty thefts, in consequence of which great numbers of them are sent to the penitentiary." In support of this contention, Andrews cited statistics showing that the ratio of annual deaths among free Baltimore blacks was one in twenty-nine, against only one in forty-four among slaves, owing to the "salutary effect of temperance and regular exercise" that were enforced on the slaves; he also noted that three out of every five prisoners in the state penitentiary were free blacks. [3]

Frederick, however, viewing the same scene from below rather than above, saw a different picture. Within months after his return he received a savage firsthand lesson in the tactics used by the "industrious" Irish to dislodge the "indolent" blacks from their jobs.

The Aulds had moved again while Frederick was away. They now lived on Fells Street (today a continuation of Thames) in one of a row of curiously built houses that were constructed on the bias because Fells meandered northeast at an angle while Shakespeare Alley, immediately behind it, ran due east and west. Here Frederick lived for most of his final two years in Baltimore. [4]

Meanwhile, Hugh Auld's status had worsened. His shipbuilding business having failed, he was reduced to working as a foreman in other yards, so that he no longer had a place of his own in which Frederick could learn a trade. Instead, he arranged to have the youth taken on as an apprentice calker at William Gardner's yard, where two large warships, the brigs *Fourth of July* and *Independence*, were under construction for the Mexican government that spring.

At Gardner's, as at other Fells Point yards, black and white workers had for many years worked side by side at the same skilled jobs for roughly equal pay. But with the influx of the Irish, the situation changed. Gardner's contract called for completion of the two warships by July, with heavy penalties for failure to meet the deadline. The white carpenters took advantage of this to walk off their jobs, saying they would not return until all the free blacks were fired.

The boycott apparently succeeded, although Gardner in fact did not meet his deadline. [5] In any event the racial animosity it engendered quickly spilled over into the ranks of the apprentices, where Frederick was the only black. Since he was a slave and what little pay he earned went to his white master, the Irish carpenters did not demand that he be fired; instead they encouraged the white apprentices to make his life miserable in numerous petty ways in hopes that he would give up trying to learn his trade. For months he had to endure contemptuous slurs against "the niggers" and listen to talk about how the blacks intended "to take the country" and all "ought to be killed." A curse accompanied most remarks made to him.

It was not all one-sided. Frederick was more than a match physically for any of the white boys, and he let them know it. One day Edward North, biggest and meanest of his tormentors, took a swing at him, whereupon Frederick picked him up and unceremoniously dumped him into the water of the dock. On another occasion he was driving bolts in the hold of a vessel with Ned Hays when one of the bolts bent. Hays, with a curse, said it was Frederick's blow that had bent the bolt; Frederick snapped back that it was Hays's fault, not his. Hays grabbed an adze—a large, arc-bladed hand axe—and rushed at him. Frederick parried his wicked swing with a heavy maul, and for a moment the two glared at each other in fury. Then their tempers cooled.

Finally—egged on, Frederick thought, by the adults—four white apprentices, North, Hays, Bill Stewart, and Tom Humphreys, came at him at once. Armed with bricks and handspikes, they closed in on him from all sides; and while he was fighting off those in front, he received from behind a savage blow from a handspike that knocked him, stunned, to the ground. All four rushed in and began to pummel him with fists and bricks. As Frederick managed to get up onto his hands and knees, one of the attackers planted a heavy kick directly into his left eye; for a time it felt as if the eyeball had burst, and soon the eye was swollen completely shut. Eventually they left him, satisfied by his puffed-up eye and bloody face that he had been punished enough.

Through all this, Frederick reported, at least fifty white adults looked

144

on, and not one said a word in his behalf. Instead there were cries of "kill him!—kill him!—kill the damned nigger! He struck a white person! Knock his brains out!" When Frederick staggered to his feet and, grabbing up a handspike, attempted to go after the four apprentices, several adults seized him and held him until the youths escaped. Now he was afraid he really would be murdered; "Judge Lynch's law," as applied in Maryland, decreed death to any black who struck a white, even though the legal penalty was only thirty-nine stripes with the lash. But he slipped out of the grasp of his captors and fled home.

There Sophia Auld burst into tears at the sight of his battered and bloody face. While she cleaned up his wounds and covered his eye with a lean piece of fresh beef, Hugh Auld listened with growing indignation to his story. Frederick had had many differences with Master Hugh, but had to admit that on this occasion he was a "manly-hearted fellow, and . . . his best nature showed itself. . . . He poured curses on the heads of the whole ship yard company, and swore that he would have satisfaction for the outrage."

As soon as Frederick was somewhat recovered, Auld took him to the office of Justice of the Peace William H. Watson in Bond Street with a view to seeking a warrant for the attackers' arrest. Watson listened to the story, and then asked:

"Mr. Auld, who saw this assault of which you speak?"

"It was done, sir, in the presence of a ship yard full of hands."

"Sir," said Watson, "I am sorry, but I cannot move in this matter except upon the oath of white witnesses."

"But here's the boy," Auld argued. "Look at his head and face. *They* show *what* has been done."

Watson patiently pointed out that a Maryland law which had been on the books since colonial times decreed that no black could bring evidence against a white person. Therefore he could do nothing unless white witnesses would come forward. Frederick's word was not acceptable; nor Auld's, either, since he had not seen the attack.

Even Auld, who usually upheld the slave code, was disgusted with this manifestation of its unfairness. When he found he could persuade none of the white witnesses to testify, he angrily withdrew Frederick from Gardner's yard and got him a job at Walter Price's; Auld was foreman there and could keep an eye on the youth.

Although Fells Point shipbuilding in general was declining, Price's yard was busy that year with a special kind of work. Price had become one of the principal suppliers of swift sailing vessels for the illegal African slave trade. By working there, Frederick made a direct although perhaps unwitting contribution to that horrendous traffic.

Almost alone among the nations, Great Britain was trying to suppress the slave trade by sending warships to blockade the West African Guinea coast. It was a thankless task, one the British ships were often unequal to; the slow old vessels usually assigned to the blockade were no match for the slavers' swift craft. As one British officer put it, "Trying to stop the slave trade with cruisers is like trying to stop a river by building a dam across its mouth."[6] The United States government, although it had officially outlawed slave imports in 1808, refused to cooperate in enforcing its own laws; the cotton states were hungry for slaves, and no one cared much whether they were smuggled or not. By the 1830s more than one hundred thousand slaves a year were pouring into Cuba and Brazil, and many of them were turning up illegally at the Savannah and New Orleans slave markets.[7]

To outrun the British blockade, the slavers sought the fastest sailing vessels they could find—and that meant, in many cases, the lean, rakish, sail-heavy schooners and brigs known as Baltimore clippers that were built at Fells Point. These had established a reputation in the War of 1812 as the swiftest craft in the history of sail. By the 1830s they were being refined even further, with sharper hulls, a greater weight of sail, and special designs to jam more African bodies aboard their crowded holds and decks. One of the suppliers of these highly profitable though illegal vessels was the Fells Point yard of Walter Price.

In 1836 and 1837, while Auld and Frederick were employed by Price, at least three vessels definitely identified as engaging in the slave trade were built at his yard. These were the schooner-rigged *Delorez*, registered August 3, 1836; the hermaphrodite brig *Teayer*, registered June 16, 1837; and the brig *Eagle*, registered December 1, 1837. There may have been others; and certainly additional slave ships were constructed at other Fells Point yards where Frederick worked—for instance, the schooner *Laura*, registered by Butler & Lambdin on March 15, 1838, at a time when by his own account Frederick was "a favorite" of Butler and even "served as his foreman on the float stage."[8]

Thus there can be little doubt that Frederick learned his skills as a calker and practiced them as a young journeyman on vessels destined to take part in some of the foulest and most horrifying episodes in the annals of slavery. For a man who hated slavery with a deep and all-consuming passion, it was an ironic turn of events.

Whether he knew the destination of the craft he worked on is another question. The facts were common knowledge at Fells Point, but perhaps they did not trickle down to the level of a teen-age black apprentice. Elaborate precautions were taken to avoid public disclosure that the ship-building that sustained the Fells Point economy through the 1830s went in large part to supply an illegal and officially condemned market.

The United States law of 1820 defined any participation in the slave trade, including shipbuilding, as piracy punishable by death. To circumvent this, the vessels built by Price and others reached their eventual owners by a complicated process. First registered to an American owner, they would sail to Havana or Brazil and there be "chartered" with their American crew by a slave trader who would put up $9,000 or more—equal to full payment for the ship—in "earnest money," plus a charter fee. With the American crew and a complement of non-American "passengers," they would proceed to Liverpool to be outfitted for the slave trade. As American-flag vessels they could not be searched by the British even though the supplies and equipment they took aboard—African trade goods, leg irons, and the like—clearly indicated their purpose. Off the African coast the "passengers" would take over, the registry and flag would be changed to Spanish, Portuguese, or Brazilian, and the slave run made. Thus the Americans were not engaging in actual slave dealing, and the foreigners were protected, except for a few hours, from search and seizure by the British. It was a neat and deadly bit of trickery, and the profits were enormous; up to eight hundred slaves, worth as much as $180,000, could be loaded aboard in a single eight-hour period. The vessels then became the property of their "charterers," and their Port of Baltimore registry was changed to read "sold at Havana" or "sold to foreigners."

If Frederick knew of his small role in this foul commerce, he never mentioned it in his later writings. Instead, his memories of the period were warmly nostalgic. What he recalled were "the pungent fragrance of boiling pitch," the look of "the seams of a ship's deck," the "ringing, cheerful sound of a calker's mallet," and the hundreds of men pouring through the Fells Point streets when the tolling of a bell signaled a change in shifts.

Many of these men stopped at the store of John Aburn, who sold groceries and whiskey, although he didn't drink himself. Frederick noted that little was done without whiskey, especially by the Irish: "Grog time was as well defined and certain as dinner time or the time to go to work." Worrell's blacksmith shop, where ships' fittings were made, and Hubbard's block and pumpmaker's shop, were "perfect beehives of activity." In the harbor stood brigs, brigantines, schooners, and ships in the Liverpool, West Indies, and South American trade that were waiting to load or unload

147

cargoes at Patterson's, Chase's, or Brown's wharf. A whipping post, considered essential to good order, stood opposite the county wharf. Frederick was never subjected to punishment there, although he did receive a whipping from Hugh Auld for spending all day watching Captain Cummins drill his "flying artillery," a militia company, at the inspection house and following these greatly admired soldiers through the streets. [9]

During the years 1836 to 1838 Frederick formed numerous close friendships with other young blacks. His earlier Fells Point street companions, the white boys who had helped him learn to read and write, by now had cut him out of their circle; they were grown men, or nearly so, working in the shipyards, where they had absorbed the prevailing antiblack prejudice. Even little Tommy had grown up; shortly after Frederick returned to Baltimore, Tommy signed on as a seaman aboard the brig *Tweed,* built in 1834 at Levin Dunkin's Fells Point yard. Remembering their warm childhood relationship, Frederick was sorry to see him go. "There were few persons to whom I was more sincerely attached than to him, and there are few in the world I would be more pleased to meet," he wrote in the 1850s. Not for many years after that did he learn that Tommy had been lost at sea on February 3, 1848, at the age of twenty-four. [10]

Nearly all his new friends were free and worked, or hoped to, in the shipyards. They included William Isaacs, Dawson Thomas, James Harris, Robert Brown, Harry Jones (a "good-hearted boy" known as "Frazier's Harry"), and John Chester, whom Frederick considered "a young man of real ability" and with whom he spent many Sundays in the shipyard, hidden away under ships' bottoms or behind piles of timbers, reading and talking about forbidden subjects. Like Frederick, most of these young men despised the racially poisoned atmosphere of Baltimore, and soon left. Isaacs wound up in Victoria, British Columbia; Thomas, in California; Harris and Brown, elsewhere in Canada; and Chester, in South America.

However, Frederick's most intimate companions were the five free youths with whom he formed a secret debating club that they named the East Baltimore Mental Improvement Society. They met at various houses, including James Mingo's little rented shack in Happy Alley, and argued hotly over topics ranging from the status of blacks in Maryland to classical theology. As the only slave among them, Frederick was technically barred from joining a secret society; but this legal quibble was overlooked, and in fact he appears to have been the club's intellectual leader and perhaps its founder. His wide-ranging mind was already looking beyond the second-class citizenship that was the lot of free blacks to a full challenge of the white establishment. During a debate one night at Mingo's house, Frederick vowed that he never intended to stop until he was a United States senator. [11] It was a bold declaration of war for a nine-teen-year-old slave boy from the Eastern Shore to be making against the sacred precepts of white supremacy.

Other club members included William E. Lloyd, William Chester, Joseph Lewis, and Henry Rolles. Frederick considered them gifted youths "who, with the advantages of education, would have made their mark in the world." He had the same opinion of Samuel Dougherty, one of his scholars in the secret classes Frederick conducted at night when Hugh Auld thought he was asleep. Dougherty was energetic and enterprising, a man who, "had he been a white man, or had he been given anything like fair play, . . . would have been one of the most successful men Balti-more ever knew." Another who showed marked potential was Daniel Keith, "a man of noble mould. His head and bearing point him out for a leader of his people, . . . one of the wisest and best that the colored people on Fells Point have ever had." [12]

Despite its serious nature, the East Baltimore Mental Improvement Society also had social gatherings, and at one of these Frederick met a girl named Anna Murray, like him a native of the Eastern Shore. Their friendship ripened into love, and by 1838 they were engaged to be married.

Anna was dark and quiet, a hard-working girl who had none of Fred-erick's intellectual ambitions but gave his soaring imagination a solid base. She was the practical one of the pair, a few years older than Frederick and much better adjusted to the hard realities of nineteenth-century black life. Beyond a few words, she could neither read nor write.

Born near Denton in Caroline County, just across Tuckahoe Creek from Frederick's birthplace, she was the eighth of twelve children of Bambarra Murray, a slave, and Mary, his slave wife. According to her daughter, Rosetta Douglass Sprague, Anna's parents were granted manumission just a month before she was born, so that she was their first free child. At the age of seventeen she joined the influx of free blacks into Baltimore, where she worked as a maid for a French family by the name of Montell for two years. She was employed as a domestic at the home of a Mr. Wells, said to have been postmaster, on South Caroline Street in Fells Point at the time she met Frederick. [13]

Meanwhile Frederick, as ever the angry young radical, had broken away from his association with the Bethel African Methodist Church on Straw-berry Alley, where he had undergone his first rapturous religious experience. His reason appears to have been disgust with the negative attitude of its lay leaders toward abolitionism, in which Frederick was already a strong believer. In 1835 five Bethel trustees had signed an open letter, which was published in *Nile's Register* and widely quoted by proslavery apologists,

Young Frederick Douglass

Anna Murray Douglass

denouncing in passionate language the efforts of northern abolitionists as a danger to free blacks as well as slaves, and calling for suppression of their "vile" publications.

The letter, signed by Nathan Montgomery, John Lauck, Stephen Lauck, James Wilson, and Thomas Saunders, took as its principal target William Lloyd Garrison's newly formed American Anti-Slavery Society, with which Frederick in a few years would be closely affiliated. It expressed the writers' "heartfelt and unconquerable abhorrence of the atrocious attempts of mistaken, hot-headed zealots to plunge the country into anarchy and discord, and to deluge it with torrents of blood." For their part, the five trustees pledged themselves "not to receive any of the vile, mischievous and incendiary publications now so industriously scattered abroad," and called on local postmasters to destroy such material on sight.

The letter may have been well intentioned, but it could not have been to Frederick's liking. Shortly after his return to Baltimore, he reportedly left the Bethel Church and joined the Sharp Street A.M.E., which was much farther from his home but more acceptable on racial matters. The Reverend John Fortie, minister at Sharp Street, had coauthored a much more moderate letter, also published in the *Register,* which called the attention of Baltimore whites to the facts that, first, among the free blacks were many "good and conscientious citizens" who supported ten churches, thirty-five or forty benevolent societies, and numerous weekday and Sabbath schools, and second, black homeowners helped support the city's financial institutions. While it disavowed any action tending to "molest or destroy the peace and harmony of the community," it did not mention the abolitionists. [14]

In the spring of 1838 Frederick made a deal with Hugh Auld that, to all extents and purposes, set him free. Henceforth he would be permitted to "hire his time"—find jobs for himself and collect his own wages—provided he paid Auld three dollars a week and furnished his own board, clothing, and calking tools. Thomas Auld, still his legal owner, had turned this proposition down during a visit to Baltimore; but when Frederick brought it up again after Thomas had left, Hugh readily agreed. [15]

It was a good arrangement both ways. Auld no doubt was glad to be rid of responsibility for this headstrong and independent youth, now twenty years old and impossible to discipline properly. Besides, the weekly three dollars was guaranteed, whether or not there was work to be found at the shipyards. Anytime Frederick did not pay up promptly on Saturday night, using savings from past earnings if necessary, the deal could be canceled.

As for Frederick, he calculated he would have to earn at least $6 a week (the prevailing wage for journeymen calkers was $1.50 a day) to meet Auld's payments plus his new expenses. That meant at least four days work per week, or even more to make up for periods when bad weather closed down the shipyards. But he was confident he could do it; he was a good and reliable workman, well liked by most of the yard bosses. In the past he had often brought home as much as $9, of which Auld had allowed him only an occasional "sixpence or a shilling" for spending money. Now, by working from sunrise to sunset six days a week, he should be able to start putting away some savings for his "freedom fund." It made the long-awaited day of escape seem infinitely nearer.

So Frederick eagerly moved out of the Fells Street house into his own lodgings—the first time in his life that he had lived independently of a master and mistress—and as spring lengthened into summer his little hoard of savings gradually grew. At the same time he continued his active role in the intellectual ferment of the black community. With Anna's encouragement he took up music, starting a lifelong love affair with the violin; together they bought three volumes of collected musical pieces, two by Dyer and one by Shaw, which would be cherished possessions for many years. [16] He kept up his teaching, and he furthered his own education by studying under blacks more advanced than he. At debating-club meetings he sharpened his skill at public speaking, using techniques gleaned from *The Columbian Orator,* and gained a reputation as a mimic for his hilarious burlesques of racist sermons by white preachers.

But always in the back of his mind was fear, a gnawing dread that his new-found freedom might be snatched away as quickly as it had been granted. While he remained in Maryland he was still a slave; and as long as he was a slave he could, without warning, be "sold south," as so many members of his family had been. Thomas Auld had sworn he would never do this, but what if something happened to him? Then Frederick would become the property of the hated Rowena; and he had no illusions as to how the mean-spirited daughter of William Hambleton, who had wanted him shot, would dispose of him. Or suppose he did something, even unwittingly, to incur the wrath of either Thomas or Hugh Auld? Both were men of violent tempers. In a single flash of anger they could decide to sell him to the southern market, and all his hopes of escaping to freedom would be gone. It was time to start thinking in concrete terms of an escape plan, one that would have a better chance of success than his abortive effort in St. Michaels. [17]

Frederick's timing could not have been better; it was part of the good fortune with which his entire life seemed to be endowed. Just a year earlier, in 1837, a railroad had been completed that ran north out of Baltimore, crossing the Susquehanna River by ferry and connecting at Wilmington with a steamboat line for Philadelphia. Precautions were taken to prevent this route from being used by escaping slaves, but the security net was not yet nearly as tight as it later would be. Thus in 1838, as never before nor afterward, it was possible for an enterprising slave, with luck, nerve, and proper-appearing papers, to ride north to freedom simply by boarding a railroad passenger car in Baltimore. This was the plan Frederick decided on; but just when he would carry it out remained indefinite—until his hand was forced early in August by an angry clash with Master Hugh.

With several friends, Frederick had arranged to spend a weekend at a camp meeting about twelve miles from Baltimore. He was delayed at his work on Saturday night, and it was so late by the time he was ready to go that, rather than hold up his friends any longer, he decided to postpone his weekly payoff visit to Hugh Auld until his return. Once at the camp meeting, he enjoyed himself so much that he stayed an extra night; and it was Monday evening by the time he showed up at the Fells Street house with his weekly three dollars. He found Auld in a rage, made all the worse by the fear that had haunted him all weekend that Frederick might be trying to escape.

There was a roaring scene. Auld shouted that he had a mind to give Frederick a whipping for daring to leave town without permission, and Frederick yelled back that he had not known their bargain included his having to get Auld's approval whenever he wanted to go anywhere. Finally Auld said, as nearly as Frederick could later recall it: "Now, you scoundrel! you have done for yourself; you shall hire your time no longer. The next thing I shall hear of, will be your running away. Bring home your tools and your clothes, at once. I'll teach you to go off in this way."

So ended Frederick's brief taste of freedom. That same night he was back at the Auld house, under Hugh Auld's watchful—and wrathful—eyes, and his opportunity to earn money for himself was gone.

In the heat of his own anger he decided to get back at Auld by refusing to work under the old conditions; and all that week he sulked around the house, not even trying to find employment. On Saturday night there was another showdown. Auld demanded his wages, and Frederick said he had earned none. Auld threatened again to whip him, and Frederick prepared to fight back; they nearly came to blows, even though Frederick knew that another fight with a white master would doom him to the slave traders for certain. At last Auld backed down, but he said with a peculiar smile that Frederick need not trouble himself any more about trying to get jobs, that Auld himself would see that he got work, and plenty of it.

Thinking things over that Sunday, Frederick wasn't sure just what those ominous-sounding words were supposed to mean. Could it be that Auld had decided he must be sold? He came to two conclusions: he had better give in at once on the matter of seeking work for himself, and he had better delay no longer in setting a target date for his escape plan. It was not, when he came right down to it, an easy thing to decide. He would be giving up everything he loved—his dear friends, the rough camaraderie of the shipyards, even the Auld family, and especially "Miss Sopha"—for the uncertainties of life in an alien and faroff world.

But it had to be done. Reluctantly he crossed his Rubicon. He made up his mind that on the morning of Monday, September 3, he would endeavor to get aboard a train and, if all went well, ride north to freedom. This decision was made on August 12, so that he had just three weeks and a day in which to make his final preparations.

The time passed all too swiftly. To allay Master Hugh's suspicions, Frederick reported early Monday morning at the yard of Butler & Lambdin on the City Block, near the drawbridge, and was hired on as a calker. He worked there and at Walter Price's for the next two weeks, earning nearly eighteen dollars all told. When he turned the money over to his master, Auld handed him back a twenty-five-cent piece, saying sarcastically, "Make good use of it." Frederick promised he would, but did not add that it would go into his slender escape fund. In the third week he worked only four days, and had only six dollars to turn over to Master Hugh, who gave him a look as if he suspected Frederick was holding out on him.

For all his efforts, Frederick had been able to save only seventeen dollars, not nearly enough to pay his fare to the north and finance him until he could get established there. But Anna came to the rescue; she sold one of her two featherbeds and dipped into her own savings to provide the needed funds.

Frederick found it impractical to borrow the freedom papers of any of his friends. Even if they were willing to take the risk involved—and it was considerable, since aiding a slave to escape was punishable by a lengthy prison term—Frederick did not look enough like any of them, with his light coloration and his Indian features, to pass a close inspection. Instead he obtained, from a retired merchant sailor named Stanley, a paper known as a "seaman's protection," which certified that the holder was a free American sailor and entitled to all rights under the American flag. The man described on it did not look much like Frederick either—he was much older and darker—but it was the best he could do.

On the fateful Monday morning he and Anna bade each other a tearful farewell. When—or if—he reached safety in New York City he planned to send for her, and they would be married there. But the *if* lay like a heavy weight between them; if he was caught the future would be bleak. He would be jailed and sold, and they would never see each other again.

Then he was off to the station, where he waited, trying to look inconspicuous, while others, black and white, bought their tickets and boarded the train. He had decided not to join the ticket line for fear the ticket-seller would take time to study the sailor's paper carefully and he would be discovered. For the same reason he had arranged with Isaac Rolles, a hackman and brother of one of his debating-club friends, to bring his baggage to the station at the last moment. Rolles arrived just in time, and Frederick grabbed his bundles and jumped aboard the train as it was pulling away.

The moments that followed were the most suspenseful of his life. The car was crowded with men of both races—Jim Crow cars had not yet been devised—and the conductor seemed to take forever as he slowly made his way down the aisle, taking tickets and carefully scrutinizing the papers of each black passenger. Under the law the railroad could be sued and he could be held personally liable if a slave slipped through undetected;

so he was making sure each black corresponded to the written description of him.

Frederick was well disguised for his masquerade, dressed in a red shirt, tarpaulin hat, and black cravat tied carelessly around his neck in sailor fashion; and from his years around the docks he could "talk sailor" like any old salt. Even so, he knew he could never pass a thorough examination; his best bet was a bluff and hearty manner that, he hoped, would draw the conductor's attention away from the details on the protection card.

In this he was helped by the fact that all of America just then was in the throes of patriotic fervor against British demands for the right to seize and search American-flag vessels. "Free trade and sailors' rights" were the hotly defended slogans of the day, and American seamen, wherever they appeared, were greeted with pats on the back, free drinks, and cheers. Ironically the dispute involved British efforts to keep American-flag vessels from being used in the African slave trade; but if Frederick was aware of this background he was willing to use it to his advantage. Right now his problem was not the plight of black slaves thousands of miles away, but of one black youth on a railroad car speeding through northeastern Maryland.

When the conductor finally reached him, Frederick looked up with what he hoped was a sailor's confident grin, and was rewarded by seeing the other's harsh countenance turn friendly at the sight of what he supposed to be an American hero of the open seas.

"I suppose you have your free papers?" the conductor asked in a diffident tone.

"No, sir," Frederick replied as casually as he could. "I never carry my free papers to sea with me."

"But you have something to show you are a free man, have you not?"

Now it was time to sound the patriotic trumpet. "Yes, sir!" Frederick said with every show of pride. "I have a paper with the American eagle on it, that will carry me around the world!" The conductor smiled in appreciation; and when Frederick handed him the bogus protection, he barely glanced at it before collecting the fare to Wilmington and moving on.

The worst was over; but there still were several hours to get through before he would be safely out of Maryland, and even then he would have to pass through another slave state, Delaware. To Frederick, the minutes seemed hours, and the hours days. "The heart of no fox or deer, with hungry hounds on his trail, in full chase, could have beaten more anxiously or noisily than did mine," he wrote of this suspenseful journey. Every white man was a potential enemy, and some of the blacks, too; blacks as well as whites had been known to turn in escaping slaves for the reward. On the train were several men he knew casually and who might at any moment

155

recognize him despite the sailor rig, and report him to the conductor. Luckily, none did; but at Havre-de-Grace, where the passengers had to leave the train and take a ferry across the Susquehanna River, he encountered a new and nearly disastrous danger.

As he boarded the ferry he was greeted with a loud and friendly hail; and to his dismay saw that one of the ferry hands was a young black man named Nichols, who knew him well and had recognized him instantly. Nichols was full of cheerful questions: What was he doing on the train? Why was he wearing that sailor getup? Where was he going? When was he coming back? Any one of them might spell disaster if somebody overheard and realized that he was not, in fact, a deep-sea sailor. Frederick answered in monosyllables, and as soon as he could he ducked away to another part of the ferry.

There were two other close calls. As he boarded the Wilmington train on the north side of the river, a southbound train arrived and stopped on the track across from it. Frederick glanced into the other train and there, seated at the window directly opposite, was a Captain McGowan, under whom he had worked only a few days before on a revenue cutter being built at Walter Price's yard. McGowan would certainly have known him; but in the hurry of the moment he did not look out the window as he gathered up his belongings and prepared to leave the train.

With a sigh of relief, Frederick settled in his seat. But then he saw another man he knew, a German blacksmith named Frederick Steen. They rode in the same car all the way to Wilmington, and several times Steen stared at Frederick intently, as if trying to place him. "I really believe he knew me, but had no heart to betray me. At any rate he saw me escaping, and held his peace," Frederick wrote in gratitude.

The last risk came when Frederick left the train at Wilmington, still in slave territory, and boarded a steamboat for Philadelphia. He was sure he would be arrested; the bounty hunters who profited by capturing escapees, he had been told, were especially vigilant at the border points. But no one paid any attention to him, and soon he was on his way up the Delaware. At Philadelphia he paused only briefly to reflect that he was on free soil; then he asked a black bystander how to get to New York City, and was directed to the Willow Street station, where he boarded a train that evening.

He reached New York at about one o'clock on the morning of September 4, 1838. He was tired, hungry, nearly broke, homeless, and friendless. His future was a blank. But at least the years of restless dreaming were over. He had done it; he was, at long last, on his way to being free. [18]

❧ Part II ❧

The Exile's Return

🌿 *Chapter Ten* 🌿

Postwar Reunions

As long as slavery endured in Maryland, Frederick could never return. He was a permanent exile—at first as a fugitive slave subject to recapture, and later, even as a free man, liable to imprisonment under the harsh Maryland code that made it a crime for a freed slave to reenter the state. Although this law was generally ignored, it would have been a tempting weapon to use against a black leader as formidable and as outspoken as he was in the 1840s and 1850s. He himself doubted if white racists would have waited for the law; perhaps overdramatizing, he declared he would have been "murdered at sight" if he had appeared on the streets of Baltimore.[1]

Taking the name of Frederick Douglass to evade pursuers, he built a new life for himself and Anna—to whom he was married in New York City on September 15, 1838—in the alien North. Gradually he rose to prominence in Massachusetts, and later, in Rochester, New York, as a powerful and gifted antislavery orator, writer, and newspaper editor. In Great Britain, which he visited twice, he became perhaps America's best-known and most-honored celebrity of either race; and even among slave-holding southerners in the United States he won grudging recognition as the acknowledged spokesman for three million enslaved blacks.

But the pain of exile never ceased. Despite his international stature, despite his honors in the North, he remained at heart a Marylander. He could not go back; but in the bitter winters of New England and upper

New York State, he yearned for the soft climate of his Eastern Shore childhood and the scenes of his Fells Point youth.

"It is not that I love Maryland less, but freedom more," he wrote from Rochester in 1848. ". . . The fact is, there are few [blacks] here who would not return to the south in the event of emancipation. We want to live in the land of our birth, and to lay our bones by the side of our fathers; and nothing short of an intense love of personal freedom keeps us from the south."[2]

The first public notice he received, within a few months after his arrival in New Bedford, Massachusetts, reflected this same deep attachment to the land of his roots. On March 29, 1839, the *Liberator*, William Lloyd Garrison's fiery abolitionist newspaper, reported that a "Mr. Douglass" had been among the speakers in favor of a resolution denouncing African colonization at a March 12 meeting of New Bedford blacks. Whether Frederick had a hand in writing the resolution is not known; but its wording bore the unmistakable imprint of his thinking and sentiments:

. . . We are *determined* to lay our unfettered bodies on the soil that gave us birth. . . .

We are American citizens, born with natural, inherent, just and inalienable rights. . . . The inordinate and intolerable scheme of the American Colonization Society, shall never entice or drive *us* from our native soil. . . . We look upon those of our free colored brethren who will consent to be banished to the pestilential shores of Africa as enemies of the sacred cause of abolition.

For Frederick, even the rock-bound coast of New England was preferable to the "pestilential shores of Africa." He was not, and never would be, a supporter of the "Afro-American" cult. But it was to Maryland, the land of his forefathers, that he gave his loyalty and his love.

Slavery in Maryland, under a new state constitution, was formally abolished on November 1, 1864. Just sixteen days later Frederick returned to Baltimore for the first time in twenty-six years.

He came home on a wave of national triumph. The Union had been saved; the war had been won for the North, and only the mopping-up remained; Lincoln had been reelected, and the end of slavery everywhere was clearly in sight. The slaveholding power in the South, which Frederick had so long and so bitterly opposed, was crushed.

For him it was also a personal triumph. He had left as Freddy Bailey, a frightened youth in a borrowed sailor's jacket, jumping unceremoniously aboard a northbound train with false credentials in his pocket. He came back as Frederick Douglass, a polished and well-to-do Victorian gentleman, world-renowned, advisor to President Lincoln, socially at ease in the society of sophisticated whites, and undisputed as black America's leading voice.

Even the setting was dramatic. He first public appearance, on the night of November 17, was an emancipation celebration at the old Bethel African Methodist Church in Fells Point where he had first imbibed religion as a boy.

The audience that greeted him that night was racially mixed, in itself a wonder he could scarcely have imagined in the Baltimore of his youth. Among them were men and women he had known then, and who had grown older as he had. At the rostrum he towered above them all, handsome and distinguished, his great shock of hair sprinkled with gray, his broad-cheeked face composed, his eyes flashing under the heavy brows.

He opened softly, as always, almost humbly, apologizing for the handbills that had described him as America's greatest orator. It was a trick to set the audience at ease that he had learned long ago from Caleb Bingham's *Columbian Orator,* the little book on the "art of eloquence" he had bought with his hard-earned first fifty cents. Then he launched into reminiscence, recalling the great black preachers he had heard at Bethel Church, "the gentle voice of Father Waters," the "thunder" of Peck and Cannon, "the eloquence of Lewis G. Wells, Joseph Wilson, William Douglass." These were the men who by example had given him his first lessons in public speaking. He recalled also his Fells Point street days, the gang fights with the "town boys," the whippings he got because he followed marching groups of militia all day and was late getting home at night.

But his listeners had not come to hear an aging ex-Baltimorean relive the days of his youth. They had come to hear the famous Frederick Douglass, orator without peer, gadfly of America's conscience, uncompromising champion of black rights. And Douglass did not disappoint them. The speech he delivered was one of the most eloquent, and certainly one of the most emotional, of his life.

In spirit and content, it was unlike any of his addresses in the past. For once there were no diatribes against the slave masters, no scornful references to Thomas and Hugh Auld, no bitter outcry against Edward Covey's whip, no denunciation of white prejudice against blacks. All that was now forgotten. He came "not to condemn the past but to commend and rejoice over the present."

What could he say? "All former experience at public speaking," he admitted, "avails me nothing here. When a man confronts Niagara, for the first time in his life, he is awed into silence by the grandeur and sublimity of the scene. ... What can I say which will be half so eloquent, commanding or touching, as the thought which now fills every mind and thrills every heart. . . . that the spirit of liberty has been here, and like the breath of the Almighty, has touched our chains and left them broken.''

In hushed tones, he told of his joy and wonder that the meeting he was addressing could even take place. His life, he said, had been distinguished by two important events. "One was my running away from Maryland, and the other is my returning to Maryland tonight. . . . I rejoice that . . . we are permitted to meet here on the soil of our birth—to meet not only as men, but as Marylanders—children of Maryland—the land at whose sparkling fountains we first quenched our thirst—the land whose fields, when we were hungry, first gave us bread—to meet here upon our own dear native soil.'' The very fact that he was there to speak, and they to listen, "with none to molest and make us afraid,'' was proof that "Maryland is now a glorious free state, that the revolution is genuine, full and complete.''

He gloried now in being a Marylander; but he had always loved the state. "Even in the gloomiest days of her history, and of my own, I have felt an inexpressable affection for my native state, and hailed with the joy of an exiled son, every indication of progress and civilization she has presented.''

It was a confession of faith that would have been a revelation—and undoubtedly a shock—to the thousands in the North and in Britain who had heard him in speech after speech condemn the viciousness and cruelty of the slaveholding South and describe his Maryland childhood as one of deprivation and brutal treatment. But to Frederick there was nothing contradictory about it; he had hated nothing about Maryland except the fact of slavery, and now that emancipation had come, his love was complete.

But he was not yet finished; there was purpose behind his confession of love for Maryland. He was far too old a hand at the art of propaganda to let it go at that. Having moved his listeners to sentimental tears for their beloved state, he proceeded to jolt them back to reality with the uncompromising moral pressure for which he was famous.

As a matter of course, he said soothingly, Maryland was destined for national leadership. Its climate, its resources, its people, its geographical position, all made that inevitable. And Maryland's Anglo-Saxon majority—with a bow to the whites in his audience—would always be dominant within the state. But some of these, he continued with mock concern, seemed to have no faith in themselves. They seemed afraid that whites could not compete with blacks on an equal basis, "that to invest the colored race with equal rights, is dangerous to the rights of white men.'' That was a "slander upon the ability of the white race,'' and he would personally defend them against it: "I deny that the black man's degradation is essential to the white man's elevation. I deny that the black man should be tied, lest he outstrip you in the race of improvement. I deny the existence of any such necessity, and affirm that those who allege the existence of any such, pay a sorry compliment to the white race." On the contrary, he affirmed, "the more men you make free, the more freedom is strengthened, and the more men you give an interest in the welfare of the State, the greater is the security of the State."

The implicit irony in his argument was vintage Douglass. By the time he finished, whites who wanted discriminatory laws were made to appear cowards who were afraid they were not as good as blacks, and Douglass himself was their protector against such nonsense.

He then proceeded to the fundamental message of this homecoming speech: a call for "absolute civil and political equality" in Maryland between blacks and whites. With slavery abolished, it was time to restore the rights to vote and hold office that the state's blacks had lost in 1801. As he put it:

If the Negro knows enough to pay taxes, he knows enough to vote; if the Negro can form an opinion respecting the claims of rival candidates and parties, and knows good from evil, as all your laws concerning his conduct imply, he knows enough to vote. If he knows an honest man from a thief, he knows enough to vote. If he knows enough to commit crime and to be hanged or imprisoned, he knows enough to vote. If he knows enough to fight for his country, . . . he knows enough to vote.

He is a man, and if he knows as much when sober as an Irishman knows when drunk, he knows enough to vote on long established American usage.[3]

Maryland's white majority was not ready to meet his challenge. Blacks would not receive the franchise until 1870—and then only under the goad of the Fifteenth Amendment to the Federal Constitution. But at least Douglass, on his homecoming night, had flung down the gauntlet.

All told, he delivered six lectures during his stay in Baltimore. And he enjoyed an affectionate reunion with his sister Eliza, who had heard about his speaking engagements and had traveled the sixty miles from Talbot County to see him. They had not met or even corresponded since he had been shipped out of St. Michaels in disgrace in the spring of 1836.

Frederick rejoiced to see her, at fifty-two, "still quite straight and vigorous," with a posture and manner that reminded him of his grandmother. A warm and motherly woman who had borne nine children, she was known as "Mammy Liza" to generations of St. Michaels blacks and whites. Although she could not read or write, she had followed his career with pride and interest; one of her daughters, born in 1856, had been named Mary Douglass Mitchell in his honor. Of members of his Bailey kin group, she reported that some, including his cousin Tom, had been set free and were still living in the St. Michaels area; but others, he was grieved to learn, had "been sold and scattered through the rebellious slave states."[4]

The contrast between brother and sister must have been evident to both. She had remained an illiterate child of the Eastern Shore, while he had become a cosmopolitan citizen of the world. Yet she possessed as much as he of the Bailey family steel. Her freedom, in fact, had been far harder-earned than his. Frederick had received his manumission as a gift from British friends; she, with the help of her husband, Peter Mitchell, had bought and paid for hers with her own labor over a period of years.

While Frederick was still living in the St. Michaels area, Thomas Auld had sold Eliza and her two children to her husband for one hundred dollars, in effect granting them their freedom by putting them under Peter Mitchell's legal control. Because the law required manumitted slaves to leave the state, Mitchell, a free man, held his entire family in technical slavery until 1844. In July of that year, the law being no longer operative, he set Eliza free.[5]

Auld may have considered his part in the transaction generous, since he could have gotten as much as six hundred dollars by selling Eliza and the children to a slave trader. But to Eliza and Peter one hundred dollars was an enormous sum. She worked as a domestic for five dollars a month, and he as a field hand for not more than fifteen, so that it must have taken them years to pay off Captain Auld.

Nevertheless they had raised nine children, most of whom were working at the menial jobs that, except for oyster tonging, were the only opportunities open to free blacks. John, Edward, and Peter, Jr., were employed as farm laborers; Susan and Mary Douglass were "out to service." Two older girls were married and gone from the household.

For housing the Mitchells were dependent on the benevolence of Peter's employers, Samuel and John N. Hambleton, bachelor brothers of William Hambleton, who had once threatened to shoot Frederick if Thomas Auld didn't remove him from the neighborhood at once. By unwritten agreement, whites refused to sell land to blacks, and thus effectively preserved the peonage system that was little or no better than actual slavery from an economic standpoint. Frederick's son Lewis, who visited Eliza's family a few months later, wrote to his father that St. Michaels was "one of the worst places in the South" in this respect. As Lewis described it:

The white people will do everything they can to keep the blacks from buying land. Large tracts of woods that the whites will neither use nor sell to the blacks lie idle and wasting. .... The whites think to control the labor by not selling land to the blacks. The highest price paid a farm hand here is fifteen dollars a month. A large number of colored men make from eighteen to twenty dollars a week oyster-ing. They have surplus money and can't use it to any advantage around here; and they do not want to move away.

When blacks attempted to retaliate by opening their own stores in town and boycotting white merchants, the whites reacted with violence. Shortly before his June, 1865, visit, Lewis reported, a meeting of blacks had been mobbed by white shopkeepers and broken up because its chief speaker "was advising the colored people to do business for themselves, those who were not able to work to open stores and the rest should trade with them."[6]

The Hambleton brothers for whom Peter Mitchell worked were con-sidered "soft" on race issues, but even they did not try to buck the white agreement against land sales to blacks. Both were United States Navy pursers—Samuel as a youth had been a hero of the Battle of Lake Erie in the War of 1812—and strong Union supporters. In contrast to their brother William, they had freed all their slaves, including Peter, many years earlier. When the Civil War began, John, at the age of sixty-three, had sworn loyalty to the Union and had continued to serve in the navy through-out the hostilities.

Their "liberalism" consisted in permitting Peter, his brothers, James and Washington Mitchell, and other former slaves to rent an acre of ground each on their estate, known as Perry Cabin Farm. There the Mitchell brothers built small houses (on what is now Mitchell Street in St. Michaels), kept pigs and chickens, and raised enough vegetables for their families. When at his death in 1870 John Hambleton bequeathed the one-acre lots on which they lived to James and Peter Mitchell and granted each a small cash gift, it was considered a dangerous precedent by many Talbot County whites.[7]

Such in sum were the economic facts of life for Eliza Bailey Mitchell and thousands of similarly situated Eastern Shore blacks as the era of "freedom" began. There would be little change for nearly a century; for most, the only escape from virtual serfdom would continue to be flight to the slums of Baltimore and Philadelphia.

During his Baltimore visit, Frederick also attempted to have a reunion with Sophia Auld, now a widow. But in this he was rebuffed. When he called at her house on Ann Street, there was an angry altercation; Benjamin Auld, younger brother to "little Tommy," brusquely ordered him from the house. Benjamin Auld, who had become a Baltimore policeman, had been reading Frederick's autobiography and was incensed by remarks Frederick had made about Sophia in that book.[8]

In truth, there was considerable justice in Benjamin's view. Frederick had built his public career around his childhood experiences as a slave; and in the course of it he had held up not only Sophia, but also Thomas and Hugh Auld, to public scorn and ridicule. Regardless of their faults, he had said things about them that he must have known were not entirely true; and he had probably exaggerated the extent and vehemence of "Miss Sopha's" opposition to his reading while underplaying her many and long-continued kindnesses. In his speeches he had treated the Aulds even more roughly than he had in his books.

From Frederick's viewpoint such exaggeration was mere hyperbole, not only justified but necessary. He was at war with slavery, and he was willing to use any weapon that came to hand against it. Slavery was inhuman; the Aulds were slaveholders; therefore, they had lost the right to be treated as human beings. It was as simple as that. In his famous "Letter to My Old Master," published in the *North Star* in 1848, he had warned Thomas Auld not to expect fair treatment from him: "I intend to make use of you as a weapon with which to assail the system of slavery—as a means of concentrating public attention on the system, and deepening the horror of trafficking in the souls and bodies of men. I shall make use of you as a means of exposing the character of the American church and clergy—and as a means of bringing this guilty nation, with yourself, to repentance." He then proceeded to assail Auld with a mixture of truth, half-truth, and outright falsehood that made superb anti-slavery propaganda but was unfair to the man at whom it was aimed.

The letter charged that the stripes on Frederick's back were scars of a whipping that had been inflicted at Auld's "direction," which was true in the sense that Auld had sent him out to Covey, knowing the man's reputation. It said Auld had caused him to be dragged fifteen miles from the Bay Side to Easton—which was doubtful because it was William Hambleton, not Auld, who had arrested the plotters—and "to be sold like a beast in the market," which was entirely false since Auld not only had refused to sell him but had sent him back to live in Baltimore.

Auld was "the guilty holder of at least three of my own dear sisters, and my only brother, in bondage." This, too, was false, and Frederick must have known it. Auld had never owned any of them except Eliza; Perry, Sarah, Kitty, and Arianna all had gone to Andrew Anthony in the slave division to which Frederick had been witness, and he could hardly have been unaware during his three years in St. Michaels that they were not Auld's slaves.

Even more shocking was the charge that Auld had cruelly mistreated

Frederick's grandmother, Betsey Bailey. "My dear old grandmother, whom you turned out like an old horse to die in the woods—is she still alive? . . . Send me my grandmother! that I may watch over and take care of her in her old age," the open letter demanded.[9] In fact, Betsey Bailey at the time when the letter was written was being cared for in Captain Auld's household. After Isaac Bailey's death, she had continued to live in their little woods cabin. When Auld learned that, in her mid-seventies, she was going blind and was nearly destitute, he sent for her and—although she was not his responsibility—saw to it that she was cared for until her death in November, 1849.[10]

Frederick's first autobiography, *Narrative of the Life of Frederick Douglass, an American Slave,* had been less a factual story of his childhood than a powerful and effective polemic against slavery. He had painted with bold strokes all the evils of slavery, portraying his youth as one of cruelty and deprivation, reciting every horror he had observed or heard about. The book had been extremely successful, selling more than 30,000 copies by 1850 in the United States, Britain, France, and Germany, and providing the basis for his international reputation. Its portrait of Frederick as the victim of brutal masters, a child who was torn from his mother's breast, forced to go naked and to eat from a trough like a pig, and con-stantly beaten, was the one by which the world knew him.

This was the public Frederick Douglass, the tortured victim risen to confront his tormenters, the wounded gladiator striking back at those who would have destroyed him. "He was cut out for a hero," wrote one admirer shortly after he took to the lecture circuit for the Massachusetts Anti-Slavery Society in 1841. "In a rising for liberty he would have been a Toussaint or a Hamilton. . . . Let the South congratulate herself that he is a fugitive. It would not have been safe for her if he had remained about the plantation a year or two longer."[11]

Douglass nurtured the image, for it was his badge of distinction. The cardinal fact of his career was that he had been a slave and that he carried on his back the scars from Covey's whip to prove it. That was what had brought him to the attention of the Garrisonian abolitionists in the first place; it was what drew crowds as he toured New England and the Mid-west in the 1840s; it was what made him an object of adulation in Great Britain. When he proclaimed himself the spokesman for black America, it was not simply as a black, but as a black who had been a slave and knew the full depths of slavery's horrors.

"I deem it neither arrogant nor presumptuous to assume to represent three millions of my brethren," he wrote in 1846. ". . . I have been one with them in their sorrow and suffering one with them in their ignorance and degradation—one with them under a burning sun and the slave-driver's bloody lash. ... Being thus so completely identified with the slaves, I may assume that an attack upon me is an attack upon them."[12]

But there was also a private Frederick, more closely attuned to the open-hearted boy who had charmed all who knew him with his smile and quick intelligence, who had seen first in Aaron Anthony and later in Thomas Auld a father image, who had hungered for affection and approval, and who had held it against Auld that he gave too little of them, that he tried too hard to be a stern master and not hard enough to be a foster parent.

This Frederick had no desire for revenge against his former owners. Indeed, he loved them; they were his family. He looked back on his Fells Point years with the nostalgia any man might feel for a happy boyhood. He might abuse the Aulds unmercifully as symbols of the slave-owning class; but he felt nothing for them as individuals but affection.

Typical of these inner feelings was a letter Frederick wrote to Hugh Auld about 1859. For public consumption he had pictured Hugh as a "foul imp of a slaveholder" who was eager to "lay his infernal clutch on me" and Sophia Auld as a woman of "tiger-like fierceness" who treated Frederick "as though I were a brute." But none of this was reflected in his private correspondence, which was in fact an almost wistful plea for reconciliation:

It is twenty years since I ran away from you, or rather not from you but from *Slavery,* and since then I have often felt a strong desire to hold a little correspondence with you and to learn something of the position and prospects of your dear children. They were dear to me—and are still—indeed I feel nothing but kindness for you all. I love you, but hate Slavery. ... Gladly would I see you and Mrs. Auld—or Miss Sopha, as I used to call her. I could have lived with you during life in freedom though I ran away from you so unceremoniously. I did not know how soon I might be sold. But I hate to talk about that.[13]

Frederick's appeal went unanswered. If he harbored no bitterness, Hugh Auld did. The picture has often been drawn of the mature Douglass, mellowed by age and success, forgiving his former masters for their cruelty to him as a slave. In fact, it was the Aulds who found it difficult to forgive him for his public statements about them. Not until 1891, when Frederick and Benjamin Auld finally patched up their old quarrel, did Frederick learn that "little Tommy," his beloved childhood companion, had become a sailor and had been lost at sea in 1848.[14]

Indicative also of the inner Frederick was the warm relationship he established with Amanda Auld Sears, daughter of Thomas and Lucretia, and maintained for many years with her children. He had fond memories of her mother, who had befriended him on the Lloyd plantation, and he had known Amanda well as a stepchild of the hated Rowena. After a lecture in Philadelphia shortly before the war, he was informed that Amanda, now married and living in Philadelphia, had been among his audience. Next day he sought out her husband, John L. Sears, a former St. Michaels teacher turned coal merchant, and arranged to visit Amanda at the Sears home.

It was a touching reunion. Frederick, anxious to "make the contrast between the slave and the free man as striking as possible," dressed in his best clothes and rode to the house in a fine hired carriage. A large crowd was present. When he recognized Amanda among the thirty or so people, she "bounded to me with joy in every feature. . . . All thought of slavery, color, or what might seem to belong to the dignity of her position vanished, and the meeting was as the meeting of friends long separated, yet still present in each other's memory and affection." Frederick's account of the meeting continued:

> Amanda made haste to tell me that she agreed with me about slavery, and that she had freed all her slaves as they had become of age. She brought her children to me, and I took them in my arms, with sensations which I could not . . . describe. . . . She had read my story and had through me learned something of the amiable qualities of her mother. She also recollected that as I had had trials as a slave she had had her trials under the care of a stepmother, and that when she was harshly spoken to by her father's second wife she could always read in my dark face the sympathy of one who had often received kind words from the lips of her beloved mother.[15]

When Thomas Auld heard about the meeting, he told Sears he had done the right thing in inviting Frederick to the house—a fact that gave Douglass great satisfaction. Both Amanda's greeting to Frederick and Auld's reaction to it reveal at least as much about the Auld family's attitude toward Frederick as they do about his attitude toward them. Clearly he was far more to them than "just another slave." He was, and always had been, a very special person.

Seven years later Frederick and Amanda met again when she brought her two children up from Baltimore to see him march in a Philadelphia procession of national Republican leaders. After that they kept in touch, and when Amanda learned late in 1877 that she was dying, she called him to her bedside. At her request, he described her mother as he recalled her; a staunch Methodist, Amanda was certain she would meet her mother beyond the grave and wanted to be sure she would recognize her. John Sears invited Frederick to her funeral and sent him a note that said "God bless you for your kindness to her."[16]

When the Sears family later ran into financial troubles, it was to Frederick that they turned for help. John Sears asked him to use his influence in getting Sears a post office job, and to lend money to the two Sears daughters, Minnie and Anna Lucretia. After John's death, his son, Thomas E. Sears, sought Frederick's aid in getting a Washington job for Anna Lucretia, who was "well educated & a good penman." How Frederick responded to all these appeals is unknown, but the fact that they continued indicates he must at least have been sympathetic.[17]

In quiet ways he helped others of the old slaveholding Eastern Shore families that had seemed so wealthy and powerful in his youth but had been reduced to near-poverty by emancipation. Nellie Jenkins was a daughter of the former Sarah Elizabeth Hambleton, sister of the hated Rowena, and a granddaughter of Frederick's one-time nemesis, William Hambleton. When she came to him seeking help in getting a job, Douglass interceded personally with Secretary of Agriculture J. M. Rusk, telling Rusk she was "a member of the family in which I was formerly a slave." Rusk found employment for her at nine dollars a week in the Agriculture Department's seed room. Later Sarah Hambleton Jenkins wrote a warm letter of thanks for Frederick's kindness in enabling her daughter "to support herself and in some way assist her family." When newspapers got hold of the story, Frederick was embarrassed.

He also showed continued interest in Fells Point, the scene of so many happy—and some unhappy—memories of his youth. After Bethel Church was abandoned by its congregation, which built a "handsome pressed brick church" a few blocks away, Frederick purchased the building for $2,200, razed it, and built housing to replace some of the miserable shacks in which Fells Point blacks had lived on Strawberry Alley, now renamed Dallas Street. Reporting the purchase in 1891, a local newspaper headlined the story: "Mr. Douglass Buys the Place of His Early Devotions," said it was there that "the power of the gospel subdued his 'stubborn heart' and he was made a regenerated follower of Christ," and commented: "It seemed to be the proudest moment of Mr. Douglass' eventful life to be the owner of the old church, and smiles swept over his countenance as he was handed the warrant of his ownership."[18]

The housing project proved not to be a paying proposition. During the economic slump following the panic of 1893, Frederick's Baltimore agent, Charles F. Bodery, sent him a check for fifty dollars in rentals but added: "On account of the stringency of the times it is very hard to collect money here now. . . . Two of the houses are now vacant."[19]

The *Narrative* had been published in May, 1845, at a time when Frederick, already a nationally known speaker, feared that his effectiveness on the platform would be destroyed because too many people refused to believe that a man with his command of language and polished diction could ever have been a slave. He was still a fugitive, but nevertheless he decided to tell who he was and where he had come from, and to give details of his slave experience. Then he went to Great Britain on an extended lecture tour, at least partly for the purpose of forestalling any possible attempt at his recapture.

The book, as he expected, produced a furor of controversy in Talbot County. Despite severe Maryland laws against dissemination of abolitionist literature, it was widely circulated in the state, and excerpts were pirated and published in a pamphlet. A correspondent wrote from Baltimore in September, 1845, that it was being read avidly, and that "five hundred copies are still wanted here." A black newsman who visited the city in November reported that he had been called on "by at least a dozen colored persons" who had known Frederick as a slave and wanted to hear the latest news of him.

Frederick was in Scotland when he learned that the *Narrative* had been denounced in a published letter as a "catalogue of lies" that had been ghost-written for him by "evil designed persons" to excite public indignation against slaveholders and the Methodist Church. The author was a former Talbot Countian with the resounding name of Absalom Christopher Columbus Americus Vespucius Thompson, called "A.C.C." for short. As a boy he had lived on a farm adjoining that rented by Covey; his father, Dr. Absalom Thompson, had maintained a medical clinic said to have been the first "hospital" on the Eastern Shore.

Most of Thompson's "refutation of falsehood" consisted merely of defense of the characters of the men Frederick had accused of various crimes and brutalities. He had known Colonel Lloyd, Gore, Thomas Auld, and the others personally, he said, and knew that they were "respectable citizens" who could not possibly be "murderers, hypocrites, and every thing else that is vile," as the *Narrative* charged.

Of Frederick he said: "About eight years ago, I knew this recreant slave by the name of Frederick Bailey, (instead of Douglass.) He then lived with Mr. Edward Covy [*sic*], and was an unlearned and rather an ordinary negro, and am confident he was not capable of writing the *Narrative* alluded to; for none but an educated man, and one who had some knowledge of the rules of grammar, could write so correctly."[20]

When Frederick read this passage in the *Liberator,* which had picked up Thompson's letter from the *Delaware Republican,* he was overjoyed. Thompson had unwittingly done him a great service; now he could silence forever the rumors that had followed him to Britain that he was an imposter who had never been a slave. Exultantly he dashed off an open letter in reply thanking Thompson for his "full, free and unsolicited testimony, in regard to my identity. ... You have done a piece of antislavery work, which no anti-slavery man could do. . . . I now stand before both the American and British public, endorsed by you as being just what I have ever represented myself to be—to wit, an American slave.'' To make sure the British public got the point, he included the entire correspondence in the third English edition of his book.[21]

In a second letter Thompson included statements from several St. Michaels area residents to buttress his claims. One of them was Thomas Auld, who said of Frederick:

> He states that I used to flog and starve him; but I can put my hand upon my Bible, and with a clear conscience swear that I never struck him in my life, nor caused any person else to do it. I never allowanced one of my slaves: but the tale would not have answered their (the Abolitionists') purposes, unless the slave had been starved, or nearly whipped to death. . . .
>
> I placed him [Frederick] in Baltimore to learn a trade, and told him that if he would behave himself and learn his trade well, when he was 25 years old I would emancipate him; and he promised me faithfully that he would do it. He does not say one word about this in his Narrative, as it would not have answered to have mentioned so much truth.[22]

In reply Frederick recalled the incident in the stable when Auld had lost his temper and lashed Frederick with a cart whip with Edward Auld as witness. "My memory, in such matters, is better than his," he added drily. He also noted that Auld had not denied Frederick's chief accusation, that he had whipped Henny until the blood ran while quoting Scripture to justify his action. As far as is known, Auld never did issue a public denial of that incident.

However, in his second autobiography, *My Bondage and My Freedom*, Frederick made some changes designed to meet Auld's objections. In describing how small the amount of food Auld's kitchen slaves had received was, he eliminated the word *allowance*, which had the special meaning on the Eastern Shore of a fixed ration on which slaves had to subsist. He included Auld's promise to free him at twenty-five, saying the only thing wrong with it was that "it seemed too good to be true." And he added several passages indicating that he realized the picture he had drawn of Auld in the *Narrative* was unfairly harsh.

"It is possible," Douglass wrote, ". . . that I do Master Thomas injustice. He . . . acted, upon the whole, very generously, considering the nature of my offense [in organizing an escape attempt]. He had the power and the provocation to send me, without reserve, into the very everglades of Florida, beyond the remotest hope of emancipation; and his refusal to exercise that power, must be set down to his credit." And again: "[He] showed much humane feeling in his part of the transaction, and atoned for much that had been harsh, cruel and unreasonable in his former treatment of me and others."[23]

In the 1855 autobiography, Frederick also modified other passages in the *Narrative*. He appears to have been making a deliberate effort to correct the record on his childhood and to present a more balanced account. Without retracting any of his major atrocity charges, he conceded for the first time that his own experience, except for the months under Covey, had not been an unhappy one. He personally had suffered "nothing cruel or shocking" at the hands of Aaron Anthony. "I was seldom whipped —and never severely—by my old master." It was the slave woman Aunt Katy, rather than his white master, who had deprived him of food and forced the children under her care to eat like pigs. In his life with the Hugh Auld family at Fells Point he had enjoyed "kind and tender treatment" for several years, not just a short time, before Sophia Auld turned bitter against him because of his reading; and even then the break between them had been as much his fault as hers. He became a sullen teenager, resentful and brooding over his condition as a slave. "I can easily believe," he wrote, "that my leaden, downcast, and discontented look, was very offensive to her. Poor lady! She did not know my trouble, and I dared not tell her." Even Hugh Auld was a "good, kind master," a "rough but manly-hearted fellow" whose "best nature" sometimes showed itself.

However, these changes in his life story went unnoticed at the time and have been largely overlooked by Douglass students ever since. Sympathetic readers want Frederick to have had a miserable childhood, and his repeated references to the fact that he had been a "favored slave" are brushed off as mere sarcasm. Probably one hundred people have read the *Narrative* for every one who has gone carefully through the early sections of *My Bondage and My Freedom* or his final autobiography, *Life and Times of Frederick Douglass*. The stark recital of horrors in the earlier book, rather than the more modified picture in the later ones, remains the essential Douglass story as the world sees it.

Further insight into the relations between Frederick and the Aulds is revealed in the chain of events through which he obtained his freedom while in Great Britain in 1846. He was still in Scotland in March of that year when word came that Thomas Auld had transferred title to him to brother Hugh. According to the abolitionist press Hugh, incensed by remarks in the *Narrative,* had vowed to seize him and "cost what it may . . . place him in the cotton fields of the South" if he ever returned to the United States.

Just when and where Hugh Auld issued such a threat—if he ever did—remains a mystery. I have been unable to find any published reference to it except in the abolitionist *Pennsylvania Freeman,* which first published it February 26, 1846, and other antislavery papers, which reprinted it. The statement has the ring of one of Auld's idle remarks, made after a few drinks, like the whippings he promised Frederick but didn't carry out. The abolitionist press, like other newspapers of the time, was not above printing unconfirmed gossip as fact.[24]

In any case Hugh Auld's later behavior does not indicate any grim determination to exact revenge, "cost what it may." Nor does Thomas Auld's motive in the transfer appear to have been a desire to help his brother get even with Frederick. If anything, it was a sop to his own conscience.

On the same day—October 25, 1845—that he sold his rights to Frederick to Hugh for one hundred dollars, Thomas Auld granted manumission effective immediately to Frederick's cousin, Thomas Bailey. He had already emancipated Henny, and sold Eliza to her husband. He retained some young slaves whom he freed later; but it seems evident that he was determined to rid himself of all his slaves.[25]

Frederick's British friends took the reported threat seriously. They first offered him a permanent home and collected a purse of $500 to bring Anna and the Douglass children to England. When he turned this down, Mrs. Anna Richardson wrote to Hugh Auld asking if he would sell Frederick's manumission, and if so what his price would be. Her letter was dated August 17, 1846. On October 6, Auld responded:

Madam

In reply to your letter dated Newcastle on Tyne 8th mo 17th 1846 I state that I will take 150£ Sterling for the manumission of my slave Frederick Bailey, alias Douglass—I am prepared to give such papers or deed of Manumission as will forever exempt him from any claims by any person or persons, in other words the papers will render him entirely and legally free.

As soon as your agent is prepared to deliver me the money I will hand him the papers.

In haste Resp'ly yours H Auld.[26]

The tone of this letter reveals Hugh Auld for what he was: a venal man more interested in money than revenge. He was far from wealthy and he had a large family to support. If he could get some cash out of Frederick, who in any case was on the other side of the Atlantic, that was fine with him. For £150 sterling, he could swallow a lot of resentment.

In fact, aside from the single unverified report in the *Pennsylvania Freeman,* there is nothing to indicate that either Hugh or Thomas Auld ever even considered selling Frederick to the Deep South. All the evidence is to the contrary. They had made no effort to recapture him during the three months between the time he revealed his identity in May, 1845, and sailed for Great Britain in August, although his whereabouts and activities were highly publicized. Earlier, as Frederick admitted, Thomas had refused to sell him when he had both provocation and opportunity in 1836. And finally, Hugh Auld's quick, almost eager, agreement to accept payment for Frederick's manumission cannot be reconciled with the abolitionist picture of him as a wicked slavemonger panting for revenge.

As soon as Auld's favorable response arrived, Mrs. Richardson and her sister-in-law, Ellen Richardson, proceeded to raise the needed funds. Anna's husband, Henry Richardson, sent a draft to his New York agent, Walter Lowrie, a former United States senator from Pennsylvania. On November 24 Lowrie wrote to Auld that he had received the money and was prepared to hand it over on receipt of the freedom papers, but would need proper evidence that the slave Thomas Auld had sold to Hugh was truly the man known as Frederick Douglass.[27]

The transfer deed of October 25, 1845, had not identified Frederick as Douglass, but merely as Frederick Bailey. Therefore Thomas Auld executed a new deed of sale, dated November 30, 1846, which contained both names, and filed it at the Talbot County Courthouse in Easton. Lowrie's Baltimore representative, attorney J. Meredith, examined this document and pronounced it satisfactory; and on December 5 Hugh Auld signed a deed of manumission declaring "'my NEGRO MAN named FREDERICK BAILEY, otherwise called DOUGLASS . . . to be henceforth free, manumitted, and discharged from all manner of servitude.'"[28]

A week later the transaction was completed. Auld handed the deeds of sale and manumission over to Meredith; Meredith handed Auld a draft for $711.66, the dollar equivalent of £150 sterling, out of which Auld paid Meredith $25 for his services. Meredith filed the papers at the Baltimore Chattel Records Office; and at 10 A.M. on December 12, 1846, by authority of A. W. Bradford, clerk, Frederick Douglass officially ceased to be a chattel and became a free human being in the eyes of the law.

Frederick's reunion with Eliza in November, 1864, was not the last he held with a member of his black family. In February, 1867, he received a letter from a man who identified himself as "Perry Downs . . . a brother of yours." Frederick had heard that Perry had been "sold South," but Perry said that was not true; his wife had been sold to Brazos County, Texas, by John P. Anthony, and he had gone there voluntarily to find her, and had stayed. He was being "treated pretty well" and was getting fifteen dollars gold wages a month as a field hand. "I have a great desire to see you if it is possible to make arrangements," he added.[29]

Frederick evidently responded; a few months later Perry and his family turned up in New Orleans, trying to make their way to Frederick's home in Rochester, New York. They were befriended by the Reverend T. W. Conway, who gave Perry a note to J. J. Spelman in New York City. With Spelman's help Perry, his wife Maria, and their four children reached Rochester early in July. Frederick found them at his home when he arrived back July 9 from a lecture tour in Virginia, and immediately wrote an ecstatic note of thanks to Spelman.

"The meeting of my brother after nearly forty years' separation is an event altogether too affecting for words to describe," he said. "How unutterably accursed is slavery, and how unspeakably joyful are the results of the overthrow! The search now being made, and the happy reunions now taking place all over the South, after years of separation and sorrow, furnish a subject of the deepest pathos."[30]

Others in the family did not share Frederick's enthusiasm. The younger Douglasses, who had grown up in middle-class freedom and had had little or no contact with slaves or slavery, were repelled by the new arrivals. Charles Remond, working at the Freedmen's Bureau in Washington, received such a bad report from Rochester that in August he wrote his father: "I don't understand in what way those people you have at home are related to you, is it that Mr. Downs is your half brother? From what I have heard of their conduct, I should be afraid to have them in the same neighborhood, and more especially when you are away in the winter months."[31]

Nevertheless, Frederick proceeded to build a home for them on his own grounds, spending most of his time that summer on the project. It was completed in September, at which time he reported to Theodore Tilton:

I have been keeping a kind of hotel all summer! My poor brother Perry—after a bondage of fifty-six years, deeply marked by the hardships and sorrows of that hateful condition; and after a separation from me during forty years, as complete as if he had lived on another planet—came to me two months ago, with his family of six, and took up his abode with me. To him—dear old fellow!—one who has carried me on his shoulders many a time (for he is older than I, though my head seems to contradict it)—one who defended me from the assaults of bigger boys when I needed defense—I have been mainly devoting myself, and gladly so.

I have now completed for him a snug little cottage on my own grounds, where my dear old slavery-scarred and long-lost brother may spend in peace, with his family, the remainder of his days.[32]

Publishing a portion of the letter in the New York *Independent,* of which he was editor, Tilton, a warm admirer of Douglass, commented: "Frederick Douglass is a true, great, and noble man, with a mind fit for a

176

senate, and with a heart fit for a child. When hundreds of the public and prominent men of this country are dead and forgotten, his name will still be remembered. And when his life comes to be written, it will hardly contain a more beautiful and romantic chapter than the pleasing story which we have just borrowed from his graphic pen."[33]

Unfortunately, the story did not end there. Perhaps the cruel Rochester winters were too much for Perry and Maria; or perhaps there were further difficulties between the Downs and Douglass families. At any rate, Perry and Maria left their "snug little cottage" in the fall of 1869 and went home to the Eastern Shore. Their grown children dispersed in various directions. Perry, "old and decrepid" (as the *Easton Gazette* spelled it), was living in Talbot County in 1878 when Frederick again made arrangements to care for him, this time at the Douglass home of Cedar Hill in Anacostia. According to one report Perry, Frederick's sister Kitty, and her son Henry all finished their lives and died at Cedar Hill.[34]

Eventually he also heard from Sarah, his older sister who had been sold to Peregrine Cohee of Mississippi in 1832. As Sarah O. Pettit, she wrote him from Louisville, Kentucky, on September 26, 1883, saying it had been a long time since they saw each other, but "still I have never forgotten that you are my Brother." She promised to write him "a good long letter if you will only drop me a few lines in reply."

Despite all these renewed contacts with his old time Talbot County associates, Frederick shied away from returning to the Eastern Shore for many years after he could have done so. He traveled to Baltimore often; among his noteworthy visits was one on May 19, 1870, to celebrate the adoption of the Fifteenth Amendment. After passing resolutions thanking God, the Republican party, and President Grant for giving them the right to vote, the assembled throng adopted, with "loud acclaim," the following: "Resolved, That recognizing in Frederick Douglass the foremost man of color in the times in which we live, and proud to claim him as one 'to the manor born,' we do here most respectfully, yet earnestly, request him to return to us, and by the power of his magnificent manhood help us to a higher, broader, and nobler manhood."[35] In July, 1871, Frederick made a sentimental return to his old shipyard haunts at Fells Point. He recounted this visit in great detail in the *New National Era*, of which he was then editor.

But something held him back from a pilgrimage to the county of his birth. Perhaps he was not yet ready; perhaps he was not yet sure of his reception—in his memory, and in the word he had received from Lewis, racial attitudes were far more vicious in Talbot County than in Baltimore. In 1865 he wrote that he would be glad to have a meeting with Thomas Auld, even though "it could not fail to be awkward," if the meeting

177

could be arranged on neutral territory. He did not relish going to St. Michaels. However, he added, "time and events have made changes and it is just possible that the Lamb may yet venture into the den of the Lion without danger of being eaten up." From Eliza he had learned that Auld had said he would be glad to see Frederick; "he has but to say so to me by letter—and considering his age, and forgetting his past, I will make him a visit." The formal invitation was not issued.[36]

When he was invited by a group of prominent Easton citizens to speak at Fourth of July ceremonies there in 1867, he turned down the opportunity, citing a prior engagement. His letter of refusal contained ironic recollections of his last visit to Easton, when the "house" he stayed in had been notable for "heavy locks, thick walls, iron gratings and unwholesome atmosphere." It would be a full decade after that before he felt ready to return to Talbot County.[37]

Just why he hesitated so long is a matter of speculation. It was not aversion to the area or its people; when he finally did go back, it was on a wave of sentimental fondness. Most likely he wanted to be certain that his return to the county of his birth would be on a note of triumph.

The 1870s were a time of increasing honors for Douglass. He was named assistant secretary of a commission to investigate the proposal that the Dominican Republic be annexed by the United States. He was nominated in 1872 for vice-president, on a ticket with Victoria Claflin Woodhull, by a radical splinter group named the Equal Rights Party, but did not campaign for the office. Instead he stumped the northeastern states so effectively for President Grant's reelection that the *New York Times* declared: "From the outset of the present contest . . . the speeches of Frederick Douglass have been among the most powerful weapons of the party." He was chosen a presidential elector from New York, and after Grant's victory was named official messenger to convey the state's election results to the president of the United States Senate. He was appointed president of the Freedmen's Bank (a dubious honor, since the bank was in deep financial trouble and soon failed, although the failure was through no fault of Douglass). Finally, after the disputed election of Rutherford B. Hayes to the presidency over Samuel J. Tilden in 1876, he was named by Hayes to the highest office ever held up to that time by an American black, United States marshal for the District of Columbia.

The appointment to this largely honorary post was one that Douglass probably should have refused, and one that brought savage criticism down on him from some other black leaders. It was part of a shameful deal in which Hayes bought the support of southern Democrats in Congress by agreeing to withdraw Federal troops from the southern states, and thus end the Radical Reconstruction era, in return for which the southerners supported his claim to enough southern electoral votes to swing the election. The Douglass appointment was a sop to the black people; in Philip S. Foner's words, "Hayes could pose as a champion of Negro rights while bargaining away the Negro's freedom."[38]

Opponents said Douglass had been "gagged" by a fat office. He denied this, pointing out that he could and did speak out against Hayes's policies, and particularly against segregation in Washington, D.C., which shocked the southerners who had helped put him in office. More importantly, he considered the appointment a personal recognition that also would prove "gratifying to a large class of the American people of all colors and races."[39]

The appointment was confirmed by the Senate on March 17, 1877, and Douglass's commission became official March 19. The slave boy from Tuckahoe Creek had become the most honored black in American history.

❧ *Chapter Eleven* ❧

Homecoming to Talbot

Now it was time to go home again. He had not been to the county of his birth in forty-one years, since the April morning when Captain Auld had taken him down to the wharf, told him sternly to behave himself, and sent him back to Baltimore to learn the calking trade. Then he had been a slave—and worse, in the eyes of his masters, a jailbird, a trouble-maker, a potential source of infection to other slaves who was under threat of being sold south or even murdered if he stayed around St. Michaels.

Now he was a somebody, a success, a whole man. Perhaps he was not yet a United States senator, as he had vowed he would become on that long-ago night at Jim Mingo's house in Happy Alley. But he had proved his case. He had traveled the whole road. He was past being anybody's chattel; or just another escaped slave whose English friends had bought his freedom; or the "prize exhibit" of the northern abolitionist intellectuals, a freak to be shown off as proof that a black man, if given a sufficient infusion of white blood, could rise above the savages; or even, as he had been regarded by Lincoln, a "credit to his race" who was to be tolerated and patronized. He was United States marshal for the District of Columbia by appointment of President Rutherford B. Hayes. And more than that. He had not simply risen higher than any American black before him; he had at last achieved full recognition in the white man's world and on the white man's terms.

Douglass, ca. 1880, about the time of his return to Talbot County

Or so it seemed in those euphoric days during the spring of 1877, when men of substance tipped their hats to him in the street and the congratulatory letters and telegrams were pouring in. "How the world wags!" his old friend, Theodore Tilton, wrote exultantly from New York. "There was a time when you would not have relished the slave catching duties of the marshal of any city in America! ... To me, the spectacle of Frederick Douglass as marshal of the Capital of the United States, is a greater evidence of human progress than if I could see either Abraham, Isaac, or Jacob elected by a returning board as mayor of Jerusalem! Your honors are deserved. God bless you in wearing them!'' [1]

"I think the Senate itself your proper place," L. A. Hammond of Syracuse wrote. From blacks came simple, heartfelt notes eulogizing him as "noblest of our race" and "the best representative of our people in this country." A Louisville man said he had pictures of Charles Sumner and Frederick Douglass hanging in his parlor, and now would put a laurel wreath around the Douglass picture, "for it is a great triumph for the cause."

There was another reason for going home: he felt he owed Thomas Auld an apology. He had made the name of Auld a symbol in four languages of the cruelty and oppressiveness of the slave-owning class; but now that there had been time for bitterness to mellow, anger to cool, old sores to heal, he realized that Captain Auld had been not an evil man but merely a weak and bewildered one, as much a victim of the slave system as Frederick had been himself. Word had come by roundabout means that Auld, now nearly eighty-two, was bedridden and might soon die. While there was still time, Frederick wanted to make peace. [2]

Messages were exchanged, quietly, through emissaries. It became clear that if Douglass wanted to see Auld, the old captain would be happy to see him. One late spring day Frederick rode the train up to Baltimore, and on the afternoon of Saturday, June 16, he boarded the steamer *Matilda* at Fells Point for an overnight journey across the bay. It was not the pleasantest of crossings. His companions were a party of black excursionists bound for a weekend in St. Michaels; and the fastidious Douglass, with his thick veneer of culture acquired in the drawing rooms of Britain and New England, found he had little in common with them beyond the color of his skin. He might be the acknowledged champion of black rights, but as always he was uncomfortable in the company of lower-class blacks.

As *Matilda* pulled away from the Fells Point wharf, the one hundred or so people who lined her two-hundred-foot deck were already laughing and singing, waving good-by to those left behind. They were joyful with good reason; like Douglass, most of them were Eastern Shore natives headed home for a reunion with relatives and old friends—and besides, they had on board the most famous black man in the world.

Soon bottles were being passed around; food baskets were opened; banjos were produced; dancing and stomping began. Old *Matilda*, a stern-wheeler built during the war, had only primitive accomodations; her passengers relieved themselves over the rail and, since there was nowhere for most of them to sleep, kept up their shouting, singing, and stomping all night long. Douglass, a teetotaler whose musical taste found expression in classical violin sonatas, sat through the night in grim disapproval.

"The one hundred colored people aboard made as much noise as five hundred whites would have done, and as long as they do these things they are inferior to the whites," he said sternly the next day. [3] But the voyage finally ended, and sunrise found *Matilda* tied up at the steamboat wharf on Navy Point in St. Michaels harbor. After forty-one years, Frederick was home again.

At a glance St. Michaels didn't appear much changed from the scruffy little harbor town he had last seen in 1836. Its population had increased only a little in the intervening years. Even its houses seemed to be the same old ones, although perhaps they had a bit more paint; Frederick remembered them as having none at all. There was a canning plant near the wharf with the name "Harrison" painted along one wall that had not been there in his day, and behind it a steam sawmill. With his practiced eye, Frederick noted that some of the boats tied up around the harbor were of a new design. They were called buckeyes or bugeyes, a refinement of the old pungies and bateaux he had known. But the streets, when he went for a stroll, still had their familiar names: Willow, Cherry, Mulberry, Cedar, Water, Carpenter's Alley. The townspeople made a living as they always had, building boats, harvesting oysters, catching crabs, trading with farmers in the area. From the names on storefronts it was clear the same old families—Hambletons, Dawsons, Harrisons, Haddaways, Dodsons, Harringtons—controlled the town's business life.

In relations between the races, it was difficult to see much change despite the end of slavery. Blacks kept their place. They lived, for the most part, in shacklike houses they had built themselves in the "section" at the northwest edge of town, or on the same farms where they had lived as slaves. Black men remained little more than serfs, working as common farm laborers for eighty-five or ninety dollars a year and a "lay-in" of corn meal and black strap molasses, while women were domestic servants at five dollars a month or worked at Harrison's canning house for not much more. Most had just enough land around their houses for a garden, a few chickens, and, if they were lucky, a pig or cow. If economic conditions for the blacks had been improved by freedom, it was hard to see how.

One change Frederick did note. There was now a "colored" school, which was kept by an earnest young black man in a rickety one-room building for which the Talbot County school commissioners grudgingly doled out a few dollars per year in upkeep money. Even that had been established only because it was required by law. With ironic amusement, Frederick remembered the schools he had conducted here—the first one broken up by an angry posse of white men, the second held in secret while the slave youths were supposed to be resting on Sunday afternoons.

Still, for all its racial barriers, the Eastern Shore was home. Although he had lived long in far places, Douglass realized with a surge of nostalgia that he had missed this gentle land more than he knew. "I am an Eastern Shoreman, with all that that name implies," he told a crowd of blacks and whites who gathered to hear him speak that afternoon. "Eastern Shore corn and Eastern Shore pork gave me my muscle. I love Maryland and the

Eastern Shore!'' It was strange talk from a man who had devoted much of his life to giving the Eastern Shore of Maryland a bad name; but there was much that seemed contradictory in what Douglass said and did that day.

First there was the business of his visit with Captain Auld. Although he denied it later, when he came under critical fire for showing ''softness'' toward his old master, Douglass made no secret at the time that the primary purpose of his trip was to meet the captain. ''I come, first of all, to see my old master, from whom I have been separated for forty-one years, to shake his hand, to look into his kind old face, and see it beaming with light from the other world,'' he said, according to the correspondent for the *Baltimore Sun*. [4]

The meeting itself was arranged with a protocol reminiscent of a confrontation between two heads of state who had been warring, but who now sought peace. A Mr. Green, Auld's personal servant, approached Douglass and formally invited him to visit the captain. Douglass, equally formally, agreed. The two then set off for the house on Cherry Street, at the corner of Locust Lane, where Auld was living with his daughter Louisa and her husband, William H. Bruff. [5]

As they strode up Willow Street from the steamboat wharf, they were followed by a mixed crowd of blacks and whites, well-wishers and curiosity seekers. Sister Eliza wasn't there—she had died a year or so before—but a flock of younger Mitchells and their kin were on hand. Half the black community of St. Michaels seemed to be related to him in one way or another. White men stopped him to shake his hand, the older ones to tell him they remembered him as a boy and had always known he would do well. Frederick smiled and nodded, courteous as always; but he must have wondered privately how many of them had been among the crowds screaming for his death as he was pulled behind horses through St. Michaels on that long-ago Easter Saturday.

Now it was different, and as he walked along, his great head with its greying mane towering above the crowd, Douglass looked more like a benign monarch—or a candidate for high political office—than a former slave. The *Sun* correspondent, who was trailing him, made note of his appearance; and on Tuesday his paper rather nervously pointed out in an editorial that Douglass had lived away from Maryland too long to be considered seriously as a candidate for the United States Senate.

At the door of the red brick house, William and Louisa Bruff were waiting to greet him, and to let both Frederick and the curious crowd know that he was welcome in their home. It was one of those moments of which Douglass experienced so many: a breaking of barriers. Undoubtedly it was the first time that a black man had ever entered a white home in St. Michaels by the front door, as an honored guest. [6]

Douglass remembered Louisa only as a toddler; she had been born in 1833, the year he came to St. Michaels to live; she was the child of Rowena, Auld's second wife, of whom he had no fond memories. Now she was crippled by arthritis, which gave her a drawn and almost hard look; but with what must have been considerable effort for a woman in her time and place, she greeted him graciously, and he was immediately conducted to Captain Auld's bedroom.

The two men faced each other at last. Auld, shrunken with age and illness, his skin waxen, his hands palsied, was almost unrecognizable as the man Frederick had known; and Douglass, whom Auld had last seen as an eighteen-year-old youth in ragged overalls, towered above him, handsome and fashionably dressed, his big frame and broad shoulders seeming to fill the room.

"Captain Auld," Frederick said in greeting; and at the same moment Auld called out in a quavering voice, "Marshal Douglass!" Then came a remark that was to cause Douglass much embarrassment in the way it was reported in the national press. As he told the story, he was simply trying to set the sick old man at ease. "Hearing myself called by him 'Marshal Douglass,' I instantly broke up the formal nature of the meeting by saying, 'not Marshal, but Frederick to you as formerly.'"[7]

However, the *Sun* correspondent, learning the story at second hand, somehow got the impression that the exchange had been between Douglass and William Bruff, and that Douglass had said, "I am Marshal Douglass in Washington; here let me be Fred. Douglass again." This gave the remark an entirely different meaning, as if Douglass had said, "Just call me Fred." The *Sun* story, which was widely reprinted, sent waves of shock through younger blacks who bitterly resented the slur of being called only by their first names.

Undoubtedly all Douglass meant to imply was that he hoped the relationship that had once existed between the two could be restored. But even that was bad enough as far as his critics were concerned. Having accepted as an article of faith all the things he had said and written about Auld's cruelty, they could not understand why he, in a manner of speaking, was now kissing his former oppressor's hand. He appeared to be repudiating a lifetime of antislavery testimony.

To a degree they were right; but Douglass was beyond caring what the public thought. Whatever he had said about his master in the bitterness of his youth, all he felt for him now was an overwhelming tenderness and love. They shook hands and Auld, deeply moved, burst into tears. Frederick was shaken also. "The sight of him, the changes which time had wrought in him, his tremulous hands constantly in motion, and all the circumstances of his condition affected me deeply," he wrote. "We both, however, got the better of our feelings, and conversed freely about the past.''

There was a lot to be said, and not much time in which to say it. Douglass plunged at once into a question that had always concerned him: How had Auld reacted to his successful escape?

The old man chose his words carefully. This went to the heart of the misunderstanding between them. He had been pictured as an ogre panting to get his chattel back into his grasp. The truth had been quite the reverse.

''Frederick,'' he said, ''I always knew you were too smart to be a slave, and had I been in your place, I should have done as you did.''

''Captain Auld, I am glad to hear you say this,'' Douglass replied, according to his own account. ''I did not run away from *you*, but from *slavery*; it was not that I loved Caesar less, but Rome more.''

Next it was time to admit error, never an easy task for Douglass. Still it had to be faced. In his 1848 open letter he had not only accused Auld falsely but had called down upon him the wrath of God: ''Your wickedness and cruelty are greater than all the stripes you have laid upon my back. . . . It is an outrage upon the soul, a war upon the immortal spirit, and one for which you must give account at the bar of our common Father and Creator.''

Now the old man was dying, and those words and all the others Frederick had spoken and written against him lay between them, as did the cruelties of which Auld could be accused with some truth. It was, as Frederick wrote, a time for ''settlement of past differences preparatory to his stepping into his grave, where all distinctions are at an end, . . . for remembrance of all his good deeds, and generous extenuation of all his evil ones.''

Just what ensued became a matter of public dispute. According to the *Sun*'s version of the scene, ''Douglass grasped the palsied hand of Capt. Auld [and] begged his forgiveness.'' Douglass didn't mention this, but said he admitted that he ''had made a mistake . . . in attributing to him ungrateful and cruel treatment of my grandmother.'' Later he complained that the newspaper account had been ''defective and colored'' and that the visit was made ''the subject of mirth by heartless triflers,'' when cartoons published in the South showed him kneeling humbly at the feet of his old master. [8]

There followed some discussion of the date of Frederick's birth, a question he was still trying to resolve. Captain Auld was pretty sure it had been in February, 1818, but Frederick thought he was a year older than that. The interview was over in twenty minutes, ''and we parted to meet no more.'' It had been a brief discussion, but it had cleared the atmosphere of forty-one years of misunderstanding. [9]

For Douglass this remarkable homecoming day was just beginning. He seemed in a mood to speak his mind at least as bluntly as he had in Rochester or Washington, and the speech he delivered that afternoon before a racially mixed throng in a picnic grove outside St. Michaels sent still more shock waves through the world of black intellectuals. If the *Sun*'s report was even near to being accurate, they had good reason to be disturbed. After his nostalgic boast of being "an Eastern Shoreman, with all that that name implies," the *Sun* reported:

Mr. Douglass then passed into a eulogy of the white race and its accomplishments, and said to the colored people that they were in contact with the most favored, the most indomitable, the most energetic race in the world, and that he would be false to his race if he did not tell them just where they stood—what an immense distance they were behind the white people. He did not believe the colored people were fundamentally and eternally inferior to the whites, but they are, nevertheless, practically inferior. "We must not talk about equality until we can do what white people can do. As long as they can build vessels and we can not, we are their inferiors; as long as they can found governments and we can not, we are their inferiors. . . .

"If twenty years from now the colored race as a race has not advanced beyond the point where it was when emancipated it is a doomed race. The question now is, will the black man do as much now for his master (himself) as he used to do for his old master? Do you, my colored friends, get up as early now to work for yourselves as you used to do to work for that stern old Roman, Samuel Hambleton?"

. . . He told the colored people that they must get money and keep it if they wished to elevate themselves. . . . A poor people are always a despised people. To be respected they must get money and property. Without money there's no leisure, without leisure no thought, without thought no progress. Their preachers should tell them more about what to do and less about what to feel. They should cultivate their brains more and their lungs less. They should not depend upon being helped, but should do for themselves. He was tired of Ethiopia's holding out her hands . . . . They should not depend upon the Lord for everything. The Lord is good and kind, but is of the most use to those who do for themselves. No man has a right to live unless he lives honestly, and no man lives honestly who lives upon another.[10]

The speech reiterated views that Douglass had expressed many times. His stubborn assumption that the "race problem" would be solved if only blacks worked hard and saved their money (as he had) was already the despair of those who were trying to cope with the plight of millions of illiterate southern field hands suddenly set free. It was never more clearly enunciated than here, on his home ground, before his relatives and old friends as well as whites whom he had held up personally to public scorn.

Blacks who heard him might have wondered how they were supposed to save up money on eighty-five dollars a year, or improve their condition when they were barred from buying farms; but whites were delighted. As they saw it, Douglass was absolving them of all responsibility for helping blacks and all blame for their poverty. It was up to the blacks themselves. As the *Sun* put it, "He gave the colored part of his audience some of the best advice and soundest instruction they have had for many a day . . . . The speech was well received, especially by the white part of the audience."

There were immediate repercussions when the story of the day's events circulated through the nation's press. Southern whites were highly amused by the spectacle, as it was presented in many areas, of the great Frederick Douglass kneeling before his old master, asking to be called "Fred" and begging forgiveness. Even moderate whites praised Douglass for his "manliness" in admitting errors in his past writings, and his "forthrightness" in criticizing black weaknesses.

Many blacks were appalled. To them it seemed that their hero had let them down, gone soft on slavery, joined up with the oppressors. John Mercer Langston, a long-time Douglass critic and rival for black leadership, led the chorus of those who accused Douglass of what today would be called "Uncle Tomism"—toadying and cringing to whites. Some blamed it on his "Caucasian blood," which had "diminished his regard for the Negro." Others thought that, in the rarified atmosphere of intellectualism, he had completely lost touch with the black masses. Not long afterward the *New York Times* concluded: "It would appear that Mr. Fred. Douglass's role as a leader of his race is about played out." [11]

Only Douglass knew what was in his heart. To his critics he angrily retorted that he did not have to apologize to anybody for his opinions, that the whipping scars on his back and the years he had spent in the antislavery struggle spoke for themselves. In writing about the Auld episode, he fell back on the theme that "time makes all things even," that once slavery was abolished he no longer had any reason to hate his old master. It was a roundabout way of saying that, except as a symbol of the slave owners, he had never hated his old master at all.

Meanwhile, there was a reaction of another kind. A short time after his visit to St. Michaels, Frederick received a letter from Louisa Bruff that contained a surprising proposal. Her husband had suffered financial reverses, Mrs. Bruff confided, and the couple had decided to sell their St. Michaels property and move to Texas. So the house he had just visited was for sale. "Perhaps you would like to buy a nice summer residence in St. Michaels," she wrote. "The house contains ten rooms besides two nice rooms in the cellar, it cost over $4,000, but I will sell it for $3,000. I know it is a small item with you, but a very considerable one with me. . . . Please to write and let me hear from you as soon as you can." [12]

What Douglass replied is not known. It was true that he was thinking of buying a house; a year later he purchased Cedar Hill in a previously all-white neighborhood of suburban Washington. But St. Michaels on the Eastern Shore, with its rigid racial code, was another matter. Even if he could entertain his white friends there, what would he do about his numerous black relatives?

Still, there was gratification in the fact that a daughter of the high and mighty Rowena Hambleton Auld was appealing for financial assistance from a former slave. However he had felt privately about Thomas Auld, he had never felt anything but dislike for the haughty Rowena. Now her own child was begging him for help.

How the world had wagged, indeed.

Seventeen months later, Frederick returned to the Eastern Shore on a second sentimental journey. This time he went to Easton, scene of his jailing and the most miserable moments of his life, and made a pilgrimage to the site of his birth on Tuckahoe Creek.

The occasion was a paid lecture sponsored by Talbot County Republicans who hoped his presence and his example would help stimulate newly enfranchised local blacks to register and vote. The staunchly Republican *Easton Gazette* gave him celebrity coverage, devoting two and a half columns to his visit; the rabidly racist *Star* scarcely mentioned him.[13]

Douglass was given a suite in the town's finest hostelry, the Brick Hotel. Even though it had recently been remodeled, it was still recognizable to him as the old Lowe's Tavern, where grinning slave buyers had traded in black flesh in the old days. The *Gazette* noted that he was breaking the color line, commenting that it was "the first time, we presume, in the history of Easton that a colored man was ever a guest in one of our principal hotels. But times have changed beyond conception and he being a gentleman of education and refinement, and standing among the principal men of the country, no one appeared to think it wrong to deviate from the old custom."

Certainly Douglass, for one, didn't think it wrong. He was in his element, traveling as a distinguished citizen and destroying traditions as he went. But it was a personal triumph rather than a race-wide one; it was also the *last* time for many years that a black man was a guest at the Brick Hotel.

He had sailed from Baltimore aboard the overnight steamer *Highland Light*, on which he had also set a precedent by being assigned a stateroom, and arrived at Easton Point early on the morning of Saturday, November 23, 1878. After breakfast at the hotel and a stroll through Easton's streets, he spoke to assembled blacks at the newly built Bethel A.M.E. Church, giving them his standard lecture about working hard and saving their money. In the afternoon he made a similar appearance at the Asbury A.M.E. Church. Between times he held court in his hotel suite, receiving white callers among whom were, according to the *Gazette*, "some of our citizens who were acquainted with him in early life."

On Monday he traveled in a hired rig the twelve miles up to Tuckahoe Creek, to the crossroads known as Tappers Corner, and to the farm, once owned by Aaron Anthony, where his grandmother's cabin had stood. Nothing remained of the little log hut; even the well that he remembered was gone. The old overseer's house was also gone, and a new house had been built by the current owners, Mr. and Mrs. Ebenezer Jackson.[14] So it was difficult to reconstruct the place as it had been when he had last seen it half a century earlier.

Frederick and Louis Freeman, who had been a slave on this farm when it was owned by Aaron's grandson, John P. Anthony, studied the lay of the land. Where a deep, curving gully ran up toward the road from Tuckahoe Creek, Freeman pointed out the spot known in his time as "Aunt Bettie's lot." It looked right, and Frederick, searching in his memory, recalled a big cedar tree that should be a little deeper in the woods, near the edge of the ravine. He plunged into the underbrush for a look.

The tree was there, and Frederick solemnly declared that he had found the exact spot where he was born. He stood for a few moments in silence. Then, ceremoniously, he scooped up several handfuls of earth to take back to his new home at Cedar Hill.[15]

That night he told the crowd that gathered to hear him speak in the main courtroom of the Talbot County Courthouse how he had collected "some of the very soil on which I first trod" during his morning outing. He also spoke of the old whitewashed jail, only a few rods from the courthouse, where he had been locked up and exposed to the jeers of the slave traders. He recalled the "kindly treatment" he had received from Sheriff Joseph Graham. The one-time sheriff, now nearly eighty, was in the audience.

The gathering was a friendly one. "The court room was tolerably well filled, there being quite as many white as colored people in attendance, including a few ladies," the *Gazette* reported. "It was pleasant to notice that after the lecture many of the best gentlemen of the county went forward and took Mr. Douglass by the hand, and that this was not confined to those who are in political accord with him. By this these gentlemen have done Mr. Douglass no special honor; but they have honored themselves by showing so much independence."

Douglass's formal address was an old standard, "Self Made Men," which he had been delivering in town halls and lecture rooms since the 1850s, and which, with three or four other set speeches, netted him $5,000 to $6,000 a year in fees. It glorified those who had risen from lowly birth to high station through their own courage and hard work. He offered himself as an example, along with Lincoln, Horace Greeley, the poet Burns, and Benjamin Bannekar, the great Maryland black inventor and astronomer of the Revolutionary era.

The high point for the *Gazette* came when he departed from his main theme and, "in a burst of oratory which for eloquence and effectiveness could hardly be surpassed," spelled out his controversial views on the race problem—views that had stirred much criticism among his black contemporaries. As the reporter recorded it, the passage went like this:

It has often been asked of me by people of the North, what do we do with the Negro? My reply always has been, "Give him fair play, and let him alone." Give him fair play! Let him have every chance that every other man has, no less and no more. Let him alone! Don't hinder him in his effort to rise. Don't help him any more than you help any one else. If he is able to stand alone, well! If he is not able to stand alone, well again! Let him perish from the face of the earth! The world will get along as well without him as with him, or better. Give him fair play, and let him alone!

Then, turning to the white portion of his audience (Easton was being liberal, but not so liberal as to let blacks and whites sit together in public), Douglass thundered: "If you see the Negro going to church, let him alone! If you see him going to school, let him alone! If you see him going to the ballot box, let him alone! Do not form your Ku Klux Klan, and your rifle clubs, to drive him from the polls!" As the *Gazette* saw it, "this appeal thrilled every bosom in the audience." [16]

For those who were not present, the newspaper offered a description of Douglass that carefully emphasized his non-Negroid characteristics.

Mr. Douglass in his delivery is quiet and deliberate. The tones of his voice are most agreeable. His enunciation is distinct. His pronunciation [is] that of a cultivated man of the North, rather than of the South. His language is chaste, correct and appropriate. It possesses none of the characteristics of the colored man. He gives evidence, by frequent quotations, of possessing very considerable acquaintance with English literature. In appearance he is a large man, of full habit, but not obese. His color is that of a bright mulatto. His features are not at all those of the negro, except that there is a slight depression of the nose, and the spreading of the nostrils. His lips are thin, and retracted rather than protuberant. His forehead is not high, nor broad, but he seems to possess a large brain. His manners are collected, easy and graceful, indication of habitual association with men moving in polite circles. [17]

In brief, doubtful readers were assured, there was no reason for them to feel prejudice against Frederick Douglass. He might be part black, but he neither looked, behaved, talked, nor (presumably) thought like a black. It was a backhanded compliment, a reverse way of expressing racial prejudice.

Another homecoming journey—and an even better chance to demonstrate how the world had wagged—came in June, 1881, when Douglass returned to that most lofty symbol of southern white culture, the Lloyd plantation, now known as Wye House.

In his books he had described the Lloyd estate as a "secluded, dark and out-of-the-way place ... where slavery, wrapt in its own congenial darkness, could and did develop all its malign and shocking characteristics, where it could be indecent without shame, cruel without shuddering, and murderous without apprehension or fear of exposure or punishment."[18] He had spelled out in detail many atrocities and at least one murder that he said had occurred there. He had pictured the master of Wye House, old Colonel Lloyd, as a cruel tyrant who wallowed in luxury while he kept his slaves half-starved.

But, as in the case of Thomas Auld, his views had mellowed with the passage of time. The scenes of his youth, where his roots were, continued to haunt him. As he grew older (he was sixty-three that February) he came more and more to feel that his childhood had somehow been the happiest period of his life. Besides, a visit to Wye House, more than any other action, would symbolize how far he had traveled since then.

The Colonel Lloyd of Frederick's boyhood had long since died, and his son, Edward Lloyd VI, also. But there was still a Colonel Edward Lloyd, as there always had been since the seventeenth century. This one was the seventh, and last, of the old breed—an autocratic southern gentleman who had supported the Rebellion with his heart and treasure, and who had seen his wealth in the form of slaves slip away with emancipation and his vast estates in Maryland, Mississippi, Arkansas, and Louisiana come to the verge of ruin. The Lloyds were not exactly poor; Edward VII, like his predecessors, was a shrewd business manager. But they were no longer the overlords they once had been.[19]

Still, Wye House remained an echo of the Old South. Jefferson Davis had been entertained there in 1867; Admiral Franklin Buchanan, the Confederacy's greatest naval commander, and Brigadier General Charles S. Winder, who had been Stonewall Jackson's right-hand man, were buried there.[20] Aging gentlemen with goatees still gathered in the drawing room, with its portraits of Lloyd ancestors by Benjamin West and Charles Willson Peale, to toast the Lost Cause in Maryland rye whiskey. And

Frederick Douglass, one-time slave, felt his homecoming would not be complete until he was greeted as an equal there.

The opportunity arose when his friend and fellow Republican, John L. Thomas, Jr., offered him a cruise on the Chesapeake aboard the United States revenue cutter *Guthrie*, which was assigned to Thomas as collector of customs for the Port of Baltimore. What more natural than that the touring party should stop in during the cruise at Wye House, which Thomas's distinguished guest had not seen since childhood?

More than mere nostalgia was involved. The visit was a calculated political maneuver as well, and a shrewd one. Whether Douglass was refused admittance or welcomed, the resulting publicity would help the Radical Republican cause—either by demonstrating that the Democratic Lloyds were still wallowing in antebellum bigotry, or by showing how far the newly enfranchised blacks had progressed.

For Douglass, however, politics was secondary. He had set his heart on a return to Wye House several years earlier, and had mentioned his desire to Thomas during a conversation the previous winter. Thomas was enthusiastic; when Douglass expressed doubt as to how the present Colonel Lloyd would view such a visit, "Mr. Thomas promptly assured me that from his own knowledge I need have no trouble on that score. Mr. Lloyd was a liberal-minded gentleman, and he had no doubt would take a visit from me very kindly."[21]

So the trip was arranged, and the *Guthrie* cast off from Baltimore at 9 A.M. on June 12, 1881, a Tuesday morning. Aboard were Thomas, Douglass, Peter Thompson of Baltimore, and Colonel Samuel E. Chamberlaine, descendant of a proud old Talbot County family with Lloyd connections. As they crossed the bay, Douglass entertained the others with accounts of his travels and recollections of the Lloyd plantation as it was when he had last seen it fifty-six years earlier.[22]

"In four hours after leaving Baltimore we were anchored off the Lloyd estate," Douglass wrote, "and from the deck of our vessel I saw once more the stately chimneys of the grand old mansion which I had last seen from the deck of the *Sally Lloyd* when a boy. I left there as a slave, and returned as a freeman; I left there unknown to the outside world, and returned well known; I left there on a freight boat, and returned on a revenue cutter; I left on a vessel belonging to Col. Edward Lloyd, and returned on one belonging to the United States."[23]

Thomas sent a note to the house, addressed to Colonel Lloyd, inviting him to come aboard the cutter, and informing him that Douglass was present and desired permission to revisit the estate where he had lived as a child. If it was a difficult decision for the Lloyds, they met it like seasoned aristocrats. The man who had welcomed Jefferson Davis to these same halls might not care to shake hands with Frederick Douglass; but the Lloyds of Wye had long been masters of the art of compromise. Out to the *Guthrie* came, not Colonel Lloyd, but his eighteen-year-old son, Howard. He explained that unfortunately the colonel had been called away to Easton on business, but that in his absence Howard would be happy to receive the visitors, including Douglass. [24]

Everyone present seemed to accept Colonel Lloyd's absence at face value, although it could hardly have been coincidence. The trip was no secret, and one can picture the colonel climbing into his carriage and setting forth for Easton the moment a lookout reported the *Guthrie* had been sighted steaming up Miles River.

Howard Lloyd and his eight-year-old brother, DeCourcy, then conducted the visitors on a leisurely tour of the grounds. It was a moment among moments for the proud Douglass, and he wrote of it with an intensity of emotion that revealed as much about his own inner feelings as it did about the estate he was visiting:

I hope I shall be pardoned for speaking with much complacency of this incident. It was one which could happen to but few men, and only once in the lifetime of any. . . . That I was deeply moved by it can be easily imagined. Here I was, being welcomed and escorted by the great-grandson of Colonel Edward Lloyd— a gentleman I had known well fifty-six years before, and whose form and features were as vividly depicted on my memory as if I had seen him but yesterday. He was a gentleman of the olden time, elegant in his apparel, dignified in his deportment, a man of few words and of weighty presence, and I can easily conceive that no governor of the State of Maryland ever commanded a larger measure of respect [than] did this great-grandfather of the young gentleman now before me. [25]

Wye House had changed remarkably little in the fifty-six years except, Douglass noted, for the absence of "the squads of little black children which were once seen in all directions, and the great number of slaves in its fields." The slaves had been largely replaced by machinery; as Howard Lloyd pointed out, ten men now did the work of seventy. But there were still a good many blacks on the place, some of them living in the same "long quarter" and other structures that had sheltered them as slaves. Most of the buildings he remembered were still there—the stable, the storehouse from which Aaron Anthony had distributed slave allowances, Uncle Abel's shoemaker shop and Uncle Tony's blacksmith shop, the huge barn in which he had once loved to watch the darting swallows and listen to their chatter, the little overseer's house once occupied by those symbols of viciousness, William Sevier and Orson Gore.

Frederick was especially delighted to find Aaron Anthony's house still standing, and even the kitchen where Aunt Katy had presided, "and where my head had received many a thump from her unfriendly hand."

With a pang, he recalled that it was there he had last seen his mother. He located the window under which he had sung for Miss Lucretia. But when he looked for the little kitchen closet in which he had slept in a bag, he found its walls had been torn down and it had been incorporated into the kitchen. The dirt floor also had been replaced by planking. Outside, the oaks and elms under which young Daniel Lloyd had divided with Frederick his cakes and biscuits were as beautiful as ever. According to one account, at this point Douglass lapsed into a mimicry of slave vernacular, saying, "Over in them woods was whar me and Mars Dan useter trap rabbits." [26]

At Douglass's request the party visited the ancient family burying ground, which contained tombs dating back two centuries. Howard Lloyd gathered a bouquet of flowers and evergreens that he presented to Frederick to take back to Cedar Hill. Finally young Lloyd led the way into the "great house" itself, and invited his guests to take seats on the veranda, and to refresh themselves with wine from the mahogany sideboard in the dining room.

For Frederick it was an hour of deep fulfillment. Here was he, Freddy Bailey, the ragged slave boy, sitting on the veranda of the Lloyd mansion, sipping Madeira and chatting with his equals just as he had seen Francis Scott Key and other distinguished visitors doing as he had peered at them from the bushes. It had been a long journey of fifty-six years, to take those few short steps from the slave quarter to the mansion; but he had made it.

On an impulse, he proposed a toast to the Lloyd family, saying (as Thomas recalled it) that "he trusted that God, in his providence, would pour out the horn of plenty to the latest generation, and that the children and descendants of the master of the old house would worthily maintain the fame and characteristics of their ancestors." Nothing was said about old Colonel Lloyd's penchant for whipping Barney, his condoning of the actions of his overseers, or the skimpy rations he had allotted his slaves. In the warm nostalgic haze, all that was forgotten.

Almost as an afterthought, Douglass stopped on the way back to the *Guthrie* and spoke to the blacks who had assembled near the wharf to greet him. Many were children and grandchildren of people he had known, with here and there a gray-haired man or woman who recalled him as a child, or claimed to. If Frederick was interested in learning how they were managing to live under freedom, there was no time for such questions. Nor did he display any curiosity at seeing so many of them still living at the old plantation, under quasi-slave conditions. "They all seemed delighted to see me, and were pleased when I called over the names of many of the old servants," he reported. "... After spending a little time with these, we bade goodbye to Mr. Howard Lloyd, with many thanks for his kind attentions, and steamed away to St. Michaels.''

Next day the *Guthrie* took him up to the Miles River estate called The Rest, where Frederick enjoyed another warm reunion. This time it was with Mrs. Franklin Buchanan, widow of the famous Confederate admiral who was buried at Wye House. In the old days Frederick had known her as Ann Catherine Lloyd, a slender girl of eighteen or so. She had scarcely been aware of his existence; but she was a daughter of the old colonel, which meant everything to Douglass. He wrote with gushing enthusiasm of her graciousness in receiving him:

She invited me to a seat by her side, introduced me to her grandchildren and conversed with me as freely and with as little embarrassment as if I had been an old acquaintance and occupied an equal station with the most aristocratic of the Caucasian race. I saw in her much of the quiet dignity as well as the features of her father. I spent an hour or so in conversation with Mrs. Buchanan, and when I left a beautiful little granddaughter of hers, with a pleasant smile on her face, handed me a bouquet of many-colored flowers. I never accepted such a gift with a sweeter sentiment of gratitude than from the hand of this lovely child. It told me many things, and among them that a new dispensation of justice, kindness, and human brotherhood was dawning not only in the North, but in the South— that the war and the slavery that caused the war were things of the past, and that the rising generation are turning their eyes from the sunset of decayed institutions to the grand possibilities of a glorious future. [27]

He would have second thoughts, and soon, about that optimistic conclusion, as a wave of lynch law throughout the South provided a savage answer to his dream of a new era of ''justice, kindness, and human brotherhood.'' But meanwhile, when the hounds of criticism came after him again, yapping that Douglass was not only fraternizing with his old enemies but even licking their boots, it mattered less than it once had. He had been accepted as an equal at Wye House, had been received graciously by a daughter of Colonel Lloyd. For him, at least, the hatreds of the past were dead and buried.

He returned to Talbot County just once more. In March, 1893, he visited Easton and St. Michaels amid widespread press reports that he was planning to buy an estate on the Miles River and spend his final years in the county of his birth. One metropolitan daily reported this was his last remaining ambition, ''that after his life work was well nigh done he might go back to the county in which he was born and reared a slave, buy one of the handsomest old plantation places there, and end his days as one of the first citizens.'' [28]

Some Talbot Countians were as ready as he was to forget the past.

Reportedly he was offered The Villa, a massive mansion near Easton built in 1840. He inquired about buying the 200-acre farm called Sharon, where Thomas Auld had lived in his later years, and was assured by Samuel A. Harper, one of Auld's heirs, that it would be "desirable as a place of residence and also for manufacturing purposes should you desire to use it in that way." Harper would be delighted to show it to him if he wished to inspect it personally. Another Auld family connection, Frank Dawson, tried to interest him in Perry Cabin, the old Hambleton place where his brother-in-law, Peter Mitchell, had been born a slave.[29]

If he was serious about retiring to Talbot County, Frederick did not admit it. "I came to drink water from the old-fashioned well that I drank from many years ago, to see the few of the old friends that are left of the many I once had, to stand on the old soil once more before I am called away by the great Master, and to thank Him for his many blessings to me during my checkered life . . . —that's all I came for," he told a St. Michaels news reporter.[30]

In any case he did not buy. If his final ambition was to end his years in Maryland and be buried "in the soil which gave him birth"—as he had said so long ago—he did not achieve it. Instead he went back to Cedar Hill. He died there February 20, 1895, and was buried at Mt. Hope Cemetery in his adopted, city of Rochester, New York.

In a lengthy obituary notice, the *Easton Gazette* editor, Wilson M. Tylor, wrote that Douglass "has occupied the most exalted position of any member of his race in the world. Talbot reveres his memory."

There is cause to wonder about that statement. In the years since, Talbot County has shown few signs that it reveres the memory of its most famous native son. Douglass has been honored in many places: in Rochester he is memorialized by a statue; in Washington an Anacostia River bridge is named for him and his home there has been turned into a National Monument. But as this is written, the only memorial to Frederick Douglass in Talbot County, where he was born, is an abandoned, formerly all-black school, in itself a monument to the segregation he struggled so valiantly to end.

A Douglass Chronology

The Maryland Years

1701 (?) BALY, presumed great-great-grandfather of Frederick, born.

1745, DECEMBER (?) Jenny, great-grandmother of Frederick, born on Skinner Plantation, Talbot County, Maryland.

1774, MAY Betsey, grandmother of Frederick, born on Skinner Plantation.

1792, FEBRUARY 28 Harriet, mother of Frederick, born on Skinner Plantation.

1797, (?) Aaron Anthony moves his slaves, including Betsey and Harriet, to Holme Hill Farm on Tuckahoe Creek, Talbot County.

1818, FEBRUARY Frederick Augustus Washington Bailey born at Holme Hill Farm.

1824, AUGUST (?) Sent to live on Lloyd Plantation, Wye River, at home of his master, Aaron Anthony.

1825, FEBRUARY 14 (?) Mother visits him for last time before her death late in 1825 or early in 1826.

1825, AUGUST 27 Aunt Jenny and Uncle Noah escape to freedom; first intimation to Frederick that escape is possible.

1826, MARCH Sent to live with Hugh Auld family in Fells Point section of Baltimore.

1826, MAY 11 Frigate launched at Fells Point shipyard of James Beacham.

1826, NOVEMBER 14 Aaron Anthony dies.

1827, OCTOBER 18 Anthony's slaves divided among his heirs; Frederick awarded to Thomas Auld, returned to Hugh Auld family in Baltimore.

1827, (?) Sophia Auld teaches Frederick his letters; later he learns to write and do arithmetic on his own initiative.

1831, (?)   Undergoes religious conversion, joins Bethel A.M.E. Church, buys first book, *The Columbian Orator.*

1832, JULY 18   Sister Sarah sold to Perry Cohee of Mississippi, one of fifteen close relatives "sold south" during Frederick's childhood.

1833, MARCH   Sent to St. Michaels to live with Thomas Auld.

1834, JANUARY 1   Begins year as field hand under Edward Covey, the "slave-breaker." Suffers many lashings.

1834, AUGUST   Fights with Covey; is not whipped thereafter.

1835, JANUARY 1   Reassigned as field hand to William Freeland.

1836, APRIL 2   Escape plot foiled; Frederick and other plotters jailed in Easton.

1836, MID-APRIL   Sent back to Baltimore by Thomas Auld.

1836–1838   Learns calking trade, is savagely beaten by white fellow apprentices, joins debating society, meets Anna Murray.

1838, SEPTEMBER 3   Escapes north by train and boat; Anna joins him and they are married in New York City on September 15.

The Middle Years

1838, SEPTEMBER 18   Arrives at New Bedford, Massachusetts. Soon after, changes name to Frederick Douglass.

1839, MARCH 12   Speaks at meeting of New Bedford blacks against African colonization.

1839, JUNE 24   Daughter Rosetta born.

1839   First hears William Lloyd Garrison, Wendell Phillips, other abolitionist leaders; is inspired by abolitionism as "new religion."

1840, OCTOBER 9   Son Lewis born.

1841, JUNE 30   Chairs meeting of New Bedford blacks that condemns Maryland Colonization Society.

1841, AUGUST 9   Garrison hears Douglass speak at New Bedford antislavery meeting; is impressed by his ability.

1841, AUGUST 11–12   Speaks three times before large, chiefly white audiences at Nantucket convention; rouses great enthusiasm; is hired as lecturer by Massachusetts Anti-Slavery Society for three-month trial period.

1841, SEPTEMBER 28   Is forcibly ejected from Eastern Railroad train for refusal to ride in "Jim Crow" car; early progenitor of nonviolent protest movement.

1841, AUTUMN   Moves family from New Bedford to Lynn, Massachusetts.

1841, OCTOBER   In first speech reported in detail, at Lynn, launches twin attack on slavery in South, racial prejudice in North.

1842, JANUARY   Is hired permanently as antislavery lecturer after 3,500-mile tour draws big crowds, high praise for his oratorical talent.

1842, MARCH 3   Son Frederick born.

1842–1843   Travels extensively in New England and New York State; is victim of many instances of northern racial bias.

1843, SEPTEMBER 16   Attacked by proslavery mob at Pendleton, Indiana; continues lecture tour despite broken right hand.

1844, OCTOBER 21   Son Charles Remond born.

1845, MAY 28   *Narrative of the Life of Frederick Douglass, an American Slave,* published, revealing his identity and presenting a stark picture of his early life in Talbot County slavery.

1845, AUGUST 16   Sails for Great Britain aboard Cunard steamer *Cambria*; forced to travel in steerage.

1845, AUGUST 27   Proslavery *Cambria* passengers threaten to throw him overboard when he attempts to deliver abolitionist speech.

1845, AUGUST 28   Arrives at Liverpool on "visit to the home of my paternal ancestors."

1845, AUGUST 31   Travels to Dublin, Ireland, for three-month speaking tour at Dublin, Cork, Limerick, Belfast before large and enthusiastic antislavery and temperance audiences.

1845, LATE SEPTEMBER   First Dublin edition of *Narrative* published; sells rapidly, helps finance British travels.

1845, OCTOBER 25   Thomas Auld sells rights to Frederick to brother Hugh for $100; later, abolitionist press claims Hugh has vowed to get vengeance by selling Frederick south "cost what it may."

1846, JANUARY–MAY   Tours Scotland, campaigning unsuccessfully against acceptance of funds from American South by Free Church of Scotland.

1846, MAY–DECEMBER   Takes antislavery crusade to England; lionized by British crowds.

1846, OCTOBER 6   Hugh Auld agrees to sell Frederick's manumission for £150 sterling (about $710) raised by British admirers.

1846, DECEMBER 12   Becomes free man when manumission papers are filed in Baltimore County Court.

1847, APRIL 20   Arrives back in Boston after highly acclaimed British tour of eighteen months.

1847, LATE SEPTEMBER   Announces plans to start newspaper, the *North Star,* despite bitter opposition from Garrison and Phillips, with funds provided by British friends.

1847, DECEMBER 3   First issue of the *North Star* is published in Rochester, New York, where he makes his home for next twenty years.

1848, FEBRUARY 1   Meets John Brown. In later discussions with him, is greatly influenced by Brown's personality and insistence that slavery cannot be ended without violence.

1848, JULY 19–20   Attends first Women's Rights Convention at Seneca Falls, New York; begins lifelong crusade for women's voting rights.

1848, SEPTEMBER 8   Publishes letter "To My Old Master, Thomas Auld" in the *North Star,* accusing Auld of abandoning his grandmother Betsey Bailey in her old age.

1849, MARCH 22   Daughter Annie born.

1849, SEPTEMBER 7   Apologizes to Auld after learning Auld had taken Betsey into his household where she is cared for until her death in November, 1849. Auld never sees apology.

1850, MAY   Attacked by gang of toughs when he walks along Battery in New York City with two British women friends, Julia and Eliza Griffiths.

1851, MAY 9   Openly breaks with Garrison over issue of political action to end slavery, which Garrison opposes; henceforth the two become bitter enemies.

1851, JUNE 26   Changes name of publication to *Frederick Douglass' Paper*, accepts subsidy from wealthy anti-Garrisonian political activist, Gerrit Smith.

1851, SEPTEMBER   Aids three fugitive Maryland slaves, wanted for murdering their former master when he tried to recapture them in Pennsylvania in escaping to Canada. The three are among hundreds Douglass helps flee to freedom as "station master" of the Rochester terminus of the Underground Railroad.

1851–1858   Becomes increasingly engrossed with politics, first with the abolitionist Liberty Party headed by Gerrit Smith, later with the new Republican Party. Endorses Republican John C. Fremont for president in 1856.

1855, AUGUST   Publishes *My Bondage and My Freedom*, a more balanced account of his early life than the *Narrative*.

1858, FEBRUARY   John Brown stays at Douglass home in Rochester while perfecting plans for encouraging slave revolt.

1859, AUGUST 20   Meets Brown secretly at stone quarry near Chambersburg, Pennsylvania; learns of plan to attack Harper's Ferry; refuses to join Brown's forces.

1859, OCTOBER 17   Flees from Philadelphia on hearing news of Harper's Ferry raid; within a week hurries to Canada to evade arrest on charge of being a Brown accomplice.

1859, NOVEMBER 12   Sails from Quebec for England, where he stays six months.

1860, MAY   Returns to United States on learning of death of eleven-year-old Annie.

1860, DECEMBER 3   Boston meeting to commemorate John Brown's execution broken up; Douglass beaten by prosouthern mob.

1861, APRIL 22   Hails news of northern determination to fight to save the Union after attack on Fort Sumter; predicts destruction of slavery or destruction of the Union can be the war's only outcome; calls for use of black troops in Union army.

1862, DECEMBER 31   Attends gathering at Boston's Tremont Temple to celebrate the issuance of the Emancipation Proclamation, effective at midnight.

1863, FEBRUARY–JULY   Travels throughout North recruiting black troops; sons Lewis and Charles Remond are among first to enlist; both see action with Fifty-Fourth Massachusetts Regiment.

1863, JULY   Visits President Lincoln, protests discrimination against black troops.

1863, AUGUST 16   Ceases publication of *Douglass' Monthly*, successor to the *North Star* and *Frederick Douglass' Paper*, ending fifteen-year career as editor.

1864, AUGUST 25   Called to White House by Lincoln for advice on problems of Lincoln's reelection campaign; reverses earlier stand and endorses Lincoln.

1864, NOVEMBER 17   Returns to Maryland for first visit in twenty-six years; delivers six lectures in Baltimore; is reunited with sister Eliza.

1865, MARCH 4   Attends second Lincoln inauguration, is personally greeted by the president at Inauguration Ball.

The Postwar Years

1865–1866   After Lincoln's assassination, denounces President Johnson's "soft" reconstruction plan; serves on black delegation that meets with Johnson and criticizes his programs; endorses Radical Republican proposals, including black suffrage throughout South.

1867, JULY   Meets brother Perry for first time in forty years, arranges for him and his family to live in Rochester.

1868, AUGUST–OCTOBER   Campaigns for Ulysses S. Grant for president.

1869, MAY   Breaks with feminist leaders when they refuse to support ratification of Fifteenth Amendment unless it includes right to vote for all women as well as black men.

1870, JANUARY   Joins staff of *New National Era* as corresponding editor; later in year becomes editor, and on December 12 buys the Washington-based paper and its printing plant.

1871, JANUARY 12   Named assistant secretary of commission of inquiry to Santo Domingo; tours Santo Domingo January 18 to March 26; later defends Grant's proposal to annex Santo Domingo.

1872, MAY 12   Nominated for vice-president of United States on ticket with Victoria C. Woodhull by the Equal Rights Party, but instead campaigns for reelection of Grant.

1872, JUNE 2   Rochester home destroyed by fire, many important papers lost. Suspecting arson, Douglass moves his family to Washington on July 1.

1874, MARCH   Named president of Freedmen's Bank, which is in deep financial trouble and soon fails.

1874, SEPTEMBER   Closes down *New National Era.*

1877, MARCH 17   Senate confirms his appointment by President Hayes as United States marshal for the District of Columbia.

1877, JUNE 17   Returns to St. Michaels after forty-one year absence; there meets with Thomas Auld, speaks to racially mixed audience.

1878   Purchases Cedar Hill, fifteen-acre estate in Anacostia, D.C.

1878, NOVEMBER 23–26   Visits Easton; there delivers lecture at courthouse; locates site of his birth on Tuckahoe Creek.

1881, MARCH   Appointed by President Garfield recorder of deeds for the District of Columbia.

1881, JUNE 12   Revisits Lloyd plantation, called Wye House.

1881, NOVEMBER   Third autobiography, *Life and Times of Frederick Douglass,* published. It is a financial failure, as is a revised edition published in 1892.

1882, AUGUST   Anna, his wife of nearly forty-four years, dies after a long and crippling illness.

1884, JANUARY 24   Marries Helen Pitts, his white former secretary.

1885–1887   Travels with Helen on extended trip to England, France, Italy, Egypt, and Greece.

1889, JULY 1   Appointed minister resident and consul general to Haiti by President Benjamin Harrison. Keeps post until July 30, 1891, when he resigns in disgust over maneuvering by State Department and American business groups to acquire Mole St. Nicolas.

1892–1893   Serves as commissioner of Haitian exhibit at World's Fair in Chicago.

1893, MARCH   Announces plans to establish Freedom Manufacturing Co., a textile manufacturing firm, on a site near Norfolk, Virginia, where he hopes to employ 300 blacks. The scheme proves to be a sham by unscrupulous promoters using his name and prestige.

1893, MARCH   Visits Talbot County for third time amid reports that he plans to buy an estate and spend his final years there. Does not buy.

1894, JANUARY   Delivers his last great address, "Lessons of the Hour," a powerful burst of his old-time fury against lynch law in the South.

1895, FEBRUARY 20   Dies of heart attack at Cedar Hill. Funeral services at Metropolitan African Methodist Church in Washington on February 25 and at Central Presbyterian Church in Rochester on February 26. Buried in Mount Hope Cemetery, Rochester.

⚹ *Appendix B* ⚹

Genealogy of Frederick Douglass

(Based on records of slaves owned by the Anthony, Skinner, and Rice families of Talbot County, Maryland.)

First Generation

BALY, b. ca. 1701; SUE, or Selah, b. ca. 1720.

Second Generation

JENNY I, b. December (?), 1745, d. after March, 1781.

Third Generation

(Jenny's presumed children)
Hester I, b. 1760
Harry-Henry I, b. 1762.
BETSEY I, b. May, 1774, d. November, 1849; m. ISAAC BAILEY.
Jenny II, b. 1776.

Fourth Generation

(Betsey's Children)
Milly, b. January 22, 1790.
HARRIET, b. February 28, 1792, d. ca. 1825.
Jenny III, b. October 28, 1799; wife of Noah; escaped north 1825.

Betty II, b. October 19, 1801; sold south 1832.
Sarah I, b. February 7, 1804, d. 1816.
Maryann, b. April, 1806; sold south 1825.
Stephen I, b. 1808, d. 1816.
Hester (Esther) II, b. August, 1810.
Augustus, b. 1812, d. 1816.
Cate, b. 1815, d. 1815.
Prissy, b. August, 1816.
Henry II, b. February, 1820.

Fifth Generation

Milly's children:
   Bill, b. 1806, d. 1813.
   Betty III, b. February 7, 1811; sold south 1825.
   Margaret, b. December 10, 1812.
   Tom, b. September 21, 1814, d. after 1865.
   Henny, b. September 2, 1816, d. after 1840.
   Nancy, b. July, 1819.
   Infant, b. ca. 1827.
HARRIET's children:
   Perry, b. January 7, 1813, d. after 1878.
   Sarah, b. August, 1814; sold south 1832; d. after 1883.
   Eliza, b. March, 1816; became wife of Peter Mitchell; 9 children; d. after 1870.
   FREDERICK AUGUSTUS, b. February, 1818; m. (1) Anna Murray, 5 children; (2) Helen Pitts; d. February 20, 1895.
   Kitty, b. March 7, 1820; at least 3 children; d. after 1849.
   Arianna, b. October, 1822; at least 2 children; d. after 1849.
   Harriet II (?), b. ca. 1825.
Jenny III's children:
   Mary, b. February 7, 1818; sold south 1825.
   Isaac II, b. August, 1819; sold south 1825.
   John, b. 1821, d. 1821.
Betty II's children:
   Stephen II, b. July, 1819; m. Caroline Wilson; 13 children; served as private in Civil War; d. Caroline County on February 25, 1894.
   Dealey, b. 1821, d. 1821.
   Angeline, b. May, 1825; sold south 1832.
   Susan II, b. 1828.
   Rowena, b. January 1, 1830.
   Lavania, b. ca. 1831, sold south 1832.
   Isaac III, b. ca. 1832, sold south 1832.

Sixth Generation

Sarah's child:
Henry III, b. ca. 1832; sold south 1832.
Eliza's children:
Jane, b. ca. 1834.
Louisa, b. 1835.
Edward Napoleon, b. 1840.
Peter II, b. ca. 1842.
John Emory, b. December, 1843.
Susan III, b. ca. 1848.
Ella, b. 1851.
Mary Douglass, b. 1856.
Richard, b. 1859.
FREDERICK's children:
Rosetta, b. June 24, 1839.
Lewis Henry, b. October 9, 1840.
Frederick, b. March 3, 1842.
Charles Remond, b. October 21, 1844.
Annie, b. March 22, 1849, d. 1860.
Kitty's children:
Sam, b. December 28, 1842; d. May 3, 1846.
Nathan, b. March, 1845.
Henry IV, b. January, 1847.
Arianna's children:
Sam II, b. January, 1844, d. 1847.
Mary, b. 1847, d. 1848.

❧ A Note on Sources ❧

Douglass wrote three autobiographies; or rather, he wrote his auto-biography three times at different periods of his life, each time covering the story of his youth and escape from slavery and then bringing his account forward to the date of writing. The three are:

Narrative of the Life of Frederick Douglass, an American Slave (Boston: Anti-Slavery Society, 1845), referred to in notes as the *Narrative*.

My Bondage and My Freedom (New York: Miller, Orton & Mulligan, 1855), referred to in notes as *Bondage and Freedom*.

Life and Times of Frederick Douglass (Hartford: Park, 1881; rev. ed., Boston: Dewolf, Fiske, & Co., 1892), referred to in notes as *Life and Times*.

All three are available in various modern editions. In my notes I have followed the original pagination for the *Narrative* and *Bondage and Freedom*, because most modern editions follow the originals page for page. But in references to *Life and Times*, I have used the page numbering in the Crowell-Collier edition (New York, 1962), primarily because it has had wide distribution and is readily available to students in an inexpensive softback.

Of the three, *Bondage and Freedom* is by far the most detailed and reliable in its treatment of Douglass's early Maryland experiences. In writing it, Douglass made a conscious effort to correct many of the errors and misapprehensions that marred the *Narrative*, published ten years earlier at a time when he was still in the process of mastering the intricacies of written English. *Life and Times*, in its treatment of the early period, follows *Bondage and Freedom* almost word for word, with some smooth-ing out of phrasing and omission of details for reasons of space. However, only in *Life and Times* did Douglass give details of his escape method and describe his homecoming visits to Talbot County in the 1870s and 1880s.

Unfortunately, *Bondage and Freedom* is also the least familiar of the three to modern readers. The tendency is first to read the *Narrative* and then, if more information on Douglass is wanted, to skip over to *Life and Times,* which covers his career from start to finish. For that reason, if for no other, I have relied heavily on *Bondage and Freedom* in this book; it is the source of any quotation or detail attributable to Douglass but not otherwise identified.

Wherever possible, however, I have turned to outside sources, rather than any of the Douglass autobiographies, in dealing with controversial subjects. Douglass was accused of exaggerating, if not deliberately lying, in his account of the contrast between the wealth, ostentation, and lavish living in the "Great House" of the Lloyd plantation and the poverty and misery in the slave quarter there. No such charge can be made against Dr. Samuel A. Harrison, Talbot County's preeminent historian, who covered much the same ground in his essay on "Edward Lloyd V (The Governor)," which appears in the *History of Talbot County Maryland, 1661–1861,* published under the name of his son-in-law, Oswald Tilghman. Despite their contrasting viewpoints, factual differences between Harrison and Douglass are minor.

None of the biographies of Douglass written since his death probes beneath the surface of his own account of his Maryland experience. Some, such as the largely fictional *There Was Once a Slave,* by Shirley Graham, create entirely false and misleading backgrounds for the Aulds, Anthonys, Freelands, and others involved in Douglass's early life, and describe the Eastern Shore in terms of the Deep South.

The best general account is Benjamin Quarles's *Frederick Douglass* (New York: Associated Publishers, 1948; college ed., New York: Atheneum, 1974). Philip S. Foner, editor of *The Life and Writings of Frederick Douglass,* 5 vols. (New York: International Publishers, 1950–1975), also provides excellent details on Douglass's later career and performs a valuable service by printing in text form hundreds of Douglass's letters, speeches, and writings. But neither of these otherwise excellent works gives more than cursory treatment to the Maryland years. An important work in progress, *The Frederick Douglass Papers,* edited by John W. Blassingame and to be published by the Yale University Press, may eventually fill the gap.

In developing the ancestral background of the Bailey kin group, I relied primarily on the Anthony family papers contained in the Dodge Collection, Gift Collections, Maryland Hall of Records, Annapolis, and on inventory accounts and other public documents available at the Hall of Records and at the Talbot County Courthouse, Easton, Maryland. The Dodge Collection is a particularly rich source. It contains tables compiled by Aaron Anthony and others that provide a maternal genealogy for Douglass; ledger books kept by Anthony with many references to Harriet Bailey (Frederick's mother), his grandparents, and other family members; a copy of *My Bondage and My Freedom* with marginal comments written about 1919 by Harriet Lucretia Anthony, Aaron's great-granddaughter; and much else of interest to Douglass students.

Those interested in black genealogy will note that in order to trace Douglass's slave ancestors, it was necessary first to establish who their legal owners were, and then to compile a genealogy for the white family. Once I established that the Bailey kin group had been the property of the Skinner-Rice family in the eighteenth century, it was a relatively simple matter to follow them through several generations by means of the property inventories required by Maryland law for every deceased property-owner. Almost complete inventory records for every Maryland county throughout the colonial period and well into the nineteenth century are on file at the Maryland Hall of Records, Annapolis. They are the best single source for information on black family history during the slave era.

The many other primary sources consulted are listed in notes as material from them appears in the text.

In reconstructing Frederick's experiences in St. Michaels and his treatment by Edward Covey, the so-called "slave-breaker," I had no choice but to follow closely his own version of events. Neither Thomas Auld nor Covey ever publicly told their side of the story, except for a denial by Auld that he had beaten Frederick or ordered Covey to do so. Although I find no reason to doubt that Douglass gave an accurate account, at least as he recalled it, it should be kept in mind that he was a biased witness, writing an antislavery testament, and he had no intention of being fair or objective. He undoubtedly overstressed the bad qualities of the two men and understated whatever good ones they possessed. As the object of their stern discipline, he could hardly be expected to view them in a favorable light.

❦ Notes ❦

Chapter One

1. "Frederick Douglass at His Old Home," *Baltimore Sun,* June 19, 1877.

2. Goods and Chattels of Richard Skinner, deceased, June 10, 1746. Maryland Inventories, Maryland Hall of Records, Annapolis, 35:330–31; Talbot County Inventories, Courthouse, Easton, Md., JB no. 3, p. 245. (Hereafter cited as Richard Skinner Inventory.)

3. First recorded mention of black slaves in Talbot County was in an appraisal of the estate of the late John Emerson, June 19, 1666. Emerson possessed "one negrow woman" and "one negrow girl." *Archives of Maryland,* 72 vols. to date (Baltimore: Maryland Historical Society, 1883–), 54:396.

4. Ibid., pp. 430, 493. A geographical district in Talbot County has been known since the seventeenth century as Bailey's Neck.

5. Valuation of the Property of Andrew Skinner, Orphan, in the Care of Hugh Rice, March 14, 1769. Talbot County Land Records, Courthouse, Easton, Md., 20:18–19. (Hereafter cited as Talbot Land Records.)

6. Ibid. The smaller house has disappeared, but the main house, incorporated into a larger structure, remained in the hands of the Skinner family until the 1900s. It is currently (1980) the property of Doris Rend.

7. Richard Skinner Inventory.

8. Until the 1840s, when chattel records were instituted, slave bills of sale were filed among Talbot Land Records. On April 7, 1772, Hugh Rice sold to Richard Parrott of Talbot County a black man named Jack, for sixty-five pounds current Maryland money (Talbot Land Records, 20:205–6). No other sale of a Skinner-Rice slave in the eighteenth century has been found.

9. *Selah* is a Hebrew word used, as in the Biblical Psalms, to indicate a musical pause or rest. However, in this instance it may have been simply a misspelling of *Sillah* or *Scilla,* short for *Priscilla.* Those two spellings occurred among blacks related to the Skinner slaves, and Betsey Bailey, Douglass's grandmother, named one of her daughters Priscilla.

10. Similar examples of the persistence of given names, indicating clan relationships, can be traced among many other Talbot County black families. Some have survived for as long as three centuries. A classic example is the name Denby or Demby, which appeared among slaves owned by the Lloyd family of Talbot County as early as 1685, in an inventory of the

213

estate of Philemon Lloyd. In 1697 a clearly defined family group, "Denby & his wife," with four young children, were living on the Lloyd's Tuckahoe Creek plantation. The name appeared again and again in Lloyd estate inventories of the eighteenth century, and in the 1820s, when Douglass lived on the Lloyd estate, it was Bill Denby or Demby who was shot by an overseer when he fled into a pond to avoid a whipping (see chapter 5). In 1980 a number of black families named Denby and Demby, undoubtedly descendants, still are living in the area.

11. Herbert G. Gutman, *The Black Family in Slavery and Freedom* (New York: Random House, 1976), pp. 329–30, 351–52.

12. Richard Skinner Inventory. These children were almost certainly the offspring of the two women. In the eighteenth century, young children were almost never separated from their slave mothers. Douglass's charge in the *Narrative* (p. 2) that it was a "common custom" on the Eastern Shore "to part children from their mothers at a very early age" referred to the nineteenth century; in any case there is no evidence that the practice was as widespread as he claimed.

13. A diligent search of Talbot County records has turned up no earlier reference to slaves named Baly or Selah. There were earlier Sues, but the name is a common one.

14. Talbot County Wills, Courthouse, Easton, Md., HB no. 2, p. 439.

15. The marriage took place on November 9, 1748 (Robert Barnes, "Maryland Marriages, 1634–1777," mss. in Maryland Historical Society, Baltimore). A complicating factor is that after Katharine's death, Hugh Rice married Anna Sutton Skinner, who was the widow of Katharine's son, Andrew Skinner III (d. 1769). In both cases, he assumed guardianship of the women's minor children and claimed ownership of their property.

16. Talbot County Inventories, JB no. A, pp. 108–10.

17. Betsey Bailey named two of her daughters Jenny and Hester (or Esther; the two names are used interchangeably), indicating a close relationship with the Jenny and Hester of 1781.

18. Anthony Family Papers, Dodge Collection, Hall of Records, Annapolis, folder 95, pp. 159, 165–66. The collection (hereafter cited as Anthony Papers) contains much other information of great value to students of Douglass's early life and his Talbot County family.

19. Douglass mistakenly thought he was "probably" born in February, 1817. For a discussion of how he fell into this error, see chapter 3.

20. In his autobiographies Douglass named Betsey's children as Harriet (his mother), Milly, Jenny, Esther or Hester, Priscilla, and Henry.

21. In her marginal comments in a copy of *Bondage and Freedom*, Dodge Collection, Hall of Records, Annapolis, Harriet Lucretia Anthony wrote (p. 34): "Several years before Fred's death I sent him from my great grandfather's records the date of his birth." However, Douglass apparently never saw the complete Anthony tables.

22. Lewis Douglass to F. Douglass, June 9, 1865, in Frederick Douglass Collection, Moorland-Spingarn Research Center, Howard University, Washington, D.C.

23. Frederick Douglass Papers, Manuscript Division, Library of Congress, Washington, D.C., container 33, microfilm reel 21. (Hereafter cited as Douglass Papers, Lib. Cong.)

24. *Bondage and Freedom*, p. 80.

25. *Life and Times*, p. 513. Among newspaper clippings that Douglass preserved was one containing a comment by C. A. Bartoe that "he [Douglass] is, perhaps the only perfectly pronounced and complete specimen in the world of his color, kin and kind. Mount Caucasus [and] the mountains of the Moon were joined with our Indian wilderness to mix the strain of blood from three races in his veins and produce a peculiar individuality with no antecedent or copy of his traits." Clipping from the *Advertiser* (no city), May 12 (no year), in Douglass Papers, Lib. Cong., container 20, microfilm reel 13.

26. *Life and Times,* p. 463.

27. *Bondage and Freedom,* p. 52. The drawing of Rameses appears on p. 157 of James Cowles Prichard's *The Natural History of Man* (London: Hippolyte Bailliere, 1845).

28. J. Thomas Scharf, *History of Maryland from the Earliest Period to the Present Day,* 3 vols. (Baltimore: J. B. Piet, 1879), 1:377.

29. Oxford Port of Entry Account Books, 1731–1742, Hall of Records, Annapolis. The vessel was the *London Friggot,* Captain John Lockett, with a cargo of 350 blacks.

30. Governor John Seymour to British Board of Trade, November 18, 1708, quoted in Scharf, *History of Maryland,* 1:376; Oxford Port of Entry Account Books; *Maryland Gazette,* Annapolis, July 8, 1746.

31. Gutman, *The Black Family,* pp. 33–34, 169, 170–71, 340–43. Far less attention than it deserves has been given to this earlier, more mature black culture, with its West Indian background, that gave slavery in Maryland, and particularly on the Eastern Shore, its distinctive quality and flavor.

32. C. Duncan Rice, *The Rise and Fall of Black Slavery* (New York: Harper & Row, 1975), pp. 59–60, 70, 80–81.

33. John Hope Franklin, *From Slavery to Freedom* (New York: Knopf, 1967).

34. Rice, *Black Slavery,* pp. 68–70.

35. Ibid., p. 68; Thomas Bacon, *Laws of Maryland* (Annapolis: Jonas Green, 1765), laws of 1729, chap. 4, sections 1–4.

36. Talbot County Inventories, 1676–1725, analyzed by author; *Heads of Families at the First Census of the United States, 1790, Maryland* (Baltimore: Genealogical Publishing Co., 1972), pp. 9, 109–14.

37. James Bordley, Jr., *The Hollyday and Related Families of the Eastern Shore of Maryland* (Baltimore: Maryland Historical Society, 1962), p. 96.

38. Mulattos, the children of one black and one *known* white parent, had a special status under Maryland law. (The word comes from the Spanish *mulato,* meaning "young mule," the offspring of a female horse and a jackass.) Free mulattos could testify in court cases involving whites and had other rights denied free blacks. In many cases mulatto children were acknowledged in their white fathers' wills. The fact that mulatto children were born of white women mated to black men was recognized in legislation providing penalties for "such shameful matches" (1664), fines for performing such marriages (1715), and a provision that mulatto children born of white women, in or out of wedlock, must serve seven years as slaves, whereas mulattos born of black women were slaves for life (1717). Cf. Jeffrey R. Brackett, *The Negro in Maryland* (1889; reprint ed., Freeport, N.Y.: Books for Libraries Press, 1969), pp. 191–96.

39. *Bondage and Freedom,* pp. 76–77, 91.

40. Bacon, *Laws of Maryland,* laws of 1729.

41. *Maryland Gazette,* June 14, 1745.

42. *Narrative,* p. 24; Bacon, *Laws of Maryland,* laws of 1717, chap. 13, p. 2. In 1846 the act was modified to strike the word *Christian,* thus including Jews among those immune to testimony by blacks and Indians.

43. Bacon, *Laws of Maryland,* laws of 1715, section 21. Historian J. Thomas Scharf cited this act as an example of the "humane and rational views" of Maryland slaveholders. But even Scharf, an apologist for slavery who had been a Confederate officer, did not go so far as to claim it ever had been enforced. See Scharf, *History of Maryland,* 3:320, note.

44. Oswald Tilghman, comp., *History of Talbot County Maryland, 1661–1861,* 2 vols. (Baltimore: Williams & Wilkins, 1915; reprint ed., Baltimore: Regional Publishing Co., 1967), 1:52–56. Lloyd complained in a letter dated December 9, 1755, that among the

slaves on Wye River "there is at least the number of 300 that may be called Roman Catholics" and that they expected the French, with whom the English were at war, "would soon set them free."

45. Ibid., 1:283. The Reverend Thomas Bacon (1700?–1768) came to Talbot County in 1745 and afterward served as rector of St. Peter's parish. A book of his sermons "upon the great and indispensable duty of all Christian masters and mistresses to bring up their negro slaves in the knowledge and fear of God" was published in England and distributed in America.

46. Under European custom, Christians could not be enslaved, and many early Marylanders refused religious instruction to their blacks for fear their conversion would make them free. The Maryland General Assembly sought to meet this objection by acts in 1664 and 1671 declaring black slaves to be slaves for life, even if they became Christians. In 1681 the provision was extended to the children of slaves. Nevertheless, resistance to teaching Christianity to blacks extended well into the eighteenth century. See Brackett, *Negro in Maryland*, chaps. 1 and 2.

47. Despite Douglass's repeated charge, there was no law in Maryland forbidding masters to teach slaves to read.

48. *Bondage and Freedom*, p. 61.

49. Scharf, *History of Maryland*, 2:46–47.

50. Between 1746 and 1797 at least seven different persons had legal ownership of some or all of the Skinner slaves. They were Richard Skinner, who died in 1746; Katharine Skinner, his widow; Hugh Rice Sr., who married Katharine; Andrew Skinner III, Richard's son, who died in 1769; Anna Sutton Skinner, Andrew's widow, who was also married to Hugh Rice Sr.; Ann Catherine Skinner, daughter of Andrew and Anna; and Aaron Anthony, who married Ann in 1797 and assumed control of her inherited slaves.

51. An example was Stephen Bailey, Frederick's first cousin. A son of Betsey's daughter, young Betty, he was born in 1819 and, like Frederick, received early training from his grandmother before being sent to live on the Lloyd estate. He later was a slave of John P. Anthony, Aaron Anthony's grandson. In 1863, at the age of forty-four, he enlisted in the Union Army, participating in major battles and serving until 1867. After the war he and his wife, Caroline (a descendant of Emblem and Phill), became farm-owners in Caroline County and leaders of the Bethel Union Church. Today descendants of their eleven children are scattered from Massachusetts to California, and include teachers, engineers, nurses, chemists, electronics experts, librarians, a pharmacist, a contractor, a bank manager, and an insurance broker. (Mrs. Arretta Cooper et al., "History of the Bailey-Casson Family" mss., 1979.)

52. *Bondage and Freedom*, pp. 36–37, 44; notes by Harriet Lucretia Anthony on her old homestead, November 2, 1919 (unpublished mss. in private possession).

53. The U.S. Census of 1820, Talbot County, Chapel District, listed "Isaac Baily, free colored," as head of a household that included nine children under the age of fourteen.

54. Writing circa 1919, Harriet Lucretia Anthony stated in a marginal note in her copy of *Bondage and Freedom* (p. 180): "There is a lot in the woods, to be sure, on my father's old farm, ... called 'Aunt Bettie's Lot,' where she, with a number of little children lived."

55. Anthony Papers, item 97, ledger book "B."

56. See property inventory of Andrew Skinner (III), dated February 18, 1769, in Maryland Inventories, 113:71–72, Hall of Records, Annapolis.

57. Anthony Papers, item 97, ledger book "B."

58. U.S. Census, 1800, Maryland, Population Schedules by Counties. Between 17 and 1825, 779 deeds of manumission covering more than 1,000 slaves were filed amoı the Talbot Land Records. Many other slaves were freed in their owners' wills. The practiı

continued, though on a reduced scale, until the Civil War. By 1860 Talbot County had more free blacks than slaves.

59. Isaac granted manumission by Christopher Spry, October 23, 1787; Isaac granted manumission by Richard Dudley, August 19, 1794; Isaac and Bet, both about forty-five years old, granted manumission by Thomas Tibbles, May 1, 1795; Isaac granted manumission by Impey Dawson, July 18, 1796.

60. Talbot Land Records, 24:95.

61. Anthony Papers, ledger "A."

62. Lloyd Papers, Maryland Historical Society, Baltimore, available in 41 microfilm rolls. Roll 7, "Land Papers—Maintenance of Property," vol. 11.

63. *Bondage and Freedom*, p. 36.

64. Anthony Papers, ledger "A."

65. *Life and Times*, p. 28.

66. *Bondage and Freedom*, p. 36; *Encyclopaedia Britannica*, 1959 ed., 21:659–60.

67. *Life and Times*, p. 27.

68. Anthony Papers, ledger "B."

69. Harriet L. Anthony, mss., November 2, 1919. Original name of the south farm was Holme Hill but this later was changed to Home House.

70. Details of the rentals of Aaron Anthony's slaves are scattered throughout his three ledgers in the Anthony Papers.

71. *Life and Times*, pp. 28–29, 36.

Chapter Two

The primary source from which details of Aaron Anthony's life have been reconstructed is the Dodge Collection, containing the Anthony Family Papers, at the Maryland Hall of Records, Annapolis. These include, along with much other material, Aaron Anthony's three ledger books, labeled "A," "B," and "C," in which he kept accounts and recorded information on his personal life from 1795 to 1826. Except where otherwise noted, factual material in this chapter came from these ledgers.

Other major sources are the Anthony family Bible, on deposit at the Oxford Museum, Oxford, Md., and a genealogical chart of the Anthony family prepared by William N. Thompson, also at the Oxford Museum.

1. The girl was Frederick's Aunt Hester or Esther. For detailed accounts of this and other alleged atrocities related in the Douglass autobiographies, see chapter 5.

2. *Narrative*, p. 2; *Bondage and Freedom*, pp. 52, 58; *Life and Times*, p. 29.

3. "Self-Made Men" was the title of one of Douglass's most popular lectures in the years after the Civil War.

4. *Bondage and Freedom*, p. 34.

5. Queen Anne's County Deeds, LK no. HA, pp. 55–57, Hall of Records, Annapolis; Jane Baldwin Cotton, ed., *The Maryland Calendar of Wills*, 8 vols. (Baltimore: W. J. C. Dulany, 1901–1928), 7:727.

6. Anthony Bible. The older children were Rachel (b. 1744), Solomon (1751), Mary (1753), Elender or Elinor (1757), Nancy (1759), and James (1762).

7. Maryland Wills, Hall of Records, Annapolis, 37:312.

8. Caroline County Land Records, book "D," p. 292; book "F," p. 87. Of Anthony's three ledger books in the Dodge Collection, the one labeled ledger "B" appears to have been the first book he acquired.

9. Dickson J. Preston, *Wye Oak: The History of a Great Tree* (Cambridge, Md.: Tidewater Publishers, 1972).

10. The marriage date is from Talbot County Marriage Records, 1794–1825, Courthouse, Easton, Md., p. 72. Andrew's birth date, February 25, 1797, is from ledger "B," Anthony Papers. There appears to be no question that both dates are accurate.

11. Thomas Auld married Lucretia Anthony on January 16, 1823 (Auld genealogical papers, mss. by Carl G. Auld). Anthony's ledgers show charges to Lloyd for Auld's board in 1823, 1824, and 1825.

12. The original Skinner estate was surveyed for only 320 acres (Talbot Land Records, 20:72), but the Skinners owned additional land in Talbot and Dorchester counties. Anthony's holdings were given as 597½ acres when his estate was divided among his surviving heirs on November 16, 1829 (Talbot Land Commission Records, 1818–1830, Courthouse, Easton, Md., pp. 307–21).

13. Talbot County Inventories, Courthouse, Easton, Md., box no. 13, pp. 5–9. The inventory was filed on January 23, 1827.

14. For a detailed architectural study of this interesting old house see H. Chandlee Forman, *Old Buildings, Gardens, and Furniture in Tidewater Maryland* (Cambridge, Md.: Tidewater Publishers, 1967), pp. 52–55.

15. Talbot County Commissioners, slave assessment lists, 1817 and 1826, Hall of Records, Annapolis.

16. The advertisement offered a reward for Jenny and Noah, two Anthony slaves who had run away (See chapter 4). It was carried in the *Star* from September, 1825 to January, 1826, but Anthony still hadn't paid for it when he died in November, 1826. The debt was finally paid by his administrators, Thomas Auld and Andrew Anthony, April 1, 1828 (Talbot County Administration Accounts, Courthouse, Easton, Md., JP no. 14, p. 264).

17. Andrew S. Anthony married Ann Wingate in Martin County, Indiana, May 5, 1823 (Anthony Bible). Richard L. Anthony bought "1 lott old Blacksmith tools" for $19.50 at the auction of his late father's personal property, February 7, 1827 (Talbot County Inventories, box no. 13, p. 206). The reference to gossip is based on Douglass's report of the "whisper" that Anthony was his father, and his detailed knowledge of Anthony's relationship with the girl Hester; both of these must have come to him from older slaves.

18. *Bondage and Freedom*, pp. 80–81, 129, 132.

19. Ibid., pp. 122–124. The overseer was Orson Gore and the slave he allegedly slew, Bill Denby or Demby (See chapter 5). Of Anthony's reaction, Douglass wrote: "The atrocity roused my old master, and he spoke out, in reprobation of it. . . . Both Col. Lloyd and my old master arraigned Gore for his cruelty in the matter." Lloyd let Gore off with a warning, but Anthony did not approve.

20. The *Republican Star & General Advertiser* of Easton carried the following orbituary notice in its issue of Tuesday, November 21: "DIED—In this county on Tuesday last, Mr. Aaron Anthony, in the 60th year of his age." In her manuscript of notes on the old family homestead, Harriet Lucretia Anthony wrote in 1919: "The grave yard was not far from the house. . . . There rest the bodies of Aaron Anthony, his sons Andrew Skinner and Richard Lee, and my father John Planner. . . . I am sorry to say that not a single grave in our old grave yard has been marked by a stone." Today (1980) the exact location of Anthony's grave is unknown.

Chapter Three

1. *Life and Times*, p. 443.

2. Douglass to Hugh Auld, October 4, 1859 (?), reprinted in *Baltimore Sun*, February

25, 1895; Douglass to Benjamin F. Auld, September 16, 1891; Benjamin F. Auld to Douglass, September 27, 1891, all in Douglass Papers, Lib. Cong. Douglass to Benjamin F. Auld, March 24, 1894, letter in private possession. *Life and Times,* pp. 443–44.

3. Douglass to Benjamin F. Auld, March 24, 1894, letter in private possession.

4. *Bondage and Freedom,* pp. 151, 185; *Life and Times,* pp. 81, 103.

5. Harriet Lucretia Anthony's annotated copy of *Bondage and Freedom,* p. 34, Dodge Collection, Hall of Records, Annapolis; Helen P. Douglass to J. C. Shaffer, November 10, 1896, Douglass Papers, Lib. Cong.

6. The site Douglass pointed out is at the edge of a wooded ravine a few hundred yards east of the Kingston Landing Road, 2.2 miles south of Queen Anne, and just south of the junction called Tappers Corner, where Md. Route 303 turns west. No marker commemorates it. Nearly 7 miles away, at a location on Md. Route 328 that has no known connection with Douglass, is a roadside marker summarizing his career that has been erected by the Maryland Historical Society. No structure dating from Douglass's time remains on the old Anthony farm, nor are the locations of the white and black graveyards known.

7. Perry Ward Stewart was the "Mr. Stewart" mentioned by Douglass in the *Narrative,* p. 2, for whom Harriet Bailey worked. Anthony ledgers "B" and "C" show that he rented Holme Hill Farm from 1817 through 1821, when he died.

8. According to the Anthony slave tables, "Augustus sun of Betts" was born in July, 1812, and died in 1816. Frederick was the next boy born in the family after his death.

9. Douglass thoroughly confused readers by his remarks in the *Narrative* (p. 2) about his mother's employment. He said: "She was hired by a Mr. Stewart, who lived about twelve miles from my home," and he coupled this with a general charge that in Maryland it was a custom "to part children from their mothers at a very early age" and hire the mothers out on a farm a considerable distance off. This gave the false impression that when he was an infant his mother was sent to work twelve miles away while he was placed under the care of his grandmother.

In fact, this was not the case at all, and Douglass tried to correct the record in *My Bondage and My Freedom.* There he made it clear that it was not until *after* he moved to the Lloyd plantation at the age of six that his mother had to travel twelve miles to visit him. The twelve miles was from the Tuckahoe Creek farm to Wye House, not from Stewart's farm to Tuckahoe Creek. Nevertheless the notion that his mother was sent away when he was but an infant, so that they could not see each other, remains firmly fixed as part of the Douglass myth. (Compare *Narrative,* p. 2, and *Bondage and Freedom,* pp. 37–38, 53–54.)

10. *Bondage and Freedom,* pp. 40–42.

11. Ibid., pp. 44–45.

12. A water mill on this site had existed at least as early as 1704. Levi Lee became its owner in 1822. Later it was known as Satterfield & Moore's Mill. Remains, probably dating from after Frederick's time, still are visible west of Md. Route 303 a short distance north of Tappers Corner.

13. An earlier Lloyd mansion had stood on virtually the same site since the 1660s. The present one was built by Edward Lloyd IV about 1785. At this writing (1980) it is still a private home, owned and occupied by Mrs. Morgan Schiller, the former Elizabeth Key Lloyd.

14. For an excellent reconstruction of the Lloyd plantation at the close of the eighteenth century, see H. Chandlee Forman, *Old Buildings, Gardens and Furniture in Tidewater Maryland* (Cambridge, Md.: Tidewater Publishers, 1967). Comparison of Dr. Forman's description with Douglass's own recollections of the plantation (*Life and Times,* pp. 39–41, 446–49) shows how accurate an observer Douglass was, even as a small child.

Chapter Four

1. Hulbert Footner, *Rivers of the Eastern Shore* (New York: Farrar & Rinehart, 1944), p. 280.
2. Ibid., p. 274.
3. Talbot County Inventories, Courthouse, Easton, Md., box no. 1, pp. 322–331, August 3, 1685; Maryland Inventories, Hall of Records, Annapolis, 3:1–10, August 27, 1719.
4. Higginson & Bird Letter Book, Galloway Papers, Lib. Cong. Higginson & Bird to Edward Lloyd, September 27, 1718.
5. Oswald Tilghman, comp., *History of Talbot County Maryland, 1661-1861,* 2 vols. (Baltimore: Williams & Wilkins, 1915; reprint ed., Baltimore: Regional Publishing Co., 1967), 1:225.
6. Details of this incident are taken from Lloyd Papers, Maryland Historical Society, Baltimore. Roll 40, "Legal Papers," contains a number of documents relating to the dispute.
7. Tilghman, *History of Talbot County,* 1:215–16.
8. See Douglass, *Bondage and Freedom,* pp. 61–64. Douglass granted that slavery in Maryland existed in its mildest form, but argued that in such "secluded and out-of-the-way places" as the Lloyd plantation, slavery could "develop all its malign and shocking characteristics" without fear of arousing public disapproval. He said the Lloyd estate was "full three hundred years behind the age, in all that relates to humanity and morals."
9. William Still, *The Underground Railroad* (Philadelphia: Porter & Coates, 1872; modern ed., Chicago: Johnson Publishing Co., 1970), p. 315.
10. *Baltimore Republican,* June 4, 1834.
11. Lloyd Papers, roll 14. The last record of tobacco shipments from the Lloyd plantations was in April and May, 1825; of 114 hogsheads shipped out that spring, nearly all were graded either as dull or second quality.
12. Lloyd Papers, roll 40. A legend persists that the original Wye House was burned by the British in March, 1781, but contemporary accounts show clearly that the mansion was not burned, and that the raiders were not British troops but privateers from the lower Chesapeake.
13. Lloyd Papers, roll 10. Douglass thought 300 to 400 slaves lived on the home plantation.
14. Lloyd Papers, roll 10; *Bondage and Freedom,* p. 73. Since Douglass wrote of catching fish, crabs, clams, and oysters for himself, it seems certain that they were also available to the adult slaves.
15. *Bondage and Freedom,* p. 101.
16. Tilghman, *History of Talbot County,* 1:207; *Life and Times,* p. 446.
17. *Bondage and Freedom,* pp. 115–16. In Aaron Anthony's record of Lloyd slaves for January 1, 1824, Wilks's age was given as thirty-two. If this was accurate he was born circa 1791. Edward Lloyd V was born on July 22, 1779. "Sall Wilks" was listed as a house servant of Edward Lloyd IV in November, 1789.
18. *Bondage and Freedom,* pp. 56, 85. When Katy, in a fit of rage, slashed her son Phil savagely with a butcher knife, Captain Anthony warned her he would give her a lashing if she did anything like it again. In 1826, when the Anthony household was broken up, Katy was rented out for the year to Wilson Saulsbury, but she behaved so badly that in June Saulsbury evicted her from the house he had provided for her and her child.
19. *Bondage and Freedom,* pp. 132–33.
20. Ibid., pp. 130–31. In 1824, Isaac Copper was seven years old, hence a year older than Frederick. The wound Frederick suffered left a permanent cross-shaped scar on his forehead.

21. Ibid., p. 77. Daniel Lloyd as an adult lived at Wye Heights Plantation, one of the mansions built by his father. His son, Henry Lloyd, was governor of Maryland from 1885 to 1888.

22. *Narrative*, p. 14.

23. Lloyd Papers, rolls 10 and 14; Talbot Land Records, 46:506. Almost all Baltimore records concerned with slaves prior to 1852 were burned by court order because of a lack of storage space in 1952.

24. *Life and Times*, pp. 448–49. Page, a native of Greenfield, Mass., died in 1832 "under painful circumstances, being distracted in mind," according to Harrison. His family claimed his estate but not his body; he was one of the few outsiders buried in the Lloyd family graveyard.

25. The village of Copperville, near Tunis Mills, is still inhabited by descendants of Lloyd slaves.

26. *Bondage and Freedom*, pp. 71–72.

27. Ibid., p. 72.

28. Ibid., pp. 109–10, 118. Jacob Gibson (Douglass spelled the name *Jepson*) lived at Marengo, an estate that bordered on Lloyd property. A colorful character noted for physical and verbal assaults on his contemporaries, he died in 1818. At the time of which Douglass wrote, Marengo was owned by his son, Fayette Gibson, to whom old Jacob had also left a large indebtedness.

29. Ibid., pp. 135–36. According to the Anthony slave tables, Tom, son of Milly, was born on September 21, 1814. In the division of slaves following Aaron Anthony's death, he became the property of Thomas Auld. He was granted manumission by Auld in 1845 and was living in the St. Michaels area under the name of Tom Bailey when Douglass's son Lewis visited there in 1865.

30. Lloyd Papers, roll 10.

31. *Bondage and Freedom*, p. 56.

32. Talbot Land Records, 46:182. In the bill of sale Richard L. Anthony appeared as vendor, but he was undoubtedly acting for his father. Price for the four slaves was $900.

33. *Life and Times*, p. 50. Frederick did not mention the escape in his 1845 and 1855 autobiographies, probably because Jenny and Noah were still subject to possible recapture as fugitives. If he ever learned where they went or what freedom names they took, he did not record it.

Chapter Five

1. *Bondage and Freedom*, pp. 79–80. For Douglass's detailed accounts of the episode, see *Narrative*, pp. 5–7; *Bondage and Freedom*, pp. 85–88, and *Life and Times*, pp. 47–49.

2. Hester's name was also given in various accounts and records as Esther and Easter. She was the seventh of Betsey Bailey's ten daughters, and was born in August, 1810. Ned Roberts's age in an 1826 tax list of Lloyd slaves is recorded as sixteen years (see Talbot County Slave Assessments, 1826, Hall of Records, Annapolis). Thus both were teenagers close to the same age when the events related by Douglass allegedly occurred. In January, 1827, when Anthony's property was inventoried, Hester had an infant child. In the slave division of October, 1827, she and the child were awarded to Thomas Auld. After that, both disappear from the records.

3. *Bondage and Freedom*, pp. 113–14. Barnett Sampson's age was recorded in Aaron Anthony's return book for January, 1824 (Lloyd Papers, roll 10), as being fifty-five years.

4. *Narrative*, p. 19. Edward S. Winder was married to Colonel Lloyd's eldest daughter,

Elizabeth Tayloe Lloyd. Their son, Confederate Brigadier General Charles Sydney Winder, died at the Battle of Cedar Mountain, August 9, 1862. Charles Lowndes, later a navy commodore, was married to Sally Scott Lloyd. Their son, Lloyd Lowndes, was governor of Maryland from 1896 to 1900. Douglass thought Nicholson was also a son-in-law of Colonel Lloyd, but he was a son of the colonel's sister Rebecca, who married Joseph Hopper Nicholson.

5. William Sevier's name appears often in the Lloyd Papers alongside his designation as a plantation employee.

6. *Bondage and Freedom*, pp. 92–96. Nelly can be identified as Nelly Kellem, aged thirty-seven in January, 1824, according to Aaron Anthony's return book for that date. Three young Kellems named Henry, age three, Wesley, ten, and Charles, sixteen, may have been the boys who pelted Sevier with stones and bit him on the leg.

7. Ibid., pp. 82–84; Talbot Land Records, 46:182. In his account, Douglass did not identify Betsey by name, but said she was "the daughter of Milly, an own aunt of mine." According to the Anthony slave tables, in which she was listed under the curious name of "Bettfarmer," she was born to Milly on February 7, 1811. Plummer, the overseer, could have been either Philemon or James Plummer, both of whom were named in the Anthony ledgers.

8. *Bondage and Freedom*, pp. 122–23; see also *Narrative*, pp. 24–25, and *Life and Times*, pp. 66–67. Douglass gave the overseer's name as *Austin* Gore, and he is so listed in 1820 and 1830 census records. However, his name is spelled *Orson* both in the Lloyd Papers and on his tombstone in Spring Hill Cemetery, Easton, Md. In Eastern Shore usage, *Orson* would have been pronounced *Aussin*, which may account for the confusion.

9. *Bondage and Freedom*, p. 124.

10. "To the Public—Falsehood Refuted," open letter by A.C.C. Thompson, first printed in the *Delaware Republican* late in 1845 and reprinted in the *National Anti-Slavery Standard* on December 25, 1845. For a detailed discussion of this letter and Douglass's response to it, see chapter 10.

11. Lloyd Papers, roll 10, vol. 35.

12. In *Bondage and Freedom* (p. 122), Douglass said the murder occurred while he was at the Lloyd plantation, and that he knew Denby well. However, he omitted these claims in rewriting the passage for *Life and Times*. From the evidence on Denby's death in the Lloyd Papers, they could not have been true.

13. *Bondage and Freedom*, p. 121.

14. Ibid., p. 127. This harsh judgment by Douglass undoubtedly contained much truth. A double racial standard for Eastern Shore justice continued until recent times.

15. *Cambridge* (Maryland) *Chronicle*, December 25, 1830.

16. "The Meaning of July Fourth for the Negro," oration by Douglass at Rochester, N.Y., July 5, 1852, reprinted in Philip S. Foner, ed., *The Life and Writings of Frederick Douglass*, 5 vols. (New York: International Publishers, 1950–1975), 2:181–204.

17. Frederic Bancroft, *Slave Trading in the Old South* (New York: Ungar, 1931), pp. 29–30.

18. William Calderhead, "Slave Trader in a Slave Economy: Austin Woolfolk, A Case Study," *Civil War History Journal*, September, 1977, pp. 195–211.

19. Fragmentary information on Woolfolk's purchases in Baltimore exists only for the first six months of 1825, when he bought ninety-eight slaves there. Other Baltimore slave records have been destroyed.

20. *Baltimore Republican*, May 8, 1835; *Cambridge Chronicle*, January 2, 1836; *Eastern Shore Whig*, May 16, 1833.

21. Benjamin Lundy, ed., *Genius of Universal Emancipation*, March, 1822.

22. The names of hundreds of Eastern Shore individuals who sold slaves to out-of-state traders are on file in Land Records of Talbot and other Eastern Shore counties, available at the county courthouses and at the Hall of Records, Annapolis. Given names and approximate ages of the slaves are also listed.

23. Calderhead, "Austin Woolfolk," pp. 199–201.

24. Bancroft, *Slave Trading*, p. 30.

25. Calderhead, "Austin Woolfolk," p. 201.

26. Ethan Allen Andrews, *Slavery and the Domestic Slave Trade in the United States* (Boston: Scholarly Publishers, 1836; facsimile ed., New York: Arno Press, no date), p. 81.

27. M. L. Dillon, *Benjamin Lundy and the Struggle for Negro Freedom* (Urbana: University of Illinois Press, 1965), p. 119.

28. Ibid., p. 120.

29. *Bondage and Freedom*, pp. 89–91.

30. On three different occasions during Frederick's youth, his owners faced major decisions that would affect his future. Each time they decided to send him to Baltimore, where he could live in comparative freedom with a privileged status in the Hugh Auld household, rather than to sell him.

Chapter Six

1. The street's name is pronounced "Alice Anna," as if it were two words. The house no longer exists. Its site has been established by research of the Baltimore City Commission on Historical and Architectural Preservation as having been on the southeast corner of Aliceanna and Durham (formerly Happy Alley) streets, presently 1815 Aliceanna Street. A commemorative plaque was authorized on October 16, 1967, by the Baltimore City Council and prepared by the Maryland Historical Society, but at this writing (1980) it has never been installed.

2. *Baltimore American & Commercial Daily Advertiser,* May 12, 1826.

3. Norman Rukert, *The Fells Point Story* (Baltimore: Bodine & Associates, 1976), p. 41.

4. For a discussion of how this error led Douglass into making other errors concerning key dates in his life, including the year of his birth, see chapter 3.

5. *Life and Times,* p. 77.

6. Writing from memory, Douglass made several misstatements in his account of this traumatic experience. In *Life and Times,* p. 95, he wrote: "In a very short time after I went to Baltimore my old master's youngest son, Richard, died, and in three years and six months after, my old master himself died, leaving, to share the estate, only his daughter Lucretia and his son Andrew."

In fact, Aaron Anthony died on November 14, 1826, only a few months after Frederick went to Baltimore. His son Richard survived him, becoming an heir to the estate along with Lucretia and Andrew. Lucretia died on July 6, 1827, before the estate was divided, and her share went to her husband, Thomas Auld. Richard died on May 18, 1828.

7. Why Douglass was not aware of Lucretia's death remains a puzzle. In all three of his autobiographies he stated that he was awarded to her in the division of Aaron Anthony's slaves, and that she sent him back to Baltimore to live. Yet all available records agree that she had died in July, 1827, three months before the slave distribution occurred. The probable explanation is simply that nobody bothered to tell Frederick about it at the time.

8. A child named Harriet, listed as being one year old in the inventory of Aaron Anthony's estate taken on January 13, 1827, is not otherwise identified. She was not mentioned in the Anthony genealogical table. In the division of Anthony's slaves in October,

1827, she was awarded to Thomas Auld, but no further record has been found. One possibility is that she was a child of Harriet Bailey (hence the name) who was born shortly before her mother's death, and that she herself died soon after the October distribution.

9. *Bondage and Freedom,* pp. 177–78.

10. Ibid., p. 176. Douglass's characterization of Andrew Anthony as "a confirmed sot" is supported by at least two independent sources. In her copy of *Bondage and Freedom,* (Dodge Collection, Hall of Records, Annapolis) Harriet Lucretia Anthony wrote in the margin opposite Douglass's remark: "As my grandfather, Andrew Skinner Anthony, died a young man I know nothing of his cruelty, but I fear Fred is right about his intemperate habits." In a letter to Douglass dated January 14, 1856, John Manross wrote that he had known Andrew Anthony well when Anthony operated a "whiskey shop" at Hillsboro between 1828 and 1831, "and I believe your description of him is quite accurate" (Douglass Papers, Lib. Cong.).

11. *Bondage and Freedom,* pp. 175–76.

12. Talbot County Distributions, Courthouse, Easton, Md., JP no. D, pp. 58–59, October 18, 1827; *Bondage and Freedom,* p. 178.

13. Like the Aliceanna Street house, the Aulds' Philpot Street house has long since been destroyed. Its exact location is unknown; much of the Philpot Street area is now inside the warehouse compound of the Allied Chemical Corporation.

14. "Colored Churches.—No. III," *North Star,* March 10, 1848.

15. *Life and Times,* p. 79. Substantially the same quotation appears in *Narrative,* p. 33, and *Bondage and Freedom,* p. 146.

16. Jeffrey R. Brackett, *The Negro in Maryland* (1889; reprint ed., Freeport, N.Y.: Books for Libraries Press, 1969), p. 197.

17. "Celebrities at Home: Frederick Douglass," *Republic,* date unknown (circa 1880), clipping preserved in Douglass Papers, Lib. Cong. In addition to Thomas (b. January 12, 1824), the Aulds had four other children during the time Frederick spent with them. They were Ann Elizabeth (b. November 16, 1826); Benjamin Franklin (December 27, 1828); Hugh Wilson (February 13, 1831); and Edward H. (December 29, 1836). Douglass helped care for these other children as well as Thomas. A sixth child, Zepporah, was born October 28, 1838, shortly after Frederick escaped to the North.

18. "The Meaning of July Fourth for the Negro," oration by Douglass, Rochester, N.Y., July 5, 1852, in Philip S. Foner, ed., *The Life and Writings of Frederick Douglass,* 5 vols. (New York: International Publishers, 1950–1975), 2:181–204. The route from Woolfolk's slave pen on Pratt Street to the Fells Point wharves crossed the drawbridge and ran down Philpot Street, directly in front of the Auld house.

19. Caleb Bingham, *The Columbian Orator* (1797; reprint ed., Philadelphia, Lippincott, 1860), pp. 240–42. The copy Frederick bought circa 1831 is preserved among his books at the Frederick Douglass Memorial Home, Cedar Hill, Anacostia, Washington, D.C. Its twenty-three-page chapter on "the ornamental and useful art of eloquence" was his principal guide in learning to speak in public.

20. Brackett, *Negro in Maryland,* p. 99.

21. *Bondage and Freedom,* pp. 124–25. Douglass recalled the name as Thomas Lanman, but the man he referred to was probably Thomas H. W. Lambdin, who later became a teacher and bailiff in St. Michaels.

22. Douglass, "Reminiscences," *Cosmopolitan* 7, no. 4 (August, 1889):376–77.

23. *Easton Gazette,* December 24, 1831. Adams presented the petitions in the House on December 12, 1831, but he said he did not personally favor them, "whatever might be his opinion of slavery in the abstract." They were referred to the Committee on the District of Columbia, which reported them adversely.

Notes to Chapter Seven

24. *Bondage and Freedom,* pp. 165–66. For a report on Baltimore's 1832 cholera epidemic, see J. Thomas Scharf's *Chronicles of Baltimore* (Baltimore: Turnbull, 1874), pp. 460–63.

25. *Genius of Universal Emancipation,* November 10, 1829, November 20, 1829; M. L. Dillon, *Benjamin Lundy and the Struggle for Negro Freedom* (Urbana: University of Illinois Press, 1965); W. P. Garrison and F. J. Garrison, *Life of William Lloyd Garrison,* 4 vols. (1885–1889; reprint ed., New York: Arno Press, 1969), 1:203–4, 212–16.

26. *Bondage and Freedom,* pp. 154, 159–61, 183.

Chapter Seven

1. Douglass erroneously stated in the *Narrative* that he arrived in St. Michaels in March, 1832, went to work on Covey's farm in January, 1833, and returned to Baltimore in 1835. All these dates were a year early, and he corrected them in his later autobiographies.

2. According to the Auld family Bible, William H. Auld, son of Thomas and Rowena, was born on March 4, 1831, and died in infancy. Sarah Louisa Auld was born on July 13, 1833. Rowena Auld died on November 24, 1842, "with consumption."

3. Thomas Graham, who lived on Cherry Street in St. Michaels, stated in 1846 that "during Mr. Auld's entire residence in St. Michaels, he was my immediate neighbor" (Quoted in letter, A.C.C. Thompson to *Albany Patriot,* reprinted in the *Liberator,* February 20, 1846). Auld's store, which he first rented and later purchased, was "at the corner of Cherry Street and the main road or Talbot Street" (Talbot Land Records, 51:457, 52:303).

4. *Life and Times,* p. 106.

5. Auld sold Eliza and her two infant daughters to Peter Mitchell for one hundred dollars on January 25, 1836 (Talbot Land Records, 52:258).

6. Douglass misspelled the name *Hambleton* as *Hamilton* in all three autobiographies.

7. Talbot Land Records, 50:192.

8. In the redistribution of slaves that followed Andrew Anthony's death, five, including "Aunt Katy," were awarded to White Barwick, who had married Anthony's widow, Ann. The other eight, including Frederick's brother Perry, his sisters Kitty and Arianna, and his grandmother, went to Anthony's minor son, John P. Anthony, in care of his guardian, Thomas O. Martin. John P. Anthony also inherited the Holme Hill farm, and his slaves remained there. Division of August 28, 1835, in Talbot County Distributions, Courthouse, Easton, Md., JB no. D, 1825–1845, pp. 185–86.

9. Thompson to *Albany Patriot,* as cited in note 3 to this chapter.

10. Douglass to William Lloyd Garrison, April 16, 1846, *Liberator,* May 15, 1846.

11. Thomas H. Sewell, "St. Michaels Methodism," mss. compiled in 1894, Hall of Records, Annapolis.

12. Ibid., p. 581; *Easton Gazette,* July 27, 1833.

13. Douglass's accounts of Auld's "conversion" and its aftermath appear in *Narrative,* pp. 53–54; *Bondage and Freedom,* pp. 193–96; and *Life and Times,* pp. 107–9.

14. *Bondage and Freedom,* p. 201. The Bible quotation is from Luke, 12:47. Afterward Auld apparently emancipated Henny; the 1840 U.S. Census lists Henny Bailey as a free black who was living alone in St. Michaels District. Douglass charged that Auld, after an unsuccessful attempt to give Henny to his sister, Sarah Cline, "set her adrift to take care of herself, . . . virtually to starve and die."

15. Scarcely to Douglass's credit is the way in which he pictured Thomas Auld as a villain before countless audiences in the United States and abroad. His references to Auld in the British Isles speeches never failed to elicit cries of "Shame! Shame!" and "expressions of horror," according to news accounts. Sometimes he portrayed Auld as a sadist who beat

Henny every morning before breakfast just for the pleasure of seeing the blood run. At Sheffield, England, on September 11, 1846, he was quoted as saying Henny's "right hand was burnt in infancy by his (Auld's) orders," and that it was Auld who had beaten Perry and "stamped on his face until it was covered with blood." In scores of speeches, he ridiculed Auld as the prime example of the slavery-condoning, Bible-quoting southern Methodists who were among his principal targets.

16. Sewell, "St. Michaels Methodism," pp. 442, 548, 553.

17. Matthew Simpson, ed., *Cyclopaedia of Methodism* (Philadelphia: 1882), p. 255; Talbot County Wills, JP no. 9, pp. 79–89.

18. In an address at Manchester, England, on October 17, 1846, Douglass said several "grey haired men" were among the pupils. This may account for the violent opposition to the school from St. Michaels whites, who bitterly objected to education of adult blacks for fear it would lead to a local "Nat Turner rebellion."

19. *Bondage and Freedom*, p. 200. What was meant by the reference to Turner is obscure, since he was hanged rather than shot.

20. Douglass misspelled the name as *Garrison West*. A sketch of West's life appears in Robert W. Todd's *Methodism of the Peninsula* (Philadelphia: James B. Rodgers, 1886), pp. 113–23.

21. Douglass said there had been another slave in the area who could read, a man named Jim who belonged to Hugh Hambleton, but that shortly after Frederick's arrival Jim "had been sold off to the far south" (*Bondage and Freedom*, p. 237).

22. The tradition that Covey conducted a professional "nigger-breaking" operation, in my opinion, is largely myth. Douglass wrote in *Bondage and Freedom* (p. 203) that Covey "enjoyed the execrated reputation, of being a first rate hand at breaking young negroes. . . . It enabled him to get his farm tilled with very little expense. . . . Like some horse breakers, noted for their skill, who ride the best horses in the country without expense, Mr. Covey could have under him, the most fiery bloods in the neighborhood, for the simple reward of returning them to their owners, *well broken*." Douglass also spoke of "scores of lads" who had been committed to service under Covey to be broken. From those statements Douglass biographers have built a picture of Covey as conducting what amounted to a slave-breaking assembly line, where rebellious blacks by the dozens vanished from view to emerge months later docile and almost zombielike as a result of beatings and torture.

However, it should be noted that during the year Frederick served under Covey he was the only black on the farm who was there for disciplinary purposes. There were only two other slaves, the woman Caroline, who was owned by Covey, and Bill Smith, hired from Samuel Harrison, who by Douglass's own account would not permit Covey to whip Smith. Nor does it seem possible that in previous years Covey could have made efficient use of "scores" of slaves on his small rented farm of 150 acres.

In addition, when Frederick begged Thomas Auld to take him away from Covey, Auld refused partly on the ground that "I should lose your wages for the entire year" (*Bondage and Freedom*, p. 231). That indicates Covey was paying a substantial sum for Frederick's services; certainly he did not have them rent free. Covey's innate cruelty and malicious character are sufficiently documented; but nothing in the record supports the claim that he conducted a large-scale slave-breaking operation.

23. For details of A.C.C. Thompson's challenge of Douglass's statements in the *Narrative*, see chapter 10 herein.

24. Harriet Lucretia Anthony's remark was written in the margin of p. 203 of her copy of *Bondage and Freedom* (Dodge Collection, Hall of Records, Annapolis). Thompson's comment appeared in an open letter to the *Delaware Republican*, reprinted in the *Liberator* on December 12, 1845.

25. Douglass mistakenly identified Mrs. Covey's sister as "Miss Kemp." Covey had married Susan Caulk (not Kemp) on November 21, 1832; and the 1850 U.S. census named Emma R. Caulk, age thirty-four, as a member of the Covey household.

26. Douglass's accounts of his adventures with the oxen and his lashing by Covey appear in the *Narrative*, pp. 58-60; *Bondage and Freedom*, pp. 208-14; and *Life and Times*, pp. 117-21.

Chapter Eight

1. *Narrative*, p. 61.

2. Ibid., p. 63.

3. Sandy Jenkins was the property of William Groome, an Easton merchant. He had been hired out for a year to work for Susan Covey's father, a Mr. Caulk, whom Douglass mistakenly identified as "Mr. Kemp." He was undoubtedly the "negro boy named Sandy," age eight, listed in an 1817 Talbot County Assessment of Negroes (Hall of Records, Annapolis) as belonging to Joseph Groome. Pot Pie Neck is still the local name for a section of Tilghman Peninsula west of Harris Creek.

4. Whether Douglass meant to say that Sandy had actually been born in Africa, or merely that he was steeped in African traditions and beliefs, is not clear.

5. *Bondage and Freedom*, pp. 242-43.

6. *Narrative*, p. 73.

7. Talbot Land Records, 52:382; U.S. Census, 1850; Talbot County Inventories, TNC no. 3, p. 578; Talbot County Administrative Accounts, Courthouse, Easton, Md., TNC no. 24, p. 374.

8. *Bondage and Freedom*, pp. 258-61. Supporting Douglass's testimony to Daniel Weeden's character is the fact that in 1839 he forced a free black man, Samuel Brooks, back into slavery by producing testimony that Brooks had served time in the Maryland penitentiary. Weeden then bought Brooks at a bargain price as his own slave (Talbot Land Records, 54:186).

9. As nearly as can be determined, the Freeland farm was located east of what is now called Old Martingham, the long-time Hambleton family seat, in an area occupied in 1980 by an expensive country club subdivision called Martingham. Elizabeth Freeland and her son, William Freeland, Jr., who figured in Frederick's experiences in 1835 and 1836, are both buried in the Hambleton graveyard at Old Martingham.

10. Douglass address, "Intemperance, Viewed in Connection with Slavery," Glasgow, Scotland, February 18, 1846; Douglass address, Paisley, Scotland, March 30, 1846, both in John W. Blassingame, ed., *The Frederick Douglass Papers*, multivol. in preparation (New Haven: Yale University Press, 1979-), 1:165-70, 205-9. Although he emphasized the Christmastide drinking, Douglass pointed out in these speeches that slaveholders also gave their blacks whiskey and apple brandy on Saturday nights throughout the year to get them drunk "because if they had time to think . . . on the Sabbath day, they might devise means by which to obtain their liberty."

11. *Bondage and Freedom*, pp. 252-53.

12. Ibid., p. 283.

13. Ibid., p. 287. If the passes had been used, Frederick's misspelling of the well-known name of Hambleton might have given the conspirators away to any reasonably literate pursuer. But in the event, it made no difference.

14. Ibid., p. 285. The dialect is given as Douglass recorded it. In common with white abolitionists, he consistently used a hackneyed version of black speech in written accounts of dialogue with other blacks.

Notes to Chapter Nine

15. By 1836, young black males for sale were so scarce on the Eastern Shore that their price had risen dramatically (see chapter 5). At least three sales during that year of males between seventeen and twenty-three for $1,000 or more have been found in Talbot County Land Records.

16. *Bondage and Freedom*, p. 306.

17. In his account in the *Narrative*, Douglass said nothing about Auld's agonizing over the situation, his refusal to sell Frederick to the slave traders at any price, or his promise to emancipate him at the age of twenty-five. These omissions were among the reasons Auld felt, with considerable justice, that Douglass had been unfair to him. Douglass included the material in *Bondage and Freedom* and *Life and Times*, and it is those versions that have been followed here.

Chapter Nine

1. *Life and Times*, p. 546.

2. Ethan Allen Andrews, *Slavery and the Domestic Slave Trade in the United States* (Boston: Scholarly Publishers, 1836; facsimile ed., New York: Arno Press, no date), pp. 94, 73.

3. Ibid., pp. 35–36, 44–45, 56–57.

4. Benjamin F. Auld to Douglass, September 27, 1891, Douglass Papers, Lib. Cong. Although Douglass never mentioned having lived on Fells Street, B. F. Auld recalled in this letter that his family had moved there about 1834, while Frederick was in St. Michaels. The oddly built houses are still standing, on what is now called Thames Street, and some are being restored. The exact house in the row in which the Aulds lived has not been identified, but it is undoubtedly the only house connected with Douglass's youth in Fells Point that still exists.

5. Port of Baltimore Custom House Records, Master Carpenter Certificates and Ship Registrations, National Archives, Washington, D.C. The *Fourth of July* was registered on August 14, and the *Independence* on September 28, 1836. Both were taken over by the Mexican government in 1837.

6. Daniel P. Mannix, *Black Cargoes: A History of the Atlantic Slave Trade* (New York: Viking, 1962), p. 191.

7. Ibid., pp. 194–95.

8. Howard I. Chapelle, *The Search for Speed Under Sail* (New York: Norton, 1967), pp. 301–3; Port of Baltimore Custom House Records, National Archives, Washington, D.C. In addition to vessels built by Price and Butler & Lambdin, Chapelle names the following craft identified with the slave trade and built at Fells Point while Frederick was working there: the schooners *Viper* (1836) and *Clara* (1838), both by John A. Robb; the schooner *Florida* and ship *Venus* (both 1838), by William & George Gardner; the schooner *Hazard* (1838), by William K. Smith; and the schooner *Emanuel* (1836), by Levin H. Dunkin. There undoubtedly were others.

9. "The Editor's Visit to the Old Shipyard in Baltimore," article by Douglass in the *New National Era*, Washington, D.C., July 6, 1871; "A Friendly Word to Maryland," lecture by Douglass at Bethel Church, Baltimore, November 17, 1864, published in pamphlet, Baltimore, 1864.

10. *Bondage and Freedom*, p. 308; Benjamin F. Auld to Douglass, September 11, 1891, Douglass Papers, Lib. Cong.; Auld family papers, privately held.

11. William E. Lloyd to Douglass, June 13, 1870, Douglass Papers, Lib. Cong.

12. "The Editor's Visit," *New National Era*, July 6, 1871.

13. Rosetta Douglass Sprague, "Anna Murray Douglass: My Mother as I Recall Her," pamphlet, Washington, D.C., 1900.

14. Both letters are quoted in full in J. Thomas Scharf's *History of Maryland from the Earliest Period to the Present Day*, 3 vols. (Baltimore: J. B. Piet, 1879), 3:322-24. Douglass never mentioned joining Sharp Street Methodist Church; the report that he did is based on Benjamin Quarles, *Frederick Douglass* (New York: Associated Publishers, 1948), and Richard T. Greener, "Reminiscences of Frederick Douglass," *Champion* 1 (February, 1917): 291. Quarles says Frederick was a member from 1836 to 1838 and became a "class leader and choir singer."

15. Permitting a slave to "hire his time"—in effect to work as a free laborer and pay part of his earnings to his master—was a common practice in Maryland despite sporadic efforts to limit or forbid it by law.

16. *Life and Times*, pp. 205-6. The three music books were among the few possessions Frederick and Anna were able to take with them when they went to New Bedford, Massachusetts, to establish a new life.

17. Douglass to Hugh Auld, dated Rochester, October 4, 1859 (?), *Baltimore Sun*, February 25, 1895. In this letter Douglass left no doubt about his immediate motive for escaping. He told Auld his reason for running away "so unceremoniously" was that "I did not know how soon I might be sold."

18. Details of Douglass's escape are taken from a variety of accounts: *Life and Times*, pp. 197-201; "Frederick Douglass," *New York Times*, December 27, 1880; "My Escape from Slavery," *Century*, November 1881; and the unedited manuscript of *Life and Times* in the Douglass Papers, Lib. Cong. For security reasons, Douglass gave no details of his escape in his first two autobiographies, written before slavery was abolished. He first revealed that he had traveled by train on March 10, 1873, in a speech at the Academy of Music in Philadelphia. His first detailed account was the one that appeared in the *New York Times* in December, 1880. The version published in *Century* was taken word for word from *Life and Times*, which was published a month later.

Chapter Ten

1. Letter to a friend in England, reprinted in New York *Independent*, March 2, 1865.

2. Letter "To My Old Master, Thomas Auld," *North Star*, September 8, 1848.

3. The Bethel Church speech was printed in full in a pamphlet, "A Friendly Word to Maryland: A Lecture, Delivered by Fred'k Douglass, Esq., in Bethel Church on the 17th of November, 1864" (Baltimore: John E. Woods, 1864).

4. Letter in New York *Independent*, March 2, 1865.

5. Talbot Land Records, 52:258; 58:234.

6. Lewis Douglass to F. Douglass, June 9, 1865, Frederick Douglass Collection, Moorland-Spingarn Research Center, Howard University, Washington, D.C.

7. Samuel Hambleton (1777-1851) is credited with having made the flag carrying the motto "Don't Give Up the Ship" during the Battle of Lake Erie. Perry Cabin Farm was named for his commanding officer, Commodore Oliver Hazard Perry. For John N. Hambleton's bequest to the Mitchell brothers, see Talbot County Wills, TNC no. 11, p. 391.

8. Benjamin F. Auld to Douglass, September 11, 1891, Douglass Papers, Lib. Cong.

9. *North Star*, September 8, 1848.

10. *Life and Times*, p. 443. In a second letter to Auld, published in the *North Star*, September 7, 1849, Douglass apologized for some of his earlier statements, admitting that he had been "unjust and unkind." Regarding his grandmother, Douglass had been informed

"that you have taken her from the desolate hut, in which she formerly lived, into your own kitchen, and are providing for her in a manner becoming a gentleman and a Christian." However, the apology, as usual, never caught up with the accusation. Douglass permitted the 1848 letter to be reprinted in the appendix of his *Bondage and Freedom* (1855) without correction; and Auld did not even know of the 1849 letter when they met at St. Michaels in 1877 (see chapter 11).

11. Nathaniel P. Rogers in Concord, N. H., *Herald of Freedom,* December 10, 1841.

12. *Liberator,* November 27, 1846.

13. *Baltimore Sun,* February 25, 1895. Benjamin F. Auld sold the original of this letter to a collector, J. C. Shaffer of Chicago, after Douglass's death. A copy in Benjamin Auld's handwriting is in the Auld family papers, privately held.

14. Benjamin F. Auld to Douglass, September 11, 1891, Douglass Papers, Lib. Cong.

15. *Life and Times,* pp. 392–95.

16. Ibid., pp. 394–95; John L. Sears to Douglass, January 10, 1878; Thomas E. Sears to Douglass, February 1, 1878, both in Douglass Papers, Lib. Cong.

17. John L. Sears to Douglass, February 23, 1882, February 18, 1885; Thomas E. Sears to Douglass, April 15, 1886, all in Douglass Papers, Lib. Cong.

18. Unidentified clipping, Douglass Papers, Lib. Cong.

19. Bodery to Douglass, May 17, 1894, Douglass Papers, Lib. Cong.

20. "To the Public—Falsehood Refuted," *Liberator,* December 12, 1845, reprinted from the *Delaware Republican.* Date of the original publication is not known.

21. Douglass to William Lloyd Garrison, January 27, 1846, *Liberator,* February 27, 1846.

22. "Narrative of Frederick Douglass," *Liberator,* February 20, 1846, reprinted from Albany *Patriot.*

23. *Bondage and Freedom,* pp. 302–3, 306.

24. Text of the report that appeared in the *Pennsylvania Freeman* on February 26, 1846, was: "We are authorized to state that Thomas Auld who by inheritance became possessed of what in slaveholder's language is denominated the legal right to Frederick Douglass—has transferred by deed of gift, his title to said Frederick to his brother Hugh—who stung by the manner in which the family has been spoken of by his quondam slave, is so bitterly incensed against him, as to have openly avowed his determination, in case Frederick ever returns to this country, to spare no pains or expense in order to regain possession of him, and—cost what it may, the utmost of his wishes is to place him in the cotton fields of the South. We imagine that these wishes will not soon be gratified." In at least one respect the report erred; Thomas Auld had not made a gift of Frederick to Hugh, but had sold his rights for one hundred dollars.

25. Bill of Sale, Thomas Auld to Hugh Auld, October 25, 1845, Douglass Papers, Lib. Cong.; Deed of Manumission, Thomas Auld to Thomas Bailey, October 25, 1845, Talbot Land Records, 59:176; Deed of Manumission, Thomas Auld to Charles Bailey et al., May 19, 1859, Talbot Chattel Records, STH no. 1, p. 488.

26. Auld family papers, privately held.

27. Lowrie to Hugh Auld, November 24, 1846, Auld family papers, privately held.

28. Bill of Sale, Thomas Auld to Hugh Auld, November 30, 1846, Talbot Land Records, 60:35–36; Douglass Papers, Lib. Cong. A copy of the second bill of sale, erroneously dated November 13, appears in *Bondage and Freedom,* p. 374, and *Life and Times,* p. 256.

29. Perry Downs to Douglass, February, 1867, Frederick Douglass Collection, Moorland-Spingarn Research Center, Howard University, Washington, D.C. Internal evidence indicates that the letter was written for Perry by a person unknown.

30. Douglass to Spelman, July 11, 1867, New York *Independent,* July 25, 1867.

31. Charles R. Douglass to F. Douglass, August 16, 1867, Douglass Papers, Lib. Cong.

32. Douglass to Tilton, September 2, 1867, Frederick Douglass Papers, New York Historical Society.

33. New York *Independent,* September 12, 1867.

34. Anna Downs to Douglass, October 5, 1869, Douglass Papers, Lib. Cong.; *Easton Gazette,* November 30, 1878; marginal note in *Bondage and Freedom,* p. 38, by Harriet Lucretia Anthony, Dodge Collection, Hall of Records, Annapolis.

35. Baltimore *Gazette,* May 20, 1870; *New National Era,* May 26, 1870.

36. Douglass to Lydia M. Child, July 30, 1865, Frederick Douglass Collection, Moorland-Spingarn Research Center, Howard University, Washington, D.C.

37. Douglass to Easton, Md., citizens, June 22, 1867, Douglass Papers, Lib. Cong. Douglass had already scheduled a series of lectures in Virginia for the week of July 4.

38. Philip S. Foner, ed., *The Life and Writings of Frederick Douglass,* 5 vols. (New York: International Publishers, 1950–1975), 4:101.

39. Douglass to John Sherman, March 13, 1877, Rutherford B. Hayes Papers, Hayes Memorial Library, Fremont, Ohio.

Chapter Eleven

1. Tilton to Douglass, March 16, 1877, Douglass Papers, Lib. Cong.

2. *Life and Times,* pp. 441–42. Editions of Douglass's autobiographies were published in French, German, and Swedish as well as English.

3. *Baltimore Sun,* June 19, 1877.

4. Ibid.

5. Auld family tradition holds that the celebrated meeting took place at Beverly, the country home of another Thomas Auld daughter, where Auld died on February 8, 1880. However, references in Douglass's text, the *Sun,* and private letters all make it clear that it was held at the Cherry Street home of William H . Bruff.

6. There have not been many such visits by blacks to white homes in St. Michaels since then. Only in recent years have its residents departed from strict adherence to southern racial traditions, and even now (1980) many traces of segregation remain. Interestingly, a collateral descendant of Douglass was a leader in breaking the color line in politics; James Thomas, a great-great-grandson of Frederick's sister Eliza, was the first black man ever elected to the St. Michaels Board of Town Commissioners, and the first ever elected its president.

7. Douglass's account of his visit to Auld, from which many of the details in this section are taken, appears in *Life and Times,* pp. 440–44.

8. At the time of their meeting, Douglass said his charge that Auld had mistreated his grandmother had appeared in the *Narrative.* This was faulty recollection on his part. In the *Narrative* he had reported that she was destitute but had not charged Auld with responsibility for it. That accusation was made in his 1848 open letter, after Auld had already sent for her and was seeing to her care.

9. Douglass was under the impression that Auld died shortly after their meeting; but in fact the tough old captain, who had survived four wives, lived on for almost three years, dying in his eighty-fifth year on February 8, 1880.

10. *Baltimore Sun,* June 19, 1877.

11. *New York Times,* September 29, 1883. The *Times* judgment was based not only on Douglass's alleged friendliness toward whites, but also on a number of issues on which he had taken stands unpopular with younger black leaders. Among them were his denunciation of efforts by charitable white organizations to help poor blacks, his opposition to black emigration into newly opened western lands, and his continued loyalty to Republican party

politics and politicians after that party had abandoned its radical position on black civil rights.

12. Sarah L. Bruff to Douglass, June 1877, Douglass Papers, Lib. Cong. Mrs. Bruff appears to have been trying to take advantage of Douglass. Talbot Land Records show that she had paid only $1,000 for the house, not $4,000 as she claimed, and that she sold it to Dr. Robert A. Dodson on October 1, 1878, for $1,200 rather than the $3,000 she had asked of Douglass (Land Records, 78:347; 86:139).

13. *Easton Gazette,* November 30, 1878. All quotations in this section attributed to the *Gazette* are from the lengthy article of this date.

14. Talbot Land Records, 72:549; 115:131. Ebenezer and Martha Jackson bought the farm from John P. Anthony in 1866 and sold it to James P. J. Hubbard in 1891. The house built by Jackson is still standing.

15. The account of Douglass's rediscovery of his birthplace is pieced together from several sources: the *Gazette* of November 30, 1878; notes by Harriet Lucretia Anthony in margins of her copy of *Bondage and Freedom,* Dodge Collection, Hall of Records, Annapolis; and an article, "Birthplace of Frederick Douglass is Confirmed," in the *Easton Star-Democrat,* May 13, 1970. The *Gazette* in its account erroneously located the birthplace as being on land owned by Nehemiah C. Fitzjarrel. His farm was south of the one the Jacksons had bought from Anthony.

16. Despite Douglass's remarks, there is little evidence that the Ku Klux Klan was active in Talbot County; nor was there interference with black voting rights. Blacks had received the franchise in 1870, when they registered in large numbers and voted without hindrance. In 1872 they had helped carry the county for President Grant; and in 1878, just before Douglass spoke, their votes had been the deciding factor in giving the Republican candidate for Congress a majority in the county over his Democratic opponent.

17. *Easton Gazette,* November 30, 1878.

18. *Life and Times,* p. 37.

19. Oswald Tilghman, comp., *History of Talbot County, Maryland, 1661-1861,* 2 vols. (Baltimore, Williams & Wilkins, 1915; reprint ed., Baltimore: Regional Publishing Co., 1967), 1:217.

20. "Confederacy President Here Just 56 Years Ago," *Easton Star-Democrat,* December 18, 1923. A reception was held at Wye House for Davis, who was promoting sales of his history of the Confederacy. Admiral Buchanan and General Winder's father, Edward S. Winder, married Lloyd daughters. Buchanan (1800–1874) had a distinguished career in both the United States and Confederate navies; Winder, who commanded Jackson's famous "Stonewall Brigade," was killed at the Battle of Cedar Mountain on August 9, 1862.

21. For Douglass's account of his Wye House visit, see *Life and Times,* pp. 444–49.

22. Interview with John L. Thomas, Jr., *Baltimore American,* June 16, 1881.

23. *Life and Times,* pp. 445–46.

24. The *Baltimore American* interview with John L. Thomas, Jr. (June 16, 1881), quoted Thomas as saying it was Edward Lloyd VIII, Howard Lloyd's elder brother, who invited the party to tour Wye House. Douglass, however, said it was Howard; and family tradition indicates this was correct.

25. *Life and Times,* p. 446.

26. *Easton Gazette,* February 23, 1895.

27. *Life and Times,* p. 450.

28. Article from a "metropolitan daily," otherwise unidentified, reprinted in *Easton Gazette,* March 25, 1893.

29. S. A. Harper to Douglass, April 2, 1893; Frank Dawson to Douglass, April 22, 1893, both in Douglass Papers, Lib. Cong.

30. *Easton Gazette,* April 1, 1893.

⚙ Index ⚙

Dickson J. Preston has worked for more than thirty years as a newspaper reporter and editor. He lives in Talbot County on Maryland's Eastern Shore, not far from the birthplace of Frederick Douglass.